PASS THE
CITIZENSHIP TEST

The Birth of Old Glory
by Percy Moran

Betsy Ross and two children presenting the "Betsy Ross flag" to
George Washington.

PASS THE CITIZENSHIP TEST

QUESTIONS AND ANSWERS FOR BOTH 2008 AND UPDATED 2020 EXAMS

BY

ROBERT C. ETHEREDGE

HISTORY COLLECTION
PUBLISHED BY

PASS THE CITIZENSHIP TEST

© Copyright 2021 by SeaWolf Press

PUBLISHED BY SEAWOLF PRESS

SeaWolf Press
P.O. Box 961
Orinda, CA 94563
Email: support@seawolfpress.com

Printed in the United States of America.

TABLE OF CONTENTS

How To Use This Book

❦

This book is designed to help anyone pass the U. S. Citizenship Test. Besides having answers to all the questions, it has the extra material that helps explain all those answers. The questions asked on the test are designed to test your overall knowledge about this country. They should not be the only things you know which is why we include detailed information about our history, government, and famous people.

Versions of the Citizenship Test

On Dec. 1, 2020, USCIS implemented a revised version of the civics test for naturalization (2020 civics test). Due to recent policy changes, some applicants required to take the 2020 civics test may now have a choice to take the 2020 test or the 2008 civics test. Please note that beginning on April 19, 2021, USCIS will only offer the 2008 civics test at the initial interview appointment regardless of filing date. This book contains the questions for both tests.

Which version should I take?

If you filed your Form N-400, Application for Naturalization on or after Dec. 1, 2020 and before March 1, 2021, and are currently scheduled for your initial examination (appointment) before April 19, 2021, you may choose to take the 2008 or 2020 civics test. All others will be required to take the 2008 civics test.

Taking the test

A USCIS officer will ask you questions and you will need to answer the questions in English. Although USCIS is aware that there may be additional correct answers to the 100 civics questions, applicants are encouraged to respond to the civics questions using the answers provided in this book for each question.

The naturalization test has two components: an English and civics test. The English portion has not changed. Whether you are taking the 2008 or 2020 test, you must demonstrate an understanding of the English language, including the ability to read, write, and speak basic English.

Reading: You must read out loud one out of three sentences correctly to demonstrate an ability to read in English.

Writing: You must write one out of three sentences correctly to demonstrate an ability to write in English.

How to use this book

1. Read the chapters and note, in the margins, the test question numbers that indicate places where you should pay extra attention. The numbers are marked according to the test version,so be sure you note the correct version.

2008 #60   **2020** #75

2. Go through the test questions for the version of the test you are taking and note all the places that ask for a name of a current official, such as President. These will include a link to the webpage that contains the information. Find the correct information for your location and write it in the appropriate box on the back side of that page. You can also enter it on the last page of the book that has a summary of your elected officials.

3. Go through the appropriate section at the front of the book. The front of each page contains the questions (with page references to the answers in the back of the book.) You can then test your knowledge and turn the page over to see the correct answers. Remember you won't know which questions the officer will be asking so you need to study them all.

Types of questions include:

1. Single answer, like "How long is the length of a senator's term?"

2. Single answer from a number of possible choices, like "What is one part of the judicial branch?" where you can answer either Supreme Court or Federal Courts.

3. More than one answer, like "Name 5 of the original 13 colonies.."

4. One from a list, "Name one American Indian tribe in the United States." where you can pick from a very long list.

5. A specific name, like the name of one of your state's senators.

2008 Citizenship Test

Applicants for naturalization with a filing date before Dec. 1, 2020, are required to take the 2008 version of the civics test. This section covers that test. The question has the reference page number and the answers are on the back of each page.

What To Expect During The Real Test

The actual civics test is NOT a multiple choice test. During the naturalization interview, a USCIS officer will ask you up to 10 questions from the list of 100 questions in English. You must **answer correctly 6 of the 10 questions** to pass the civics test.

Residents 65 or older

If you are 65 years old or older and have been a lawful permanent resident of the United States for 20 or more years, you may study just the 20 questions that have been marked with an asterisk.

Principles of American Democracy

1. What is the supreme law of the land? *(p. 148)* *(p. 171)*

2. .What does the Constitution do? *(p. 173)*

3. The idea of self-government is in the first three words of the Constitution. What are these words? *(p. 148)*

4. What is an amendment? *(p. 159)*

5. What do we call the first 10 amendments to the Constitution? *(p. 159)*

* 6. What is 1 right or freedom from the First Amendment? *(p. 159)*

7. How many amendments does the Constitution have? *(p. 167)*

8. What did the Declaration of Independence do? *(p. 142)*

9. What are two rights in the Declaration of Independence? *(p. 142)*

10. What is freedom of religion? *(p. 159)*

2008 U. S. CITIZENSHIP TEST
ANSWERS

Principles of American Democracy

1. What is the supreme law of the land?
- the Constitution

2. What does the Constitution do?
- sets up the government
- defines the government
- protects basic rights of Americans

3. The idea of self-government is in the first three words of the Constitution. What are these words?
- We the People

4. What is an amendment?
- a change (to the Constitution)
- an addition (to the Constitution)

5. What do we call the first ten amendments to the Constitution?
- the Bill of Rights

6. What is one right or freedom from the First Amendment?*
- speech
- religion
- assembly
- press
- petition the government

7. How many amendments does the Constitution have?
- twenty-seven (27)

8. What did the Declaration of Independence do?
- announced our independence (from Great Britain)
- declared our independence (from Great Britain)
- said that the United States is free (from Great Britain)

9. What are two rights in the Declaration of Independence?
- life
- liberty
- pursuit of happiness

10. What is freedom of religion?
- You can practice any religion, or not practice a religion.

* 11.   What is the economic system in the United States? *(p. 192)*

  12.   What is the "rule of law"? *(p. 176)*

System of Government

* 13.   Name one branch or part of the government. *(p. 174)*

  14.   What stops one branch of government from becoming too powerful?

     (p. 176)

  15.   Who is in charge of the executive branch? *(p. 174)*

  16.   Who makes federal laws? *(p. 175)*

* 17.   What are the two parts of the U.S. Congress? *(p. 175)*

  18.   How many U.S. Senators are there? *(p. 175)*

  19.   We elect a U.S. Senator for how many years? *(p. 175)*

* 20.   Who is one of your state's U.S. Senators? *(www.senate.gov)*

2008 U. S. CITIZENSHIP TEST
ANSWERS

11. What is the economic system in the United States?*
- capitalist economy
- market economy

12. What is the "rule of law"?
- Everyone must follow the law.
- Leaders must obey the law.
- Government must obey the law.
- No one is above the law.

System of Government

13. Name one branch or part of the government.*
- Congress or legislative
- President or executive
- the courts or judicial

14. What stops one branch of government from becoming too powerful?
- checks and balances
- separation of powers

15. Who is in charge of the executive branch?
- the President

16. Who makes federal laws?
- Congress
- Senate and House (of Representatives)
- (U.S. or national) legislature

17. What are the two parts of the U.S. Congress?*
- the Senate and House (of Representatives)

18. How many U.S. Senators are there?
- one hundred (100)

19. We elect a U.S. Senator for how many years?
- six (6)

20. Who is one of your state's U.S. Senators now?

District of Columbia residents and residents of U.S. territories should answer that they have no U.S. Senators.

2008 U. S. CITIZENSHIP TEST
ANSWERS ON NEXT PAGE

21. The House of Representatives has how many voting members? *(p. 175)*

22. We elect a U.S. Representative for how many years? *(p. 175)*

23. Name your U.S. Representative. (www.house.gov)

24. Who does a U.S. Senator represent? *(p. 175)*

25. Why do some states have more Representatives than other states? *(p. 175)*

26. We elect a President for how many years? *(p. 174)*

* 27. In what month do we vote for President? *(p. 182)*

* 28. What is the name of the President of the United States now? (www.whitehouse.gov)

29. What is the name of the Vice President of the United States now? (www.whitehouse.gov)

30. If the President can no longer serve, who becomes President? *(p. 179)*

31. If both the President and the Vice President can no longer serve, who becomes President? *(p. 179)*

32. Who is the Commander in Chief of the military? *(p. 174)*

2008 U. S. CITIZENSHIP TEST
ANSWERS

21. The House of Representatives has how many voting members?
- four hundred thirty-five (435)

22. We elect a U.S. Representative for how many years?
- two (2)

23. Name your U.S. Representative.

_____

[Residents of territories with nonvoting Delegates or Resident Commissioners may provide the name of that Delegate or Commissioner. Also acceptable is any statement that the territory has no (voting) Representatives in Congress.]

24. Who does a U.S. Senator represent?
- all people of the state

25. Why do some states have more Representatives than other states?
- (because of) the state's population
- (because) they have more people
- (because) some states have more people

26. We elect a President for how many years?
- four (4)

27. In what month do we vote for President?
- November

28. What is the name of the President of the United States now?

_____

29. What is the name of the Vice President of the United States now?

_____

30. If the President can no longer serve, who becomes President?
- the Vice President

31. If both the President and the Vice President can no longer serve, who becomes President?
- the Speaker of the House

32. Who is the Commander in Chief of the military?
- the President

2008 U. S. CITIZENSHIP TEST

ANSWERS ON NEXT PAGE

33. Who signs bills to become laws? *(p. 174)*

34. Who vetoes bills? *(p. 174)*

35. What does the President's Cabinet do? *(p. 177)*

36. What are two Cabinet-level positions? *(p. 177)*

37. What does the judicial branch do? *(p. 176)*

38. What is the highest court in the United States? *(p. 176)*

39. How many justices are on the Supreme Court? *(p. 176)*

40. Who is the Chief Justice of the United States? (www.supremecourt.gov)

2008 U. S. CITIZENSHIP TEST
ANSWERS

33. Who signs bills to become laws?
- the President

34. Who vetoes bills?
- the President

35. What does the President's Cabinet do?
- advises the President

36. What are two Cabinet-level positions?
- Secretary of Agriculture
- Secretary of Commerce
- Secretary of Defense
- Secretary of Education
- Secretary of Energy
- Secretary of Health and Human Services
- Secretary of Homeland Security
- Secretary of Housing and Urban Development
- Secretary of the Interior
- Secretary of Labor
- Secretary of State
- Secretary of Transportation
- Secretary of the Treasury
- Secretary of Veterans Affairs
- Attorney General
- Vice President

37. What does the judicial branch do?
- reviews laws
- explains laws
- resolves disputes (disagreements)
- decides if a law goes against the Constitution

38. What is the highest court in the United States?
- the Supreme Court

39. How many justices are on the Supreme Court?
- Nine (9)

40. Who is the Chief Justice of the United States now?

2008 U. S. CITIZENSHIP TEST
ANSWERS ON NEXT PAGE

41. Under our Constitution, some powers belong to the federal government. What is one power of the federal government? *(p. 181)*

42. Under our Constitution, some powers belong to the states. What is one power of the states? *(p. 181)*

43. Who is the Governor of your state? (www.nga.org)

* 44. What is the capital of your state? *(p. 134)*

* 45. What are the two major political parties in the United States? *(p. 185)*

46. What is the political party of the President now? (www.whitehouse.gov)

47. What is the name of the Speaker of the House of Representatives now? (www.house.gov)

Rights and Responsibilities

48. There are four amendments to the Constitution about who can vote. Describe one of them. *(p. 183)*

2008 U. S. CITIZENSHIP TEST
ANSWERS

41. Under our Constitution, some powers belong to the federal government. What is one power of the federal government?
- to print money
- to declare war
- to create an army
- to make treaties

42. Under our Constitution, some powers belong to the states. What is one power of the states?
- provide schooling and education
- provide protection (police)
- provide safety (fire departments)
- give a driver's license
- approve zoning and land use

43. Who is the Governor of your state now?

_____

[District of Columbia residents should answer that D.C. does not have a Governor.]

44. What is the capital of your state?*

_____

[District of Columbia residents should answer that D.C. is not a state and does not have a capital. Residents of U.S. territories should name the capital of the territory.]

45. What are the two major political parties in the United States?*
- Democratic and Republican

46. What is the political party of the President now?

_____

47. What is the name of the Speaker of the House of Representatives now?

_____

Rights and Responsibilities

48. There are four amendments to the Constitution about who can vote. Describe one of them.
- Citizens eighteen (18) and older (can vote).
- You don't have to pay (a poll tax) to vote.
- Any citizen can vote. (Women and men can vote.)
- A male citizen of any race (can vote).

2008 U. S. CITIZENSHIP TEST
ANSWERS ON NEXT PAGE

* 49. What is one responsibility that is only for United States citizens? *(p. 187)*

50. What are two rights only for United States citizens? *(p. 187)*

51. What are two rights of everyone living in the United States? *(p. 159)*

52. What do we show loyalty to when we say the Pledge of Allegiance? *(p. 192)*

53. What is one promise you make when you become a United States citizen? *(p. 187)*

* 54. How old do citizens have to be to vote for President? *(p. 167)*

55. What are two ways that Americans can participate in their democracy? (inside back cover) *(p. 204)*

49. What is one responsibility that is only for United States citizens?

- serve on a jury
- vote in a federal election

50. Name one right only for United States citizens.

- vote in a federal election
- run for federal office

51. What are two rights of everyone living in the United States?

- freedom of expression
- freedom of speech
- freedom of assembly
- freedom to petition the government
- freedom of religion
- the right to bear arms

52. What do we show loyalty to when we say the Pledge of Allegiance?

- the United States
- the flag

53. What is one promise you make when you become a United States citizen?

- give up loyalty to other countries
- defend the Constitution and laws of the United States
- obey the laws of the United States
- serve in the U.S. military (if needed)
- serve (do important work for) the nation (if needed)
- be loyal to the United States

54. How old do citizens have to be to vote for President?

- eighteen (18) and older

55. What are two ways that Americans can participate in their democracy?

- vote
- join a political party or help with a campaign
- join a civic group or a community group
- give an elected official your opinion on an issue
- call Senators and Representatives
- publicly support or oppose an issue or policy
- run for office
- write to a newspaper

* 56. When is the last day you can send in federal income tax forms? *(p. 180)*

57. When must all men register for the Selective Service? *(p. 183)*

American History

58. What is one reason colonists came to America? *(p. 1)*

59. Who lived in America before the Europeans arrived? *(p. 129)*

60. What group of people was taken to America and sold as slaves? *(p. 3)*

61. Why did the colonists fight the British? *(p. 7)*

62. Who wrote the Declaration of Independence? *(p. 142)*

63. When was the Declaration of Independence adopted? *(p. 142)*

64. There were 13 original states. Name three. *(p. 129)*

2008 U. S. CITIZENSHIP TEST
ANSWERS

56. When is the last day you can send in federal income tax forms?
- April 15

57. When must all men register for the Selective Service?
- at age eighteen (18) and twenty-six (26)

American History

58. What is one reason colonists came to America?
- freedom
- political liberty
- religious freedom
- economic opportunity
- practice their religion
- escape persecution

59. Who lived in America before the Europeans arrived?
- American Indians
- Native Americans

60. What group of people was taken to America and sold as slaves?
- Africans
- people from Africa

61. Why did the colonists fight the British?
- because of high taxes (taxation without representation)
- because the British army stayed in their houses (boarding, quartering)
- because they didn't have self-government

62. Who wrote the Declaration of Independence?
- (Thomas) Jefferson

63. When was the Declaration of Independence adopted?
- July 4, 1776

64. There were 13 original states. Name three.

New Hampshire	Massachusetts
Rhode Island	Connecticut
New York	New Jersey
Pennsylvania	Delaware
Maryland	Virginia
North Carolina	South Carolina
Georgia	

65. What happened at the Constitutional Convention? *(p. 148)*

66. When was the Constitution written? *(p. 148)*

67. The Federalist Papers supported the passage of the U.S. Constitution. Name one of the writers. *(p. 12)*

68. What is one thing Benjamin Franklin is famous for? *(p. 195)*

69. Who is the "Father of Our Country"? *(p. 107)*

* 70. Who was the first President? *(p. 108)*

71. What territory did the U.S. buy from France in 1803? *(p. 16)*

72. Name one war fought by the United States in the 1800s. *(p. 18) (p. 26) (p. 30) (p. 44)*

73. Name the U.S. war between the North and the South. *(p. 30)*

74. Name one problem that led to the Civil War. *(p. 30)*

2008 U. S. CITIZENSHIP TEST
ANSWERS

65. What happened at the Constitutional Convention?
- The Constitution was written.
- The Founding Fathers wrote the Constitution.

66. When was the Constitution written?
- 1787

67. The Federalist Papers supported the passage of the U.S. Constitution. Name one of the writers.
- (James) Madison
- (Alexander) Hamilton
- (John) Jay
- Publius

68. What is one thing Benjamin Franklin is famous for?
- U.S. diplomat
- oldest member of the Constitutional Convention
- first Postmaster General of the United States
- writer of "Poor Richard's Almanac"
- started the first free libraries

69. Who is the "Father of Our Country"?
- (George) Washington

70. Who was the first President?*
- (George) Washington

71. What territory did the United States buy from France in 1803?
- the Louisiana Territory
- Louisiana

72. Name one war fought by the United States in the 1800s.
- War of 1812
- Mexican-American War
- Civil War
- Spanish-American War

73. Name the U.S. war between the North and the South.
- the Civil War
- the War between the States

74. Name one problem that led to the Civil War.
- slavery
- economic reasons
- states' rights

* 75. What was 1 important thing that Abraham Lincoln did? *(p. 114)*

76. What did the Emancipation Proclamation do? *(p. 197)*

77. What did Susan B. Anthony do? *(p. 196)*

* 78. Name one war fought by the United States in the 1900s. *(p. 50)* *(p. 61)* *(p. 68)* *(p. 76)* *(p. 87)*

79. Who was President during World War I? *(p. 50)*

80. Who was President during the Great Depression and World War II? *(p. 119)*

81. Who did the United States fight in World War II? *(p. 61)*

82. Before he was President, Eisenhower was a general. What war was he in? *(p. 120)*

83. During the Cold War, what was the main concern of the United States? *(p. 67)*

84. What movement tried to end racial discrimination? *(p. 70)*

* 85. What did Martin Luther King, Jr. do? *(p. 196)*

2008 U. S. CITIZENSHIP TEST
ANSWERS

75. What was one important thing that Abraham Lincoln did?
- freed the slaves (Emancipation Proclamation)
- saved (or preserved) the Union
- led the United States during the Civil War

76. What did the Emancipation Proclamation do?
- freed the slaves
- freed slaves in the Confederacy
- freed slaves in the Confederate states
- freed slaves in most Southern states

77. What did Susan B. Anthony do?
- fought for women's rights
- fought for civil rights

78. Name one war fought by the United States in the 1900s.
- World War I
- World War II
- Korean War
- Vietnam War
- (Persian) Gulf War

79. Who was President during World War I?
- (Woodrow) Wilson

80. Who was President during the Great Depression and World War II?
- (Franklin) Roosevelt

81. Who did the United States fight in World War II?
- Japan, Germany, and Italy

82. Before he was President, Eisenhower was a general. What war was he in?
- World War II

83. During the Cold War, what was the main concern of the United States?
- Communism

84. What movement tried to end racial discrimination?
- civil rights (movement)

85. What did Martin Luther King, Jr. do?
- fought for civil rights
- worked for equality for all Americans

86. What major event happened on September 11, 2001 in the United States? *(p. 92)*

87. Name one American Indian tribe in the United States. *(p. 129)*

Geography

88. Name one of the two longest rivers in the United States. *(p. 133)*

89. What ocean is on the West Coast of the United States? *(p. 133)*

90. What ocean is on the East Coast of the United States? *(p. 133)*

91. Name one U.S. territory. *(p. 135)*

92. Name one state that borders Canada. *(p. 137)*

93. Name one state that borders Mexico. *(p. 136)*

2008 U. S. CITIZENSHIP TEST
ANSWERS

86. What major event happened on September 11, 2001, in the United States?
- Terrorists attacked the United States.

87. Name one American Indian tribe in the United States.

Cherokee	Navajo	Sioux
Chippewa	Choctaw	Pueblo
Apache	Iroquois	Creek
Blackfeet	Seminole	Cheyenne
Arawak	Shawnee	Mohegan
Huron	Oneida	Lakota
Crow	Teton	Hopi
Inuit		

Geography

88. Name one of the two longest rivers in the United States.
- Missouri (River)
- Mississippi (River)

89. What ocean is on the West Coast of the United States?
- Pacific (Ocean)

90. What ocean is on the East Coast of the United States?
- Atlantic (Ocean)

91. Name one U.S. territory.
- Puerto Rico
- U.S. Virgin Islands
- American Samoa
- Northern Mariana Islands
- Guam

92. Name one state that borders Canada.

Maine	New Hampshire
Vermont	New York
Pennsylvania	Ohio
Michigan	Minnesota
North Dakota	Montana
Idaho	Washington
Alaska	

93. Name one state that borders Mexico.

California	Arizona
New Mexico	Texas

2008 U. S. CITIZENSHIP TEST
ANSWERS ON NEXT PAGE

* 94.   What is the capital of the United States? *(p. 15)*

* 95.   Where is the Statue of Liberty? *(p. 41)*

Symbols

96.   Why does the flag have 13 stripes? *(p. 191)*

* 97.   Why does the flag have 50 stars? *(p. 191)*

98.   What is the name of the national anthem? *(p. 200)*

Holidays

* 99.   When do we celebrate Independence Day? *(p. 189)*

100.   Name two national U.S. holidays. *(p. 188)*

94. What is the capital of the United States?
* Washington, D.C.

95. Where is the Statue of Liberty?
* New York (Harbor)
* Liberty Island
* Also acceptable are New Jersey, near New York City, and on the Hudson (River)

Symbols

96. Why does the flag have 13 stripes?
* because there were 13 original colonies
* because the stripes represent the original colonies

97. Why does the flag have 50 stars?
* because there is one star for each state
* because each star represents a state
* because there are 50 states

98. What is the name of the national anthem?
* The Star-Spangled Banner

Holidays

99. When do we celebrate Independence Day?
* July 4

100. Name two national U.S. holidays.
* New Year's Day
* Martin Luther King, Jr. Day
* Presidents' Day
* Memorial Day
* Independence Day
* Labor Day
* Columbus Day
* Veterans Day
* Thanksgiving
* Christmas

2020 U. S. CITIZENSHIP TEST
ANSWERS ON NEXT PAGE

2020 Citizenship Test
Applicants for naturalization with a filing date before Dec. 1, 2020, are required to take the 2008 version of the civics test. All applicants for naturalization with a filing date on or after December 1, 2020, will be required to take the 2020 version of the civics test. This section covers the 2020 exam. The question has the reference page number and the answers are on the back of each page.

What To Expect During The Real Test
The actual civics test is NOT a multiple choice test. During the naturalization interview, a USCIS officer will ask you up to 20 questions from the list of 128 questions in English. You must **answer correctly 12 of the 20 questions** to pass the civics test.

Residents 65 or older
If you are 65 years old or older and have been a lawful permanent resident of the United States for 20 or more years, you may study just the 20 questions that have been marked with an asterisk. You will be asked to answer 10 of those questions and must answer at least 6 correctly.

American Government

A: Principles of American Government

1.　What is the form of government of the United States? *(p. 171)*

* 2.　What is the supreme law of the land? *(p. 171)*

3.　Name one thing the U.S. Constitution does. *(p. 173)*

4.　The U.S. Constitution starts with the words "We the People." What does "We the People" mean? *(p. 148)*

5.　How are changes made to the U.S. Constitution? *(p. 159)*

6.　What does the Bill of Rights protect? *(p. 159)*

* 7.　How many amendments does the U.S. Constitution have? *(p. 167)*

8.　Why is the Declaration of Independence important? *(p. 142)*

2020 U. S. CITIZENSHIP TEST
ANSWERS

American Government

A: Principles of American Government

1. What is the form of government of the United States?
- Republic
- Constitution-based federal republic
- Representative democracy

2. What is the supreme law of the land?
- (U.S.) Constitution

3. Name one thing the U.S. Constitution does.
- Forms the government
- Defines powers of government
- Defines the parts of government
- Protects the rights of the people

4. The U.S. Constitution starts with the words "We the People." What does "We the People" mean?
- Self-government
- Popular sovereignty
- Consent of the governed
- People should govern themselves
- (Example of) social contract

5. How are changes made to the U.S. Constitution?
- Amendments
- The amendment process

6. What does the Bill of Rights protect?
- (The basic) rights of Americans
- (The basic) rights of people living in the United States

7. How many amendments does the U.S. Constitution have?
- Twenty-seven (27)

8. Why is the Declaration of Independence important?
- It says America is free from British control.
- It says all people are created equal.
- It identifies inherent rights.
- It identifies individual freedoms.

9. What founding document said the American colonies were free from Britain? *(p. 142)*

10. Name two important ideas from the Declaration of Independence and the U.S. Constitution. *(p. 169)*

11. The words "Life, Liberty, and the pursuit of Happiness" are in what founding document? *(p. 142)*

* 12. What is the economic system of the United States? *(p. 192)*

13. What is the rule of law? *(p. 176)*

14. Many documents influenced the U.S. Constitution. Name one. *(p. 139)*

15. There are three branches of government. Why? *(p. 174)*

2020 U. S. CITIZENSHIP TEST
ANSWERS

9. What founding document said the American colonies were free from Britain?
- Declaration of Independence

10. Name two important ideas from the Declaration of Independence and the U.S. Constitution.
- Equality
- Liberty
- Social contract
- Natural rights
- Limited government
- Self-government

11. The words "Life, Liberty, and the pursuit of Happiness" are in what founding document?
- Declaration of Independence

12. What is the economic system of the United States?
- Capitalism
- Free market economy

13. What is the rule of law?
- Everyone must follow the law.
- Leaders must obey the law.
- Government must obey the law.
- No one is above the law.

14. Many documents influenced the U.S. Constitution. Name one.
- Declaration of Independence
- Articles of Confederation
- Federalist Papers
- Anti-Federalist Papers
- Virginia Declaration of Rights
- Fundamental Orders of Connecticut
- Mayflower Compact
- Iroquois Great Law of Peace

15. There are three branches of government. Why?
- So one part does not become too powerful
- Checks and balances
- Separation of powers

16. Name the three branches of government. *(p. 174)*

17. The President of the United States is in charge of which branch of government? *(p. 174)*

18. What part of the federal government writes laws? *(p. 175)*

19. What are the two parts of the U.S. Congress? *(p. 175)*

* 20. Name one power of the U.S. Congress. *(p. 175)*

21. How many U.S. senators are there? *(p. 175)*

22. How long is a term for a U.S. senator? *(p. 175)*

23. Who is one of your state's U.S. senators now? *(www.senate.gov)*

24. How many voting members are in the House of Representatives? *(p. 175)*

25. How long is a term for a member of the House of Representatives? *(p. 175)*

2020 U. S. CITIZENSHIP TEST
ANSWERS

B: System of Government

16. Name the three branches of government.
- Legislative, executive, and judicial
- Congress, president, and the courts

17. The President of the United States is in charge of which branch of government?
- Executive branch

18. What part of the federal government writes laws?
- (U.S.) Congress
- (U.S. or national) legislature
- Legislative branch

19. What are the two parts of the U.S. Congress?
- Senate and House (of Representatives)

20. Name one power of the U.S. Congress.
- Writes laws
- Declares war
- Makes the federal budget

21. How many U.S. senators are there?
- One hundred (100)

22. How long is a term for a U.S. senator?
- Six (6) years

23. Who is one of your state's U.S. senators now?

_____

Answers will vary. [District of Columbia residents and residents of U.S. territories should answer that D.C. (or the territory where the applicant lives) has no U.S. senators.]

24. How many voting members are in the House of Representatives?
- Four hundred thirty-five (435)

25. How long is a term for a member of the House of Representatives?
- Two (2) years

26. Why do U.S. representatives serve shorter terms than U.S. senators? *(p. 175)*

27. How many senators does each state have? *(p. 175)*

28. Why does each state have two senators? *(p. 175)*

29. Name your U.S. representative. (www.house.gov)

* 30. What is the name of the Speaker of the House of Representatives now? (www.house.gov)

31. Who does a U.S. senator represent? *(p. 175)*

32. Who elects U.S. senators? *(p. 175)*

33. Who does a member of the House of Representatives represent? *(p. 175)*

34. Who elects members of the House of Representatives? *(p. 175)*

35. Some states have more representatives than other states. Why? *(p. 175)*

* 36. The President of the United States is elected for how many years? *(p. 174)*

2020 U. S. CITIZENSHIP TEST
ANSWERS

26. Why do U.S. representatives serve shorter terms than U.S. senators?
- To more closely follow public opinion

27. How many senators does each state have?
- Two (2)

28. Why does each state have two senators?
- Equal representation (for small states)
- The Great Compromise (Connecticut Compromise)

29. Name your U.S. representative.

_____

Answers will vary. [Residents of territories with nonvoting Delegates or Resident Commissioners may provide the name of that Delegate or Commissioner. Also acceptable is any statement that the territory has no (voting) representatives in Congress.]

30. What is the name of the Speaker of the House of Representatives now?

_____

31. Who does a U.S. senator represent?
- Citizens of their state

32. Who elects U.S. senators?
- Citizens from their state

33. Who does a member of the House of Representatives represent?
- Citizens in their (congressional) district
- Citizens in their district

34. Who elects members of the House of Representatives?
- Citizens from their (congressional) district

35. Some states have more representatives than other states. Why?
- (Because of) the state's population
- (Because) they have more people
- (Because) some states have more people

36. The President of the United States is elected for how many years?
- Four (4) years

2020 U. S. CITIZENSHIP TEST
ANSWERS ON NEXT PAGE

37. The President of the United States can serve only two terms. Why? *(p. 174)*

* 38. What is the name of the President of the United States now? (<u>www. whitehouse.gov</u>)

* 39. What is the name of the Vice President of the United States now? (<u>www.whitehouse.gov</u>)

40. If the president can no longer serve, who becomes president? *(p. 179)*

41. Name one power of the president. *(p. 174)*

42. Who is Commander in Chief of the U.S. military? *(p. 174)*

43. Who signs bills to become laws? *(p. 174)*

* 44. Who vetoes bills? *(p. 174)*

45. Who appoints federal judges? *(p. 174)*

46. The executive branch has many parts. Name one. *(p. 174)*

47. What does the President's Cabinet do? *(p. 177)*

2020 U. S. CITIZENSHIP TEST
ANSWERS

37. The President of the United States can serve only two terms. Why?
- (Because of) the 22nd Amendment
- To keep the president from becoming too powerful

38. What is the name of the President of the United States now?

_____

39. What is the name of the Vice President of the United States now?

_____

40. If the president can no longer serve, who becomes president?
- The Vice President (of the United States)

41. Name one power of the president.
- Signs bills into law
- Vetoes bills
- Enforces laws
- Commander in Chief (of the military)
- Chief diplomat

42. Who is Commander in Chief of the U.S. military?
- The President (of the United States)

43. Who signs bills to become laws?
- The President (of the United States)

44. Who vetoes bills?
- The President (of the United States)

45. Who appoints federal judges?
- The President (of the United States)

46. The executive branch has many parts. Name one.
- President (of the United States)
- Cabinet
- Federal departments and agencies

47. What does the President's Cabinet do?
- Advises the President (of the United States)

48. What are two Cabinet-level positions? *(p. 177)*

49. Why is the Electoral College important? *(p. 181)*

50. What is one part of the judicial branch? *(p. 176)*

51. What does the judicial branch do? *(p. 176)*

* 52. What is the highest court in the United States? *(p. 176)*

53. How many seats are on the Supreme Court? *(p. 176)*

54. How many Supreme Court justices are usually needed to decide a case? *(p. 176)*

2020 U. S. CITIZENSHIP TEST
ANSWERS

48. What are two Cabinet-level positions?
- Attorney General
- Secretary of Agriculture
- Secretary of Commerce
- Secretary of Defense
- Secretary of Education
- Secretary of Energy
- Secretary of Health and Human Services
- Secretary of Homeland Security
- Secretary of Housing and Urban Development
- Secretary of the Interior
- Secretary of Labor
- Secretary of State
- Secretary of Transportation
- Secretary of the Treasury
- Secretary of Veterans Affairs
- Vice President (of the United States)

49. Why is the Electoral College important?
- It decides who is elected president.
- It provides a compromise between the popular election of the president and congressional selection.

50. What is one part of the judicial branch?
- Supreme Court
- Federal Courts

51. What does the judicial branch do?
- Reviews laws
- Explains laws
- Resolves disputes (disagreements) about the law
- Decides if a law goes against the (U.S.) Constitution

52. What is the highest court in the United States?
- Supreme Court

53. How many seats are on the Supreme Court?
- Nine (9)

54. How many Supreme Court justices are usually needed to decide a case?
- Five (5)

55. How long do Supreme Court justices serve? *(p. 176)*

56. Supreme Court justices serve for life. Why? *(p. 176)*

57. Who is the Chief Justice of the United States now? (www.supremecourt.gov)

58. Name one power that is only for the federal government. *(p. 181)*

59. Name one power that is only for the states. *(p. 181)*

60. What is the purpose of the 10th Amendment? *(p. 160)*

* 61. Who is the governor of your state now? (www.nga.org)

62. What is the capital of your state? *(p. 134)*

2020 U. S. CITIZENSHIP TEST
ANSWERS

55. How long do Supreme Court justices serve?
- (For) life
- Lifetime appointment
- (Until) retirement

56. Supreme Court justices serve for life. Why?
- To be independent (of politics)
- To limit outside (political) influence

57. Who is the Chief Justice of the United States now?

_____

58. Name one power that is only for the federal government.
- Print paper money
- Mint coins
- Declare war
- Create an army
- Make treaties
- Set foreign policy

59. Name one power that is only for the states.
- Provide schooling and education
- Provide protection (police)
- Provide safety (fire departments)
- Give a driver's license
- Approve zoning and land use

60. What is the purpose of the 10th Amendment?
- (It states that the) powers not given to the federal government belong to the states or to the people.

61. Who is the governor of your state now?

_____

Answers will vary. [District of Columbia residents should answer that D.C. does not have a governor.]

62. What is the capital of your state?

_____

Answers will vary. [District of Columbia residents should answer that D.C. is not a state and does not have a capital. Residents of U.S. territories should name the capital of the territory.]

C: Rights and Responsibilities

63. There are four amendments to the U.S. Constitution about who can vote. Describe one of them. *(p. 183)*

64. Who can vote in federal elections, run for federal office, and serve on a jury in the United States? *(p. 187)*

65. What are three rights of everyone living in the United States? *(p. 159)*

* 66. What do we show loyalty to when we say the Pledge of Allegiance? *(p. 192)*

67. Name two promises that new citizens make in the Oath of Allegiance. *(p. 187)*

68. How can people become United States citizens? *(p. 187)*

2020 U. S. CITIZENSHIP TEST
ANSWERS

C: Rights and Responsibilities

63. There are four amendments to the U.S. Constitution about who can vote. Describe one of them.
- Citizens eighteen (18) and older (can vote).
- You don't have to pay (a poll tax) to vote.
- Any citizen can vote. (Women and men can vote.)
- A male citizen of any race (can vote).

64. Who can vote in federal elections, run for federal office, and serve on a jury in the United States?
- Citizens
- Citizens of the United States
- U.S. citizens

65. What are three rights of everyone living in the United States?
- Freedom of expression
- Freedom of speech
- Freedom of assembly
- Freedom to petition the government
- Freedom of religion
- The right to bear arms

66. What do we show loyalty to when we say the Pledge of Allegiance?
- The United States
- The flag

67. Name two promises that new citizens make in the Oath of Allegiance.
- Give up loyalty to other countries
- Defend the (U.S.) Constitution
- Obey the laws of the United States
- Serve in the military (if needed)
- Serve (help, do important work for) the nation (if needed)
- Be loyal to the United States

68. How can people become United States citizens?
- Naturalize
- Derive citizenship
- Be born in the United States

69. What are two examples of civic participation in the United States? *(p. 204)*

70. What is one way Americans can serve their country? *(p. 187)*

71. Why is it important to pay federal taxes? *(p. 180)*

72. It is important for all men age 18 through 25 to register for the Selective Service. Name one reason why. *(p. 183)*

American History

A: Colonial Period and Independence

73. The colonists came to America for many reasons. Name one. *(p. 1)*

69. What are two examples of civic participation in the United States?
- Vote
- Run for office
- Join a political party
- Help with a campaign
- Join a civic group
- Join a community group
- Give an elected official your opinion (on an issue)
- Contact elected officials
- Support or oppose an issue or policy
- Write to a newspaper

70. What is one way Americans can serve their country?
- Vote
- Pay taxes
- Obey the law
- Serve in the military
- Run for office
- Work for local, state, or federal government

71. Why is it important to pay federal taxes?
- Required by law
- All people pay to fund the federal government
- Required by the (U.S.) Constitution (16th Amendment)
- Civic duty

72. It is important for all men age 18 through 25 to register for the Selective Service. Name one reason why.
- Required by law
- Civic duty
- Makes the draft fair, if needed

American History

A: Colonial Period and Independence

73. The colonists came to America for many reasons. Name one.
- Freedom
- Political liberty
- Religious freedom
- Economic opportunity
- Escape persecution

2020 U. S. CITIZENSHIP TEST
ANSWERS ON NEXT PAGE

* 74. Who lived in America before the Europeans arrived? *(p. 129)*

75. What group of people was taken and sold as slaves? *(p. 3)*

76. What war did the Americans fight to win independence from Britain? *(p. 7)*

77. Name one reason why the Americans declared independence from Britain. *(p. 7)*

* 78. Who wrote the Declaration of Independence? *(p. 142)*

79. When was the Declaration of Independence adopted? *(p. 142)*

80. The American Revolution had many important events. Name one. *(p. 7) (p. 8) (p. 9) (p. 10)*

2020 U. S. CITIZENSHIP TEST
ANSWERS

74. Who lived in America before the Europeans arrived?
- American Indians
- Native Americans

75. What group of people was taken and sold as slaves?
- Africans
- People from Africa

76. What war did the Americans fight to win independence from Britain?
- American Revolution
- The (American) Revolutionary War
- War for (American) Independence

77. Name one reason why the Americans declared independence from Britain.
- High taxes
- Taxation without representation
- British soldiers stayed in Americans' houses (boarding, quartering)
- They did not have self-government
- Boston Massacre
- Boston Tea Party (Tea Act)
- Stamp Act
- Sugar Act
- Townshend Acts
- Intolerable (Coercive) Acts

78. Who wrote the Declaration of Independence?
- (Thomas) Jefferson

79. When was the Declaration of Independence adopted?
- July 4, 1776

80. The American Revolution had many important events. Name one.
- (Battle of) Bunker Hill
- Declaration of Independence
- Washington Crossing the Delaware (Battle of Trenton)
- (Battle of) Saratoga
- Valley Forge (Encampment)
- (Battle of) Yorktown (British surrender at Yorktown)

81. There were 13 original states. Name five. *(p. 129)*

82. What founding document was written in 1787? *(p. 148)*

83. The Federalist Papers supported the passage of the U.S. Constitution. Name one of the writers. *(p. 12)*

84. Why were the Federalist Papers important? *(p. 12)*

85. Benjamin Franklin is famous for many things. Name one. *(p. 195)*

* 86. George Washington is famous for many things. Name one. *(p. 108)*

87. Thomas Jefferson is famous for many things. Name one. *(p. 109)*

2020 U. S. CITIZENSHIP TEST
ANSWERS

81. There were 13 original states. Name five.

New Hampshire	Massachusetts
Rhode Island	Connecticut
New York	New Jersey
Pennsylvania	Delaware
Maryland	Virginia
North Carolina	South Carolina
Georgia	

2. What founding document was written in 1787?

- (U.S.) Constitution

83. The Federalist Papers supported the passage of the U.S. Constitution. Name one of the writers.

- (James) Madison
- (Alexander) Hamilton
- (John) Jay
- Publius

84. Why were the Federalist Papers important?

- They helped people understand the (U.S.) Constitution.
- They supported passing the (U.S.) Constitution.

85. Benjamin Franklin is famous for many things. Name one.

- Founded the first free public libraries
- First Postmaster General of the United States
- Helped write the Declaration of Independence
- Inventor
- U.S. diplomat

86. George Washington is famous for many things. Name one.

- "Father of Our Country"
- First president of the United States
- General of the Continental Army
- President of the Constitutional Convention

87. Thomas Jefferson is famous for many things. Name one.

- Writer of the Declaration of Independence
- Third president of the United States
- Doubled the size of the United States (Louisiana Purchase)
- First Secretary of State
- Founded the University of Virginia
- Writer of the Virginia Statute on Religious Freedom

88. James Madison is famous for many things. Name one. *(p. 110)*

89. Alexander Hamilton is famous for many things. Name one. *(p. 195)*

B: 1800s

90. What territory did the United States buy from France in 1803? *(p. 16)*

91. Name one war fought by the United States in the 1800s. *(p. 18) (p. 26) (p. 30) (p. 44)*

92. Name the U.S. war between the North and the South. *(p. 30)*

93. The Civil War had many important events. Name one. *(p. 31) (p. 32) (p. 33) (p. 34)*

* 94. Abraham Lincoln is famous for many things. Name one. *(p. 114)*

2020 U. S. CITIZENSHIP TEST
ANSWERS

88. James Madison is famous for many things. Name one.
- "Father of the Constitution"
- Fourth president of the United States
- President during the War of 1812
- One of the writers of the Federalist Papers

89. Alexander Hamilton is famous for many things. Name one.
- First Secretary of the Treasury
- One of the writers of the Federalist Papers
- Helped establish the First Bank of the United States
- Aide to General George Washington
- Member of the Continental Congress

B: 1800s

90. What territory did the United States buy from France in 1803?
- Louisiana Territory
- Louisiana

91. Name one war fought by the United States in the 1800s.
- War of 1812
- Mexican-American War
- Civil War
- Spanish-American War

92. Name the U.S. war between the North and the South.
- The Civil War

93. The Civil War had many important events. Name one.
- (Battle of) Fort Sumter
- Emancipation Proclamation
- (Battle of) Vicksburg
- (Battle of) Gettysburg
- Sherman's March
- (Surrender at) Appomattox
- (Battle of) Antietam/Sharpsburg
- Lincoln was assassinated.

94. Abraham Lincoln is famous for many things. Name one.
- Freed the slaves (Emancipation Proclamation)
- Saved (or preserved) the Union
- Led the United States during the Civil War
- 16th president of the United States
- Delivered the Gettysburg Address

95. What did the Emancipation Proclamation do? *(p. 197)*

96. What U.S. war ended slavery? *(p. 34)*

97. What amendment gives citizenship to all persons born in the United States? *(p. 162)*

98. When did all men get the right to vote? *(p. 163)*

99. Name one leader of the women's rights movement in the 1800s. *(p. 196)*

C: Recent American History and Other Important Historical Information

100. Name one war fought by the United States in the 1900s. *(p. 50)* *(p. 61)* *(p. 68)* *(p. 76)* *(p. 87)*

101. Why did the United States enter World War I? *(p. 50)*

2020 U. S. CITIZENSHIP TEST
ANSWERS

95. What did the Emancipation Proclamation do?
- Freed the slaves
- Freed slaves in the Confederacy
- Freed slaves in the Confederate states
- Freed slaves in most Southern states

96. What U.S. war ended slavery?
- The Civil War

97. What amendment gives citizenship to all persons born in the United States?
- 14th Amendment

98. When did all men get the right to vote?
- After the Civil War
- During Reconstruction
- (With the) 15th Amendment
- 1870

99. Name one leader of the women's rights movement in the 1800s.
- Susan B. Anthony
- Elizabeth Cady Stanton
- Sojourner Truth
- Harriet Tubman
- Lucretia Mott
- Lucy Stone

C: Recent American History and Other Important Historical Information

100. Name one war fought by the United States in the 1900s.
- World War I
- World War II
- Korean War
- Vietnam War
- (Persian) Gulf War

101. Why did the United States enter World War I?
- Because Germany attacked U.S. (civilian) ships
- To support the Allied Powers (England, France, Italy, and Russia)
- To oppose the Central Powers (Germany, Austria-Hungary, the Ottoman Empire, and Bulgaria)

102. When did all women get the right to vote? *(p. 164)*

103. What was the Great Depression? *(p. 55)*

104. When did the Great Depression start? *(p. 55)*

105. Who was president during the Great Depression and World War II? *(p. 56)*

106. Why did the United States enter World War II? *(p. 61)*

107. Dwight Eisenhower is famous for many things. Name one. *(p. 120)*

108. Who was the United States' main rival during the Cold War? *(p. 67)*

109. During the Cold War, what was one main concern of the United States? *(p. 67)*

110. Why did the United States enter the Korean War? *(p. 68)*

111. Why did the United States enter the Vietnam War? *(p. 76)*

2020 U. S. CITIZENSHIP TEST
ANSWERS

102. When did all women get the right to vote?
- 1920
- After World War I
- (With the) 19th Amendment

103. What was the Great Depression?
- Longest economic recession in modern history

104. When did the Great Depression start?
- The Great Crash (1929)
- Stock market crash of 1929

105. Who was president during the Great Depression and World War II?
- (Franklin) Roosevelt

106. Why did the United States enter World War II?
- (Bombing of) Pearl Harbor
- Japanese attacked Pearl Harbor
- To support the Allied Powers (England, France, and Russia)
- To oppose the Axis Powers (Germany, Italy, and Japan)

107. Dwight Eisenhower is famous for many things. Name one.
- General during World War II
- President at the end of (during) the Korean War
- 34th president of the United States
- Signed the Federal-Aid Highway Act of 1956 (Created the Interstate System)

108. Who was the United States' main rival during the Cold War?
- Soviet Union
- USSR
- Russia

109. During the Cold War, what was one main concern of the United States?
- Communism
- Nuclear war

110. Why did the United States enter the Korean War?
- To stop the spread of communism

111. Why did the United States enter the Vietnam War?
- To stop the spread of communism

112. What did the civil rights movement do? *(p. 70)*

* 113. Martin Luther King, Jr. is famous for many things. Name one. *(p. 196)*

114. Why did the United States enter the Persian Gulf War? *(p. 87)*

* 115. What major event happened on September 11, 2001 in the United States? *(p. 92)*

116. Name one U.S. military conflict after the September 11, 2001 attacks. *(p. 92) (p. 93)*

117. Name one American Indian tribe in the United States. *(p. 129)*

118. Name one example of an American innovation. *(p. 194)*

2020 U. S. CITIZENSHIP TEST
ANSWERS

112. What did the civil rights movement do?
- Fought to end racial discrimination

113. Martin Luther King, Jr. is famous for many things. Name one.
- Fought for civil rights
- Worked for equality for all Americans
- Worked to ensure that people would "not be judged by the color of their skin, but by the content of their character"

114. Why did the United States enter the Persian Gulf War?
- To force the Iraqi military from Kuwait

115. What major event happened on September 11, 2001 in the United States?
- Terrorists attacked the United States
- Terrorists took over two planes and crashed them into the World Trade Center in New York City
- Terrorists took over a plane and crashed into the Pentagon in Arlington, Virginia
- Terrorists took over a plane originally aimed at Washington, D.C., and crashed in a field in Pennsylvania

116. Name one U.S. military conflict after the September 11, 2001 attacks.
- (Global) War on Terror
- War in Afghanistan
- War in Iraq

117. Name one American Indian tribe in the United States.

Apache	Blackfeet	Cayuga	Cherokee
Cheyenne	Chippewa	Choctaw	Creek
Crow	Hopi	Huron	Inupiat
Lakota	Mohawk	Mohegan	Navajo
Oneida	Onondaga	Pueblo	Seminole
Seneca	Shawnee	Sioux	Teton
Tuscarora			

118. Name one example of an American innovation.
- Light bulb
- Automobile (cars, internal combustion engine)
- Skyscrapers
- Airplane
- Assembly line
- Landing on the moon
- Integrated circuit (IC)

2020 U. S. CITIZENSHIP TEST
ANSWERS ON NEXT PAGE

Symbols and Holidays

A: Symbols

119. What is the capital of the United States? *(p. 15)*

120. Where is the Statue of Liberty? *(p. 41)*

* 121. Why does the flag have 13 stripes? *(p. 191)*

122. Why does the flag have 50 stars? *(p. 191)*

123. What is the name of the national anthem? *(p. 200)*

124. The Nation's first motto was "E Pluribus Unum." What does that mean? *(p. 193)*

B: Holidays

125. What is Independence Day? *(p. 189)*

* 126. Name three national U.S. holidays. *(p. 188)*

2020 U. S. CITIZENSHIP TEST
ANSWERS

Symbols and Holidays

A: Symbols

119. What is the capital of the United States?
- Washington, D.C.

120. Where is the Statue of Liberty?
- New York (Harbor)
- Liberty Island [Also acceptable are New Jersey, near New York City, and on the Hudson (River).]

121. Why does the flag have 13 stripes?
- (Because there were) 13 original colonies
- (Because the stripes) represent the original colonies

122. Why does the flag have 50 stars?
- (Because there is) one star for each state
- (Because) each star represents a state
- (Because there are) 50 states

123. What is the name of the national anthem?
- The Star-Spangled Banner

124. The Nation's first motto was "E Pluribus Unum." What does that mean?
- Out of many, one
- We all become one

B: Holidays

125. What is Independence Day?
- A holiday to celebrate U.S. independence (from Britain)
- The country's birthday

126. Name three national U.S. holidays.
- New Year's Day
- Martin Luther King, Jr. Day
- Presidents Day (Washington's Birthday)
- Memorial Day
- Independence Day
- Labor Day
- Columbus Day
- Veterans Day
- Thanksgiving Day
- Christmas Day

2020 U. S. CITIZENSHIP TEST
ANSWERS ON NEXT PAGE

127.   What is Memorial Day? *(p. 189)*

128.   What is Veterans Day? *(p. 190)*

2020 U. S. CITIZENSHIP TEST
ANSWERS

127. What is Memorial Day?

- A holiday to honor soldiers who died in military service

128. What is Veterans Day?

- A holiday to honor people in the (U.S.) military
- A holiday to honor people who have served (in the U.S. military)

CHAPTER 1.

TIMELINE OF AMERICAN HISTORY

Adventurers initially came for exploration, but then settlers came for religious or political freedom, to escape persecution, and for economic opportunities.

| 2008 | #58 |
| 2020 | #73 |

1000 — **Vikings land in North America**
Leif Ericson lands in Newfoundland.

1100 — **Anasazi Indians thrive in southwest North America**
Supported by agriculture, they build roads and massive cliff dwellings that will endure for 1000 years.

1492 — **Christopher Columbus "discovers" America**
He lands on San Salvador Island in the Bahamas, but thinks it is in the "East Indies" and calls the natives "Indians."

1497 — **English explorer John Cabot reaches North America**
The first European since the Vikings lands in North America at what is now Newfoundland, Canada.

1 5 0 0

1507 — **The new continent is named *America***
World maps now label the new continent "America" after the Italian explorer Amerigo Vespucci.

1513 — **The Spanish discover Florida**
The explorer Juan Ponce de Leon discovers Florida in search of treasure and the fabled Fountain of Youth.

1524 — **The Italians discover New York Harbor**
The Italian explorer Giovanni da Verrazano is the first European to see New York Harbor.

1565 — **Spain creates the first permanent settlement in America**
St. Augustine, Florida becomes the first permanent European settlement in North America.

1579 — **The English discover San Francisco Bay**
Sir Francis Drake supposedly lands at Drakes Bay, north of San Francisco, and claims the area for England.

1590 — **The English "Lost Colony" fails at Roanoke**
The settlement in North Carolina is found deserted with only the word "Croatoan" carved on a tree. The settlement had seen the birth of the New World's first English child, Virginia Dare.

I 6 0 0

1607 — **First permanent English settlement—Jamestown, Virginia**
Godspeed, Discovery, and *Susan Constant* bring 144 settlers to the James River. Captain John Smith helps 38 settlers survive the first winter and befriends Pocahontas. The winter of 1609 reduces the number of settlers from over 200 to only 60. They discover a new cash crop, tobacco, which saves the colony by giving it a lucrative crop to trade.

1619 — **Virginia hosts a colonial government**
The Jamestown House of Burgesses is the first representative meeting in America. It will move to Williamsburg in 1699. The first slaves in the new world are brought by Dutch traders, and a large number of single women arrive.

1620 — ***Mayflower* brings Pilgrims to Plymouth Rock**
Separatist Pilgrims fleeing religious persecution in England arrive at Plymouth, Massachusetts. The settlers sign the *Mayflower Compact* establishing local government and majority rule. Half the settlers die during the first year, but Indians help them plant crops, and together they celebrate the first Thanksgiving. Their descendants will include eight U.S. Presidents and millions of Americans.

1622 — ***Indian Massacre of 1622* in Virginia**
The Powhatan Indians launch surprise attacks on English settlers near Jamestown, killing 347 men, women, and children. This is one-quarter of the population of Jamestown.

1624 — **Dutch West India Company founds New Amsterdam**
They settle Manhattan and build a fortress wall at the future site of Wall Street. Two years later, they formally buy Manhattan from the Indians for $24 in goods, taking advantage of the Indians' general lack of the concept of "ownership."

1629 — **Religious differences reach the New World**
The 1629 grant of the Massachusetts Bay Colony charter leads to tens of thousands of new settlers in the Northeast. The 1600s will see many other religious settlements and events. Catholic colonists settle Maryland in 1632 and pass laws calling for freedom of religion. In 1636, Quakers under Roger Williams found Rhode Island based on religious freedom. William Penn will found Quaker Pennsylvania in 1682. His "Great Law" states that man cannot be deprived of life, liberty, or property, except by fair trial. The strict Puritan life leads to the Salem Witch Trials which put 19 people to death.

Roots of American democracy
New England town meetings are some of America's first democratic institutions. Every church member has a vote.

1636 — **Massachusetts founds Harvard**
The first institute of higher learning in America educates leaders and ministers. It is named for John Harvard who donates his library and half of his estate.

1645 — Minutemen selected from local militia
Towns in Massachusetts select portions of their militias to be "Minutemen" who will be ready to fight on a moment's notice. They will be crucial in skirmishes against the British in the next century.

1660 — Britain passes the Navigation Acts
Colonists must import and export goods only on ships built in Britain with crews that are at least 75% British.

1664 — New Amsterdam becomes New York City
British warships capture New Amsterdam without a fight and rename it New York in honor of the Duke of York.

1675 — *King Phillip's War* destroys New England settlements
The Indian chief known as King Phillip leads tribes in bloody battles against New England towns, leading to a huge loss of life and property. In proportion to the population, this will be the costliest war in the country's history. The settlers win only when they combine forces to form a united front. The war is caused by the Indian loss of life due to European disease, and their loss of property due to confiscation by settlers.

1676 — *Bacon's Rebellion* in Virginia
Nathaniel Bacon leads a thousand Virginians against Governor Berkeley, angry over his friendly treatment of Indians. The mob attacks and burns Jamestown.

1689 — *King William's War*
Indians, backed by the French, attack English settlements. The English capture Port Royal in Nova Scotia. The Treaty of Ryswick in 1697 ends the conflict and restores the borders that existed before the war.

Triangle Trade benefits everyone (except the slaves)
The Triangle Trade involves Britain, Africa, the Caribbean, and the American colonies. It will be a cornerstone of the economy for 100 years, with over half a million slaves brought from Africa. It generally consists of:

- **Britain**: supplies finished goods and a market for American products;

- **Africa**: provides slaves;

- **Caribbean Islands**: buy slaves, and provide sugar cane and molasses;

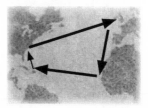

2008 #60
2020 #75

- **Colonies**: buy slaves, sugar, and molasses to make rum. Sell rum, tobacco, and other goods to England.

1693 — College of William and Mary founded
The second oldest college in America opens in Williamsburg, Virginia. It will educate Thomas Jefferson, James Monroe, and sixteen signers of the Declaration.

1 7 0 0

1701 — *Queen Anne's War*

The English capture St. Augustine, destroy Spanish towns, and wipe out the Apalachee Indians. French and Indian allies then massacre English settlers. The war ends with the Treaty of Utrecht which gives England control of Newfoundland, Acadia, and Hudson Bay.

Europe continues to fight its wars in America
The British and French use North America as a battleground for their conflicts, each side employing native Indians as needed. This leads to long-lasting resentment against the Indians from the English settlers.

1703 — First American *Mardi Gras* in Mobile, Alabama
New Orleans will start their celebration in a few decades.

1711 — Fighting in the Carolinas
The Tuscarora Indians attack after settlers take their land. Hundreds are killed on both sides. South Carolina provides military help, wiping out the entire tribe.

1718 — French found New Orleans
Jean-Baptiste Le Moyne de Bienville picks the site on important trade routes and calls it *Nouvelle-Orléans*.

1733 — Former convicts settle Georgia
James Oglethorpe imports former British prisoners, many who were in jail for non-payment of debts. He outlaws slavery, but slaves are eventually brought in to help with farming.

1737 — St. Patrick's Day makes its debut in Boston
The religious holiday honors the patron saint of Ireland.

1744 — *King George's War*
Another European war is fought in the Americas. The British capture the French fortress of Louisbourg in Nova Scotia. The war ends with the 1748 Treaty of Aix-la-Chapelle.

1754 — **"Join or Die" becomes a rallying cry**
Benjamin Franklin prints the first political cartoon in America which becomes an icon for the revolution.

French and Indian War
Friction between British forts in the Ohio Valley and French settlements leads to war. The British and colonials fight against the French and their Indian allies. George Washington commands a British Army that is defeated at Fort Necessity, losing half his troops. British General Braddock is repulsed at Fort Duquesne the next year, but the British gain control of the territory by taking Quebec in 1759. The Treaty of 1763 gives control of Canada back to the British along with everything east of the Mississippi. Spain cedes control of Florida to England.

Prelude to war
A century of continual conflicts in America sets the scene for the upcoming Revolution. Great Britain has doubled their national debt and needs help paying it, so King George keeps levying new taxes on the colonies. France has lost a large portion of their American holdings and wants revenge. With new land opening up in the West, the settlers turn more in that direction, away from England.

1763 — **Proclamation of 1763**
To placate the Indians and keep the settlers stuck on the coast, the British forbid settlement west of a boundary set by the King. This thwarts the colonial desire to move westward, and inflames their animosity towards the Indians.

1764 — **Sugar Act of 1764**
Along with the earlier Molasses Act of 1733, this act tries to raise revenue and assist British growers in the Caribbean by taxing sugar and molasses coming into the Colonies.

Currency Act
This British act restricts colonists from issuing their own currency and using it for payment of debts.

1765 — **Stamp Act**
Requires special stamps on all documents. This leads to the cry of "no taxation without representation."

Quartering Act of 1765
Forces colonists to house and feed British soldiers.

Sons of Liberty founded in Boston
The group is formed to oppose Britain, and quickly spreads to the other colonies.

1766 — **Declaratory Act**
Relenting to colonial protests, this repeals the Stamp Act, but reasserts the British right to tax the colonies.

1767 — **Townshend Acts**

These impose more taxes, punish non-compliance with the Quartering Act, and reinforce the right of Britain to tax and pass laws governing the colonies.

Mason-Dixon Line survey finished

Charles Mason and Jeremiah Dixon finish their survey of the border between Pennsylvania, Maryland, Delaware, and West Virginia. The line will separate the *North* from the *South*.

1769 — **First Mission built in San Diego, California**

Father Junipero Serra builds the first mission in what will become a chain of missions along California's El Camino Real.

1770 — **Boston Massacre—March 5**

Friction between British troops stationed in Boston and angry colonists leads to an altercation resulting in the death of 5 civilians. As a result, Britain repeals the Townshend Acts, **except for the tax on tea.** John Adams subsequently represents the British soldiers at their trial to ensure fairness, and gets them acquitted. The first man killed in the Revolution is the former slave, Crispus Attucks, shown in this picture. News of the massacre quickly spreads to all of the other colonies.

1773 — **Boston Tea Party—December 16**

With the tax on tea still in place, the colonies turn away tea-carrying ships at Philadelphia and New York, but not at Boston. Sam Adams and Paul Revere, along with colonists disguised as Indians, board ships in Boston Harbor and dump 342 chests of tea into the harbor, worth about $1 million today.

1774 — **Intolerable Acts**

In reaction to the destruction of tea, Britain passes a series of five laws that lead directly to the formation of the Continental Congress in America. These new laws:

- Close Boston Harbor until the destroyed tea is paid for.
- Allow Britain to appoint members of the Massachusetts Legislature.
- Allow Britain to move trials from America to other locations, including England.
- Enlarge the boundaries of Canada to include land previously belonging to the colonies.

1774 — **First Continental Congress meets in Philadelphia**
Formed to protect the rights of the colonies against an increasingly oppressive England, it issues a list of grievances 2008 #61
to the Crown, along with an ultimatum. The complaints include taxation without representation, onerous laws, quar- 2020 #77
tering of troops, and loss of the right to self govern. All the members risk being charged with treason and beheaded. Patrick Henry states, "I am not a Virginian, but an American."

(Now—let's see what happens when a government imposes too many taxes and laws on its people...)

1775 — *The Shot Heard 'Round the World* **- Lexington and Concord**
Britain orders the arrest of dissidents John Hancock and John Adams, and the confiscation of arms and ammunition. Paul Revere rides to alert the colonists of the danger. On April 19, fifty Minutemen meet 700 British soldiers at Lexington where eight colonials are killed. The British  proceed to Concord to seize arms, and are attacked again by 500 militiamen. More than 250 British soldiers are killed or wounded, compared to only 90 colonials. A number of black Minutemen participated. The British retreat to Boston where they are surrounded by over 15,000 colonial militiamen. They will remain there until forced out the next year. The war to win independence from Britain has started. 2020 #76

THE AMERICAN REVOLUTION HAS BEGUN

Fort Ticonderoga attacked—May 10
In the first victory for the colonies, the Green Mountain 2020 #80
Boys, under the command of Ethan Allen and Benedict Arnold, successfully attack this vital Lake Champlain fort.

Continental Army formed on June 14
The Continental Congress authorizes the army and appoints George Washington as Commander. The present-day U.S. Army honors this day as their birthday.

Battle of Bunker Hill, Boston—June 17
 General Gage leads 3,000 British troops 2020 #80
attacking colonials on Breed's Hill (it wasn't really Bunker Hill). The colonials are instructed *"Don't fire until you see the whites of their eyes"* and kill or wound almost half of the British force, one of their highest losses of the Revolution.

December failure at Quebec
Forces under General Montgomery and Colonel Benedict Arnold attack Quebec but are defeated with heavy losses, ending the colonial attempt to make Canada an ally.

1776

Thomas Paine writes *Common Sense*
This 50-page pamphlet lays out the case for separation from England. Paine feels strongly that the colonists have to fight for more than just a cessation of unfair taxes.

Colonel Knox helps end the siege at Boston
The British are still surrounded in Boston when Colonel Henry Knox hatches a plan to help end the siege. On his own initiative, he travels to Fort Ticonderoga and hauls back 60 cannon. Under cover of darkness, Washington secretly hauls them to the top of Dorchester Heights. The next morning, the British awake to see their position compromised, and shortly thereafter leave Boston.

#80 2020

The Declaration of Independence—July 4th
Thomas Jefferson finishes the document, but southern states remove his condemnation of slavery (5000 blacks would fight for the rebel cause during the war.) The founders sign the document at Independence Hall in Philadelphia—a treasonable act punishable by death. British troops have landed in New York, less than 100 miles away. There is no time for further debate or refinements—the formation of a new country is too important. America announces her separation from England...now she must fight to guarantee it.

British force Washington out of New York
General Howe moves his troops from Boston to New York and trap Washington's army on Long Island. Only a miracle allows Washington to successfully evacuate his entire force under cover of night and a fortuitous fog. He almost loses his army again on Manhattan, and again at Fort Washington where 3,000 colonial soldiers surrender.

Submarine *Turtle* attacks British warships
David Bushnell invents a small submarine that attempts to place explosives on the hulls of British warships in New York Harbor. None of the attacks are successful.

Washington retreats across the Delaware River
Washington's meager force of 19,000 is reduced to less than 4000, with enlistments due to expire for half of those men.

British hang Nathan Hale as a spy in New York City
His last words are, "I only regret that I have but one life to lose for my country."

1776
Washington rows across the Delaware
Early December 26, Washington rows his troops across the river to attack the Hessian troops in Trenton, catching them by complete surprise. He captures or kills 1,000 soldiers with only 6 American casualties. The victory is a huge morale booster for America.

2020 #80

1777
Victory at Princeton
Washington follows up his victory at Trenton with a successful surprise attack on the British at Princeton.

Another defeat for the British at Saratoga
British General Burgoyne retakes Fort Ticonderoga, but is forced out and defeated at the battle of Saratoga. However, Washington suffers defeats at Brandywine and Germantown, and retreats to Valley Forge, Pennsylvania for the winter. The British occupy Philadelphia in November.

2020 #80

Articles of Confederation adopted on November 15
Approved by the Second Continental Congress, they must be ratified by the states which will not happen until 1781. They will be used to guide the government until then.

Winter at Valley Forge
Washington and his troops spend a dismal winter in Pennsylvania, lacking proper food, clothing, and shelter. It is the low point of the Revolution with 2,500 of his 11,000 troops dying from exposure or disease.

2020 #80

1778
France joins the fight
Benjamin Franklin and the Marquis de Lafayette convince the French King to fight the British in America. French help will be instrumental in the final American victory.

1779
British capture Georgia and South Carolina
The "Swamp Fox" Francis Marion harasses enemy troops in South Carolina, eventually forcing the British northward to Virginia where Cornwallis will meet his final defeat.

John Paul Jones wins an American victory at sea

In command of the *Bonhomme Richard* fighting the British frigate *Serapis*, he issues his famous line, "I have not yet begun to fight" before defeating the enemy ship.

2020 #80

1780
Surrender of Charleston is worst American defeat of war
On May 12, Major General Lincoln surrenders his entire army of 10,000 to the British in loyalist-leaning South Carolina. Lincoln gets his revenge the next year when he accepts the British surrender at Yorktown.

1780 **Pivotal battle of Kings Mountain, South Carolina**
Following the humiliating defeat of the Americans by Lord Cornwallis at Camden, the rebels strike back. A band of patriot mountain men wipe out a loyalist army led by the British Major Ferguson. The colonial soldiers then head back into the mountains to their homes.

1781 **Battle of Cowpens a colonial success**
Daniel Morgan ambushes a superior British force under Lt. Col. Tarleton, killing or capturing almost all of his men. Tarleton is known as "The Butcher" after he killed colonial troops that had surrendered at the Battle of Waxhaws. He escapes capture.

LT. COL. TARLETON

Cornwallis surrenders at Yorktown

#80 **2020**

Cornwallis is trapped in Virginia with the York River and French fleet to his back, and the Colonial Army to his front. The British surrender on October 19 to the combined American and French forces as their band plays "The World Turned Upside Down."

1783 **Washington stops the Newburgh Conspiracy in New York**
At Newburgh, Continental Army officers demand back pay and benefits, and threaten to disband and leave the country without an army. Washington denounces their actions, but meets them and urges calm. Reading a letter outlining the country's financial problems, he finds he needs his glasses, and states his regret that he has grown old in the service of his country. His men, not even knowing he needs glasses, are deeply moved realizing the sacrifices Washington himself has made for his country. He finishes the letter and leaves, and his men unanimously agree to accept the government's terms. The nation is saved.

Revolution officially ends with the Treaty of Paris
After fighting continues for two more years, the English Parliament decides that it has had enough, and sues for peace. America finally wins her independence.

1784 **Articles of Confederation prove unworkable**
The articles were passed in 1777 and ratified in 1781, but there are still major deficiencies, including:
• No president, no navy or army, and no courts to interpret laws. States can make their own money.
• States have one vote each and most power is left to the states, under a mostly ineffective federal government.
• The government cannot levy taxes or regulate commerce.

1786 — **Shays' Rebellion tests the Confederation**
Daniel Shays leads an armed rebellion in Massachusetts, primarily fueled by debts and government taxes. The rebellion underscores the problems with the Confederation's lack of an effective central government, and helps bring attention to the need for a new constitution. Thomas Jefferson writes to a friend and says, "The tree of liberty must be refreshed from time to time with the blood of patriots and tyrants."

1787 — **Northwest Ordinance establishes the path to statehood**
Passed under the Articles of Confederation, this act establishes guidelines for new states and prohibits slavery in the Northwest territories. The procedures are:

- First, a territory is appointed a governor and judges.
- When the adult male population reaches 5,000, they can vote for their own legislature.
- When the population reaches 60,000, they can write their own constitution and apply for statehood.
- Slavery is outlawed in the territory and freedom of religion is guaranteed.

Constitutional Convention meets in Philadelphia
George Washington heads the convention convened to fix the problems of the Articles of Confederation. However, an entirely new form of government is proposed by Virginia's Edmund Randolph and James Madison. This leads to months of heated debate until the final Constitution is agreed on in September. Highlights of the final debate and agreement include:

- The Virginia plan relies on a strong central government and limited state sovereignty.
- The Great Compromise gives each state two Senators and a House representation proportional to state population.
- The new government contains an executive branch, judicial branch, and a bicameral legislative branch.
- A slavery compromise allows slavery importation until 1808, lets southern owners reclaim runaway slaves, and counts slaves as only 3/5 of a person to prevent southern states from acquiring too many seats in the House.
- The president will be elected by electors, not directly by the citizens.
- States are prohibited from issuing their own currency.
- A national bank and currency is approved.
- The civilian president is made Commander-in-Chief over the armed forces.
- Federal and state governments get the ability to tax.

1788 **Constitution finally ratified**

#67 2008
#83, 84 2020

The Constitution must be ratified by at least nine states to take effect. There are still concerns about granting a central government too much power. Alexander Hamilton, John Jay, and James Madison write *The Federalist Papers* to make the case for a strong central government and support the Constitution. Virginia agrees to ratify the Constitution only after being promised a Bill of Rights to protect individual and state rights. New Hampshire is the 9th state to ratify, and the Constitution takes effect on March 4, 1789.

★1789★ GEORGE WASHINGTON 1

CANDIDATE	PARTY	ELECTORAL VOTE	POPULAR VOTE
George Washington	*(no party)*	69	38,818
John Adams	*(no party)*	34	
Various	*(no party)*	35	

The Constitution gives each elector two votes. The candidate who receives the most votes becomes president; the runner-up becomes vice president. All 69 electors vote for Washington—he remains the only unanimous choice in our history. Adams receives the second largest number and becomes vice president. Washington takes the oath of office on April 30, 1789 in New York City.

1789 **"The Father of Our Country" sets the tone**

The government temporarily moves to New York City before a move to Philadelphia a year later. Washington sets the tone for the entire government since the Constitution does not specify every detail of government. He names Cabinet members, establishes a precedent for dealing with Congress, and sticks to his belief that a president should serve only two terms, a tradition upheld until 1940.

1790 **U.S. Coast Guard established as part of Treasury Department**

1791 **Bill of Rights added to Constitution**

The Constitution works by "enumerated powers" meaning it can exercise only those powers specifically granted to it by the Constitution. The Constitution is finally ratified only because the writers promise to add more protection for state and individual rights. These protections are added in the first 10 amendments to the Constitution, known as the Bill of Rights. These are penned by James Madison, modeled after Jefferson's Statute for Religious Freedom in Virginia, and are the cornerstone of what the Constitution guarantees every U.S. citizen.

1791

BILL OF RIGHTS

★ 1ˢᵗ AMENDMENT ★

Congress will not establish or prohibit any religion. Freedom of speech and press; right to assemble and petition the government.

★ 2ᴺᴰ AMENDMENT ★

Right to keep and bear arms.

★ 3ᴿᴰ AMENDMENT ★

Bars the government from housing soldiers in citizen homes.

★ 4ᵀᴴ AMENDMENT ★

Prohibits unreasonable searches and seizures. Establishes requirements for search warrants based on probable cause.

★ 5ᵀᴴ AMENDMENT ★

Establishes rules for grand jury indictment and eminent domain, establishes right to due process, prohibits double jeopardy and self-incrimination.

★ 6ᵀᴴ AMENDMENT ★

Establishes the right to a fair and speedy trial by jury, the right to be confronted by one's accuser and notified of the accusations, the right to obtain witnesses, and the right to legal counsel.

★ 7ᵀᴴ AMENDMENT ★

Establishes the right to a jury trial for certain civil cases.

★ 8ᵀᴴ AMENDMENT ★

Prohibits excessive fines and bail; prohibits cruel and unusual punishment.

★ 9ᵀᴴ AMENDMENT ★

Asserts rights of citizens to retain unenumerated rights.

★ 10ᵀᴴ AMENDMENT ★

Limits the powers of the federal government to those stipulated in the Constitution.

1792

New York Stock Exchange starts
The stock exchange informally starts under a tree on what is now Wall Street when 24 brokers sign the *Buttonwood Agreement*. The Exchange is formalized in 1825.

1792 ─ **U.S. Post Office Department is created**

★1792★ GEORGE WASHINGTON RE-ELECTED

CANDIDATE	PARTY	ELECTORAL VOTE	POPULAR VOTE
George Washington	Federalist	132	13,332
John Adams	Federalist	77	
George Clinton	Anti-federalist	50	

A record low turnout unanimously picks Washington, but attempts are made to make Clinton the vice president. Political parties are already involved in the elections.

1793 ─ **French Revolution**
King Louis XVI is executed and France declares war on Britain, Spain, and the Netherlands. The U.S. issues a Proclamation of Neutrality, being too weak to get involved.

Eli Whitney invents the cotton gin
The gin is a machine that quickly separates cotton fiber from the seeds. The South becomes dependent on cotton...and cotton is dependent on slavery.

1794 ─ **Britain seizes neutral shipping trading with France**
U.S. approves construction of more Navy ships, realizing a strong Navy is critical to their survival.

1795 ─

★ 11ᵀᴴ AMENDMENT ★
Grants states immunity from lawsuits from out-of-state citizens, or from foreigners not living inside the state.

★1796★ JOHN ADAMS 2

CANDIDATE	PARTY	ELECTORAL VOTE	POPULAR VOTE
John Adams	Federalist	71	35,726
Thomas Jefferson	Dem-Rep	68	31,115
Thomas Pinckney	Federalist	59	
Aaron Burr	Dem-Rep	30	

This is the first contested presidential election, and the only one to pick a vice president from an opposing party. Adams wins the vote for president, but his running mate, Pinckney, receives fewer votes than Jefferson, so Jefferson becomes the vice president, even though he is running for president.

1798

France attempts to extort money from the U.S.

The discovery of the *XYZ* affair leads to a mini-war with France at the height of their Revolution. X, Y, and Z are aliases for three French agents who try to extort money from the U.S. in return for continuing peace negotiations.

U.S. Marine Corps and U.S. Navy officially established

Alien and Sedition Acts

These unpopular acts give the government power over determining citizenship, and lead to the arrest of foreigners and even civil dissenters. They are strongly opposed, though the Alien Enemies Act stays in effect and is used to justify the internment of Japanese citizens in World War II.

1 8 0 0

1800

Government moves to Washington, D.C.

The new capital, designed by French architect Pierre L'Enfant, is finished and the government moves in. Originally named Federal City, it is created with no representation in Congress, but with 3 electors in the Electoral College. John Adams is first to occupy the White House (shown).

| 2008 | #94 |
| 2020 | #119 |

★1800★   THOMAS JEFFERSON   3

Candidate	Party	Electoral Vote	Popular Vote
Thomas Jefferson	Dem-Rep	73	41,330
Aaron Burr	Dem-Rep	73	
John Adams	Federalist	65	25,952
Charles Pinckney	Federalist	64	

The 1800 election is extremely contentious. Thomas Jefferson, with Aaron Burr as his vice president, runs against John Adams, with Charles Pinckney as his vice president. Electors vote for any two candidates, resulting in a tie between Jefferson and his own running mate Burr, each with 73 electoral votes. Adams finishes third with 65 votes. The Constitution stipulates that ties are decided by the House of Representatives, which must now decide between Jefferson and Burr. The Federalists control the lame-duck Congress and support Burr. Alexander Hamilton detests Burr and works to get Jefferson elected. The House deadlocks for 35 ballots until finally picking Jefferson. As stipulated, Burr becomes his vice president, and is ignored by Jefferson during his administration. Burr kills Hamilton in a duel, though he is not prosecuted. The main outcome of this discord is the passage of the 12th amendment which changes how electors elect the president.

1800 — **Congress establishes Library of Congress**
The British burn the library in 1814, after which Thomas Jefferson sells Congress his 6,000-book collection which becomes the core of the new library. Today, the library contains more than 140 million items, adding 10,000 new items a day.

1803 — ***Marbury v. Madison* establishes principle of "judicial review"**
Historic Supreme Court case is the first time a court has ever invalidated a law because it is unconstitutional.

Jefferson buys Louisiana Territory
France sells 828,800 square miles for $15 million to help pay off war debts, doubling the area of the U.S.

#71 | 2008
#90 | 2020

U.S. battles the Barbary Pirates in Tripoli
The USS *Philadelphia* is captured when she runs aground, and the captain and crew are taken hostage.

1804 — **Lewis and Clark Expedition heads West**
Meriwether Lewis and William Clark lead an expedition of 30 people from Illinois to chart a route to the Pacific. They will return, after a successful trip, in September of 1806.

U.S. Marines launch a daring raid in Tripoli
Lt. Decatur leads Marines in Tripoli harbor to burn the captured frigate USS *Philadelphia*.

Aaron Burr kills Alexander Hamilton in a duel

Vice President Aaron Burr mortally wounds Alexander Hamilton in a duel. Hamilton, who lost his son in a duel, purposely fires in the air. Burr, however, aims and shoots Hamilton in the stomach. He dies the next day.

★ **12ᵀᴴ Amendment** ★

Outlines the procedure to elect the president using the electoral college. Candidates will run for either president or vice president, and electors vote for each position separately.

★1804★ Thomas Jefferson re-elected

Candidate	Party	Electoral Vote	Popular Vote
Thomas Jefferson George Clinton	*Dem-Rep*	162	104,110
Charles Pinckney Rufus King	*Federalist*	14	38,919

The Twelfth Amendment establishes new rules for elections requiring electors to specify their choices for president and vice president. Jefferson selects Clinton to replace Burr as his vice president. Jefferson's popularity has improved with his Louisiana Purchase. His 45% popular vote victory margin will remain the highest in any contested election.

1806 ⊢ **Webster publishes first American dictionary**

Noah Webster publishes the first edition of what would later become the *American Dictionary of the English Language.* It standardizes spelling in America, changing many British spellings to shorter American versions, such as *program* instead of *programme,* and *flavor* instead of *flavour.* He also includes technical and scientific terms. He will spend the next 20 years improving the dictionary.

1807 ⊢ **Congress prohibits import of slaves**

Jefferson signs law at earliest date allowed by Article 1 of the Constitution. It takes effect on January 1, 1808.

Robert Fulton builds steamboat

The first commercial steamboat in America, the *Clermont,* makes a 150-mile trip in New York, averaging 5 miles-per-hour.

★1808★   JAMES MADISON   4

CANDIDATE	PARTY	ELECTORAL VOTE	POPULAR VOTE
James Madison George Clinton	Dem-Rep	122	124,732
Charles Pinckney Rufus King	Federalist	47	62,431
George Clinton James Monroe	Dem-Rep	6	4,848

George Clinton runs as Madison's running mate, but is also a candidate for president, receiving six electoral votes from electors dissatisfied with Madison. Clinton becomes vice president when Madison wins. It is one of only two times in our history when a sitting vice president continues to serve under a new president.

1809 ⊢ **Non-Intercourse Act of 1809**

This act, and the earlier Embargo Act of 1807, prohibits trade with France and Great Britain, but results in great harm to the U.S. economy.

1811 ⊢ **Chief Tecumseh organizes Indian rebellion**

The Indians continue to fight the relentless westward U.S. expansion. Future president William Henry Harrison defeats the Indians at Tippecanoe, Indiana.

1811 **New Madrid earthquakes**

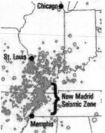

The first in a series of huge earthquakes hits the Mississippi River town of New Madrid. The quakes continue into 1812, causing damage across an enormous area. They remain the strongest earthquakes to ever hit the eastern U.S. The threat of another massive earthquake will continue into the 21ˢᵗ century. This map shows earthquake activity in the area from 1974 to 2010.

1812 **War of 1812 with Great Britain**

#72

#91

Britain has been interfering with American shipping for years. They also support the Spanish who claim a large part of the American Southwest. And, of course, Britain is at war again with France. The U.S. declares war even though she is not prepared, having only a 12,000 man army, and a Navy of 14 ships, compared to a British Navy of 1,000 ships.

USS *Constitution* defeats HMS *Guerriere*
Cannonballs bounce off her thick oak sides earning her the name *Old Ironsides*.

★1812★ James Madison re-elected

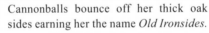

Candidate	Party	Electoral Vote	Popular Vote
James Madison Elbridge Gerry	Dem-Rep	128	140,431
DeWitt Clinton Jared Ingersoll	Federalist	89	132,781

The 1812 election takes place shortly after war is declared on Great Britain. DeWitt Clinton is the nephew of the former vice president who had died before the election. He actually changes his campaign in each region, trying to appear anti-war in the North, while pro-war in the South and West. The Federalists oppose the war, but Madison declares war in the summer before the election.

1813 ***Don't give up the ship!***

The HMS *Shannon* captures the USS *Chesapeake* whose captain, James Lawrence, lies mortally wounded. His last words are "Don't give up the up the ship!" Admiral Perry also issues memorable words as he defeats the British fleet on Lake Erie, sending the message "We have met the enemy and they are ours." This drawing depicts Perry transferring his command to the *Niagara*.

1814 — **The British burn Washington**
British troops capture Washington D.C. and set fire to the White House and Capitol. The arrival of a rare hurricane forces them to leave the Capitol and helps douse the fires.

Francis Scott Key writes *The Star Spangled Banner*
Imprisoned on a British ship watching the battle for Ft. McHenry in Baltimore, Key pens the words to our anthem. This is a picture of the actual flag that flew over the fort.

The Treaty of Ghent ends the war
The British sign the treaty in Belgium on December 24, 1814, ending all hostilities.

1815 — **Andrew Jackson wins the Battle of New Orleans**

His ragtag army soundly beats the British at the Battle of New Orleans. He has no idea that a peace treaty had been signed two weeks earlier. Jackson's outnumbered troops lose 13 fighters, but inflict 2,000 casualties on the British.

★1816★   JAMES MONROE   5

Candidate	Party	Electoral Vote	Popular Vote
James Monroe Daniel Tompkins	Dem-Rep	183	76,592
Rufus King John Howard	Federalist	34	34,740

Four Federalist candidates for vice president receive electoral votes, but Monroe easily wins the election. The Democratic-Republican party receives credit for a successful end to the War of 1812, while the Federalists have been opposing the war. Madison has also implemented economic steps that were favored by Federalists.

1817 — **First public gas street light in U.S. in Baltimore**

1819 — **Jefferson founds University of Virginia**
Thomas Jefferson designs and builds the famous university in sight of his classic home, *Monticello,* in Charlottesville, Virginia.

Florida, California, and Oregon territories added to country
Spain cedes Florida to the U.S., and a treaty with Russia gives us California and Oregon, but Russia keeps Alaska.

1820 — **Missouri Compromise—Maine and Missouri admitted**

Maine is admitted as a free state to balance the new slave state of Missouri, and slavery is prohibited in new territories north of 36°30', except for Missouri.

★1820★ James Monroe re-elected

Candidate	Party	Electoral Vote	Popular Vote
James Monroe Daniel Tompkins	Dem-Rep	228	108,359
John Q. Adams	Dem-Rep	1	

Monroe is the only candidate to essentially run unopposed, other than George Washington. There are issues around the Panic of 1819 and the recently passed Missouri Compromise, but Monroe easily wins. Only a vote for John Quincy Adams from a New Hampshire elector prevents the election from being unanimous. Missouri's vote is contested with opponents saying she is not officially a state yet. Monroe would have 231 electoral votes if Missouri is counted.

Whaleship *Essex* sunk by a whale

The Nantucket whaler is in the Pacific Ocean harpooning whales, when a large whale appears and rams the ship. The whale then retreats several hundred yards away, turns around, and then speeds directly toward the  ship. She rams the bow, causing the ship to almost immediately sink. The crew board their three small whaleboats, but most die before being rescued. This incident later inspires Herman Melville to write *Moby Dick*.

1823 — **Monroe Doctrine protects the western hemisphere**

Monroe's policy states that the U.S. will not interfere with Europe, European colonies, or in European wars. In return, the U.S. makes it clear that it will not tolerate any interference in the western hemisphere by any European power.

★1824★   JOHN Q. ADAMS   6

CANDIDATE	PARTY	ELECTORAL VOTE	POPULAR VOTE
John Q. Adams John Calhoun	Dem-Rep	84	113,122
Andrew Jackson John Calhoun	Dem-Rep	99	151,271
William Crawford Nathaniel Macon	Dem-Rep	41	40,856
Henry Clay Nathan Sanford	Dem-Rep	37	47,531

The Federalist party has collapsed, and the Democratic-Republican party runs four candidates. It will soon split into the Democratic, Republican, and Whig parties. Adams is the son of the 2nd President, and Jackson is the hero of the Battle of New Orleans. No candidate receives a majority votes, so the House of Representatives has to decide the election. Only the top 3 candidates are considered, which is interesting since the 4th candidate is Henry Clay, the Speaker of the House, who detests Jackson. Adams is picked, even though Jackson has more electoral and popular votes. Calhoun becomes vice president after easily getting the most votes for vice president.

1825 ┼ **Erie Canal opens in New York**
This ushers in the building of hundreds of canals to facilitate transportation and commerce. Hundreds of workers die, mainly of disease, building the 363-mile canal. Travel time from Buffalo to Albany is shortened from 3 weeks to 1 week.

1826 ┼ **Thomas Jefferson and John Adams die on July 4**
These two signers of the Declaration and ex-presidents both die on July 4, 1826—50 years to the day after signing the Declaration. John Adams' last words are "Thomas Jefferson still survives." He doesn't know Jefferson has died hours before.

★1828★   ANDREW JACKSON   7

CANDIDATE	PARTY	ELECTORAL VOTE	POPULAR VOTE
Andrew Jackson John Calhoun	Democratic	178	642,553
John Q. Adams Richard Rush	Natl. Republican	83	500,897

Jackson uses broad public support and backing of Vice President Calhoun, to win an easy electoral victory. The campaign is marked by a number of personal attacks, including one concerning Jackson's wife. Jackson, meanwhile, accuses Adams and Clay of a corrupt bargain in the previous election that gave Adams the victory. Jackson's wife dies weeks after the election, leading to Jackson blaming Adams for her death.

1830 Indian Removal Act
The government moves eastern Indian tribes to western lands, usually against their wishes. The government often makes treaties with one small part of a tribe, and then applies that to the entire tribe.

Railroads open up the country
The Baltimore and Ohio is the first public U.S. railroad.

1831 Slave rebellion in Virginia
Nat Turner leads a violent slave rebellion in Virginia but is caught and hung. Virginia passes tougher slavery laws in response. William Lloyd Garrison publishes *The Liberator* which pushes for an end to slavery.

★1832★ ANDREW JACKSON RE-ELECTED

CANDIDATE	PARTY	ELECTORAL VOTE	POPULAR VOTE
Andrew Jackson Martin van Buren	Democratic	219	701,780
Henry Clay John Sergeant	Natl. Republican	49	484,205
John Floyd Henry Lee	Nullifier	11	picked by legislature
William Wirt Amos Ellmaker	Anti-Masonic	7	100,715

The process of nominating candidates for each party changes to using national party conventions. The Anti-Masonic Party holds the first national nominating convention in our history. His opponents portray Jackson as a tyrant trampling the Constitution, but he easily wins another term.

1834 Cyrus McCormick invents the grain reaper

The mechanical grain reaper revolutionizes agriculture. There is a competing design from Obed Hussey, and McCormick incorporates some of Hussey's innovations in 1850 to produce a truly effective machine.

1835 Indian *Trail of Tears*
The government forcibly relocates tens of thousands of Native Americans to the Indian Territory (Oklahoma). Thousands die on the march. The Choctaw had been moved in 1831, the Cherokee will be moved in 1838, and most tribes are relocated by 1855.

1836 **Texas Revolution and the Alamo**

Mexico gained her independence from Spain in 1821, but American settlers had poured into Texas and now outnumber the Mexicans 10 to 1. Texas finally declares independence from Mexico. In response, Mexican President Santa Anna and 2,400 troops march north and surround 189 Texans at the Alamo. After a week-long battle, they capture the fort and kill every defender, including Davy Crockett and Jim Bowie. The Mexicans suffer more than 600 casualties. Three weeks later, Colonel Fannin surrenders his 300-man force of Texans to Mexican General Urrea at Goliad, Texas. Under orders from Santa Anna, Urrea executes all the Texans and burns their bodies, though some escape to tell the story.

On April 21, Sam Houston defeats the Mexican Army at the Battle of San Jacinto in a fight that lasts only 15 minutes, amidst shouts of "Remember the Alamo!" and "Remember Goliad!" The fight kills 630 Mexicans and the rest are taken prisoner. The captured Santa Anna grants Texas its independence in exchange for his life. Texas wants to become a state but, since that will upset the balance of free and slave states, statehood is put off until 1845.

Colt revolver patented
Samuel Colt's new revolver mechanism makes his handgun an instant legend.

1836

MARTIN VAN BUREN   8

CANDIDATE	PARTY	ELECTORAL VOTE	POPULAR VOTE
Martin Van Buren Richard Johnson	Democratic	170	764,176
William H. Harrison Francis Granger	Whig	73	550,816
Hugh White John Tyler	Whig	26	146,107

This is the last election until 1988 that results in an incumbent vice president becoming president. The Whigs run several candidates in different areas of the country hoping to force a stalemated election that the House of Representatives will then decide. This ploy is unsuccessful and the Democrat Van Buren wins. The vice presidential race is decided by the Senate for the only time in history when Richard Johnson initially comes up one vote short. Two other Whig candidates, Daniel Webster and Willie Mangum, also receive electoral votes, .

1838 **Mormons driven from Missouri**
Governor Boggs issues an executive order to use military force to drive the Mormons from Missouri.

★1840★   WILLIAM HENRY HARRISON   9

CANDIDATE	PARTY	ELECTORAL VOTE	POPULAR VOTE
William Henry Harrison John Tyler	Whig	234	1,275,390
Martin Van Buren Richard Johnson	Democratic	60	1,128,854

The Panic of 1837 hurt Van Buren's popularity. The Whig Party unifies behind the war hero Harrison, and campaign with the popular slogan, "Tippecanoe and Tyler, too" referring to Harrison's victory at the Battle of Tippecanoe in 1811. James Polk receives one electoral vote resulting in an election with four former or future presidents receiving votes—Polk, Harrison, Tyler, and Van Buren. The Whigs make two big mistakes: their presidential pick, Harrison, is too old and will soon die; and their vice-presidential pick, Tyler, does not agree with their platform, which will soon be a problem when he becomes president.

★1841★   JOHN TYLER   10

President Harrison delivers an almost two-hour inaugural address in freezing rain and snow, and dies one month later from pneumonia, resulting in Vice President Tyler becoming president. He is the first vice president to become president this way. However, the path of succession is not clear, and many in Congress treat Tyler as only a temporary president. The exact succession procedure will not be codified until the 25th amendment, but Tyler sets the example used until then. However, Tyler's policies align more with the Democratic-Republican Party than the Whigs. Most of his cabinet resigns. Days before leaving office in 1845, he succeeds in formalizing the annexation of Texas.

First emigrant train to California
John Bidwell leads a wagon train on a 5-month trip to California, unleashing a continual flood of pioneers westward. Their large *Conestoga* wagons were also called *Prairie schooners*.

1844 **Samuel Morse starts telegraph service**
The line opens between Baltimore and the Washington, D.C. Samuel Morse sends the words, "What hath God wrought" from the Supreme Court chamber in the U.S. Capitol building.

1844 **Angry mob kills Mormon leader Joseph Smith**
Besides being a religious leader,
Smith is a mayor and presidential
candidate. He is in a Carthage, Illinois jail on charges of destroying the facilities of a newspaper
that had exposed his polygamist

views. An angry mob storms the jail (shown above), shoot-
ing and killing Joseph and his brother, Hyrum.

★1844★ JAMES POLK 11

CANDIDATE	PARTY	ELECTORAL VOTE	POPULAR VOTE
James Polk
George Dallas	Democratic	170	1,339,494
Henry Clay
Theodore Frelinghuysen	Whig	105	1,300,004

Tyler had been kicked out of the Whig Party and finally
decides not to run. Clay opposes the annexation of Texas,
while Polk supports it and more territorial expansion, including Oregon. The popular vote is very close, and this election
sees perhaps the first role of a third party as a "spoiler." The
anti-slavery Liberty Party receives more than enough votes
in New York to keep Clay from winning that state, which he
loses by only 5,100 votes. If Clay had New York's 36 electoral votes instead of Polk, he would have won the election.

1845 **U.S. annexes Texas**
This happens six days before Polk takes office, giving Tyler
a significant accomplishment for his time in office.

U.S. Naval Academy opens in Annapolis, Maryland.

1846 **Baseball starts**
The first official baseball game is held with the New York
Nine defeating the New York Knickerbockers, 23-1.

Oregon Territory is acquired from England
The U.S. now spreads from sea to sea, achieving its Manifest Destiny. Oregon will become a state in 1859.

Mormons move to Salt Lake City, Utah
Forced westward mainly by
anger against their practice
of polygamy, Brigham Young
leads his followers to Salt
Lake City. Their solitude is
permanently broken two years

later when gold is discovered
in California. By 1861, they will have constructed 300 irri-
gation canals and made thousands of miles of desert bloom.

1846 ┤ **Donner Party meets disaster**

A party of 87 settlers, led by George Donner, leaves Wyoming for California using a new route called the "Hastings Cutoff." The route is a disaster and they arrive in the Sierra Nevadas perilously  late in the year. They are one day too late and are turned back by snowstorms. Stuck for the winter, half the party dies. Some even resort to cannibalism to stay alive.

Texas annexation touches off the Mexican-American War

#72 2008
#91 2020

The annexation of Texas touches of a 2-year war with Mexico. The U.S. invades the area of New Mexico, California and parts of northern Mexico. The U.S. Marines capture Mexico City in 1847 to end the war and add the phrase "the halls of Montezuma" to the Marines' Hymn. The Treaty of Guadalupe Hidalgo in 1848 gives the territory of California, Nevada, Utah, New Mexico, and Arizona to the U.S., and sets the Rio Grande as the new border. In return, Mexico receives $15 million in payment. Many Americans worry that the treaty will add more slave states to the union.

1848 ┤ **California Gold Rush**

James Marshall discovers gold at Sutter's Mill in California, forever changing the state and the country. Thousands of miners cross the country or sail around Cape Horn to find their fortune. Few make money, but grocers and shop owners prosper. The California population booms to almost 400,000 by the start of the Civil War.

Seneca Falls Convention in New York

A major meeting of supporters of women's rights, this is the first shot in the battle for women's suffrage that will end with the passage of the 19th amendment in 1919. The convention produces a *Declaration of Sentiments*, that declares, "We hold these truths to be self-evident: that all men and women are created equal…"

★1848★   ZACHARY TAYLOR   12

CANDIDATE	PARTY	ELECTORAL VOTE	POPULAR VOTE
Zachary Taylor Millard Fillmore	Whig	163	1,361,393
Lewis Cass William Butler	Democratic	127	1,223,460
Martin Van Buren Charles Adams	Free Soil	0	291,501

Polk accomplished many of his goals, but is in bad health and decides not to run for re-election. He dies four months after leaving office. Polk had ended the Mexican-American War, and the Whigs pick a popular hero from that war, Zachary Taylor. This election is the first presidential election held on the same day in every state. Taylor wins with less than 50% of the popular vote due to the showing of the Free Soil Party.

1850— Underground Railroad

The escaped slave Harriet Tubman uses the Underground Railroad to help escaped slaves. This network of people and safe houses was started by the Quakers in the 1790s, and will save 60,000 slaves during its lifetime.

★1850★   MILLARD FILLMORE   13

President Taylor dies from an illness less than halfway through his term and Vice President Fillmore takes over. He will be the last Whig to hold the high office.

Compromise of 1850

California is admitted as a free state; Utah and New Mexico's slave status will be decided by their voters; and the slave trade is outlawed in Washington, D.C. The compromise also contains the Fugitive Slave Act which requires all runaway slaves be arrested and returned to their masters.

1851— *America's Cup* competition starts

The U.S. sailboat *America* wins a yacht race in England, starting an international competition for the trophy now known as the *America's Cup*.

1852 **Uncle Tom's Cabin is published**
Harriet Beecher Stowe writes the famous anti-slavery book
that helps ignite anti-slavery sentiment.

1852 FRANKLIN PIERCE 14

CANDIDATE	PARTY	ELECTORAL VOTE	POPULAR VOTE
Franklin Pierce William King	Democratic	254	1,607,510
Winfield Scott William Graham	Whig	42	1,386,942

The Whigs nominates Mexican-American War hero General
Scott instead of the incumbent Fillmore. The Democrats have
a unknown candidate in Pierce, whose obscurity the Whigs try
to use in their campaigning. Other parties also run candidates,
including the Free Soil, Union, and Southern Rights parties.

1854 **Gadsden Treaty**
A treaty with Mexico gives U.S. territory in Arizona and
New Mexico in return for $10 million. The U.S. hopes to
build a railroad through the territory. It is the last major
acquisition of land by the U.S.

Kansas-Nebraska Act
The government creates the territories of Kansas and Nebraska, allows those territories to determine their own slavery laws, and repeals the Missouri Compromise.

Republican Party founded as an anti-slavery party
The new party opposes slavery and believes in the modern-
ization of the America, free land for farmers, modern banking, and industry. They believe that free labor is superior to
slave labor. John Fremont is their first candidate in 1856.

1856 JAMES BUCHANAN 15

CANDIDATE	PARTY	ELECTORAL VOTE	POPULAR VOTE
James Buchanan John Breckinridge	Democratic	174	1,836,072
John Fremont William Dayton	Republican	114	1,342,345
Millard Fillmore Andrew Donelson	Know-Nothing	8	873,053

The incumbent Pierce loses the nomination to Buchanan,
the UK Ambassador. The new Republican party selects California Senator and Governor John Fremont. He campaigns
against the Kansas-Nebraska Act and expansion of slavery,
while Buchanan warns that Fremont's actions will lead to
civil war. The *Know-Nothing Party* ignores slavery and runs
on an anti-immigration platform. Fremont receives almost no
votes from any slave state.

1857 **Supreme Court *Dred Scott* decision**

The slave Dred Scott has lived with his owner in free states and believes himself free. The Supreme Court rules that slaves and their descendents are not protected by the Constitution and thus cannot be citizens. It also rules that Congress cannot prohibit slavery in territories, and that slaves cannot be taken away from their legal owners. The decision comes to be known as one of the worst Supreme Court decisions in history.

First passenger elevator
Elisha Otis installs the world's first passenger elevator in a 5-story building in New York City. (The original elevator is still in working condition in the building.)

1859 **Silver Comstock Lode in Nevada**
A huge silver discovery is made under Virginia City, Nevada, sparking another mad rush similar to the Gold Rush of the decade before. Huge fortunes are made and much of the wealth flows to San Francisco. The mines last into the 1870s.

John Brown's Revolt at Harper's Ferry

The white, radical abolitionist John Brown and his followers seize a federal armory at Harper's Ferry, Virginia, intending to arm slaves and start an insurrection. He is captured, tried for treason by Virginia, and executed. His abolitionist activities, capture, and subsequent execution are important events leading to the Civil War, and he is a hero to many in the North. An abolitionist song about Brown, *John Brown's Body*, is the basis for the stirring song *The Battle Hymn of the Republic,* written by Julia Ward Howe.

1860 **Pony Express**

William Russell starts a service to deliver mail from Missouri to Sacramento in 10 days, using 500 horses ridden by 80 riders, 40 in each direction. The service goes bankrupt in two years due to the invention of the telegraph.

★1860★   Abraham Lincoln   16

CANDIDATE	PARTY	ELECTORAL VOTE	POPULAR VOTE
Abraham Lincoln Hannibal Hamlin	Republican	180	1,865,908
Stephen Douglas Herschel Johnson	Democratic	12	1,380,201
John Breckinridge Joseph Lane	Southern Democratic	72	848,019
John Bell Edward Everett	Constitutional Union	39	590,901

The 1860 election is dominated by the impending civil war. The issues of slavery and states' rights divide the Democratic Party into a Northern and Southern faction. Douglas is the first presidential candidate to campaign in person throughout the country. Remnants of the Whig and Know-Nothing parties form the Constitutional Union Party. The country is split right down regional lines—Lincoln does not receive a single electoral vote from a southern state. He is not even on the ballot in ten southern states. Within a month of his election, southern states start seceding from the Union.

South Carolina secedes from the Union on December 20
Lincoln receives no electoral votes from any Southern state, and South Carolina wastes no time in leaving the nation.

1861 **The Civil War engulfs the nation**

#72, 73 2008

#91 2020

The war pits the North, a commercial and industrial region that has outlawed slavery and relies on immigrants, against the South, which relies on farming, cotton, and slaves. However, the South has many great military leaders, including their new top general, the Virginian Robert E.

#74 2008

#92 2020

Lee. Foreign countries rely on Northern exports and markets, but use the South mainly as a source of cotton. The South also views the slavery issue as a state's right issue.

Photography documents the Civil War
It is the first war to be documented by the new technology of photography, used by photographers like Mathew Brady.

Telegraph connects the coasts
A transcontinental telegraph wire is connected allowing telegrams to be sent from coast to coast. The Western Union Telegraph Company runs one line eastward from Carson City, and another line westward from Omaha, Nebraska. Stringing three to eight miles of wire a day, the lines meet in Salt Lake City.

1861

The fighting begins at Fort Sumter

The rest of the South secedes: Mississippi, Florida, Alabama, Arkansas, Louisiana, Georgia, Texas, Virginia, North Carolina, and Tennessee—most before Lincoln's inauguration. They form the the Confederate States of America (CSA) with Jefferson Davis as president, and Richmond, Virginia their capital. Eleven Southern states with a population of 9 million (including 3 million slaves) confront 23 Northern states with a population of 22 million. The Union troops wear blue uniforms, while the South wears gray. The American Civil War (War Between the States) starts with the Confederate attack on Fort Sumter, South Carolina on April 12, 1861. Major Anderson surrenders the fort after 4,000 rounds have been fired...but no one is killed.

`2020` #93

First Battle of Bull Run (First Battle of Manassas)

The first major engagement takes place near Washington. "Stonewall" Jackson leads the rebels to defeat the overconfident Northern troops. Sightseers from Washington, anticipating an easy northern victory, clog the roads while fleeing back to Washington.

1862

Ironclads *Monitor* and *Virginia*

The South's new ironclad *Virginia* (built from the burned hull of the USS *Merrimack*) destroys Union ships in Chesapeake Bay with impunity, killing 240 sailors. The just-finished Northern ironclad, *Monitor*, steams into battle the next day and fights the *Virginia* to a stalemate. The era of ironclad ships has arrived.

`2020` #93

Battle of Shiloh, Tennessee

A Union army under Ulysses Grant meets the Confederates in Tennessee in a bloody battle that kills 3,600 soldiers.

`2020` #93

Homestead Act of 1862

The government encourages settlement of the West by offering 160 acres of public land in return for living on the land for 5 years and improving it.

Indian attacks continue

The Santee Sioux kill hundreds of Minnesota settlers but surrender the next year. Thirty-eight Indians are convicted and hung by the government. The Indian attacks in the West continue throughout the Civil War.

1862

#93 2020
Battle of Antietam, Maryland
The first major clash on Northern soil results in the bloodiest one-day battle in American history with 23,000 casualties.

First *Medal of Honor* presented
America's first *Medal of Honor* is given to Private Jacob Parrott for his bravery in commandeering the Confederate railroad engine *General* in Georgia.

1863

#95 2020
Emancipation Proclamation takes effect on January 1
Lincoln frees all slaves in the outlaw confederate states and areas still in rebellion. It does not address slavery anywhere else...this has to wait until the 13th amendment is passed.

New York City Draft Riots
A week of violent rioting breaks out in New York City in what will be the worst civil insurrection in our history. Anywhere from 120 to 2,000 people are killed, and 11 blacks are lynched. President Lincoln has just issued the Emancipation Proclamation, and many worry about the loss of jobs due to freed slaves fleeing northward. The government issues a new draft law, making all males between 20 and 35, and unmarried men between 35 and 45, subject to military conscription. The men are entered into a national lottery, but can pay the government $300 to be exempt, or can hire a substitute. Blacks are exempt from the lottery, since they are not considered citizens. The rioters are initially angry at the unfair draft law which targets the poorer working class, but the riots soon turn racial, and many blacks are killed. Lincoln sends in federal troops to restore order.

Battle of Gettysburg

#93 2020

General Robert E. Lee meets the Union troops in July at a sleepy town in Pennsylvania in what is to be the high-water mark for the Confederacy in the war. The bloody 3-day battle results in casualties of 25,000 on each side. On the last day of battle on July 3, General Pickett leads a suicidal charge up Cemetery Ridge resulting in thousands of casualties. General Lee retreats to Virginia, and only the lack of pursuit by the Northern General George Meade keeps Lee's army from being completely destroyed.

1863 — **Mississippi River controlled by North**
Grant defeats the rebels at Vicksburg, giving the North control of the river, and splitting the South in two.

Gettysburg Address
President Lincoln delivers one of the most memorable speeches in our history at the dedication of the Gettysburg cemetery. His two-minute speech follows Edward Everett's two-hour talk which truly will be little noted nor long remembered.

2020 #93

1864 — **Lincoln appoints U.S. Grant leader of the Northern Army**
Grant proceeds to use brute force to wear down and defeat the South. The Battle of the Wilderness results in 18,000 Union casualties, and the Spotsylvania Courthouse Battle kills or wounds another 18,000 troops.

CSS *Hunley* sinks the USS *Housatonic*
The Confederate submarine *Hunley* attacks and sinks the Union ship in Charleston harbor, but is lost with her crew of eight and never  found again until 1995. This is the first time in history a submarine sinks a enemy ship.

First burial in Arlington Cemetery
Considering General Lee a traitor, the Union converts his estate outside the capital to a military cemetery. (Today, it holds 300,000 graves, including one for President John Kennedy, and the Tomb of the Unknown Soldier.)

Battle of Mobile Bay
 Admiral Farragut leads Union ships against the Confederate fort at Mobile Bay, Alabama. The water is heavily mined (mines were then called torpedoes) and one of his ships strikes a mine, sinking with heavy loss of life. The attack falters, but Farragut seizes the initiative and commands, "Damn the torpedoes! Full speed ahead!" The Union ships proceed to win the battle.

Sherman's "March to the Sea"
The Union General William T. Sherman marches through Georgia all the way to the ocean, destroying everything in his path and burning Atlanta. His memory will forever be reviled by true Southerners.

2020 #93

★1864★ Abraham Lincoln re-elected

Candidate	Party	Electoral Vote	Popular Vote
Abraham Lincoln Andrew Johnson	National Union	212	2,218,388
George McClellan George Pendleton	Democratic	21	1,812,807

The Republican party is divided over slavery, and War Democrats join with some Republicans to form the National Union Party which nominates Lincoln. The Democrats are also divided, and run General McClellan as a "peace candidate" pushing for a negotiated peace. The Republicans run John Fremont until he withdraws, fearing that his entry will help McClellan. Confederate victories make the election outcome uncertain, but the victory in Atlanta in September turns sentiment towards Lincoln and final victory against the South. Lincoln wins the election with strong support from the military, who are allowed to vote from the field for the first time. His slogan is "Don't change horses in the middle of a stream."

1865 — The Civil War ends at Appomattox Courthouse, April 9

#93 2020

#96 2020

General Grant finally captures the Confederate capital of Richmond. General Lee surrenders the Army of Northern Virginia at Appomattox Courthouse, Virginia. Grant chooses not to humiliate the losers since they are now his countrymen again. He allows Lee's men to keep their horses and sidearms, and return home freely. The bloody struggle ends. More than 500,000 lives have been lost. Southern states will have to accept the 13th amendment ending slavery as a condition to being re-admitted to the Union. By the end of the war, more than ten percent of the Union soldiers are black.

President Lincoln assassinated

#93 2020

On April 14, John Wilkes Booth, an actor and southern sympathizer, shoots Lincoln in the head at Ford Theater. The shooting is part of simultaneous plans to kill the Vice President and Secretary of State. President Lincoln dies, and Secretary Seward is seriously injured. Booth escapes to Virginia after being treated by Dr. Samuel Mudd for a broken leg. He is surrounded a few days later by troops and killed. Lincoln's loss is a severe blow to the reconstruction of the South, and has enormous, negative long-term consequences. Dr. Mudd is imprisoned for four years for his actions.

1865 ANDREW JOHNSON 17

After Lincoln's assassination, Vice President Johnson becomes president. He will preside over Reconstruction for the next four years. He had been a Southern Senator before the war and his pro-South policies will anger Republicans.

Steamboat *Sultana* blows up

The steamboat returning Union veterans from the South blows up on the Mississippi River in the worst U.S. maritime disaster, killing 1,700.

★ 13ᵀᴴ AMENDMENT ★

Abolishes slavery and involuntary servitude except as punishment for a criminal conviction.

1866

Transatlantic cable is completed

Cyrus W. Field, after a number of failed attempts, finally lays a 2000-mile transatlantic cable  using the world's largest steamship, the *Great Eastern*. Europe and America are finally connected by telegraph.

Reconstruction of the South begins

President Johnson is sympathetic to the South. His rush to welcome southern states back into the Union, and his vetoes of civil rights bills (he vetoes the *Civil Rights Act of 1866*), make him unpopular. The reconstruction of the South is extremely difficult since the former slaves were the backbone of the economy.

1867

Seward's Folly—the purchase of Alaska

Secretary of State Seward (who narrowly escaped assassination when Lincoln was shot) purchases Alaska from the Russians for only $7.2 million. He is publicly ridiculed for the purchase. Pictured is the original check given to the Russians for the purchase.

1868

Impeachment of President Andrew Johnson

Johnson is unpopular even before he replaces some cabinet members illegally, thus violating the Tenure of Office Act. He is impeached, becoming the first sitting U.S. President to be impeached. He is acquitted by a margin of one vote.

Confederates are pardoned

President Johnson grants an unconditional pardon to former Confederate soldiers.

1868

> ### ★ 14ᵀᴴ AMENDMENT ★
> Ensures that all ex-slaves have full citizenship rights and deals with other post-Civil War issues.

★1868★   ULYSSES S. GRANT   18

CANDIDATE	PARTY	ELECTORAL VOTE	POPULAR VOTE
Ulysses S. Grant Schuyler Colfax	Republican	214	3,013,650
Horatio Seymour Francis Blair, Jr.	Democratic	80	2,708,744

Three former Confederate states are unable to vote in this election as they are not yet restored to the Union. Johnson's impeachment prevents the Democrats from nominating him. They pick Horatio Seymour instead. The Republican Party regroups, knowing they need a strong figure to defeat the Democrats who are also strong in the North. The Republicans back radical reconstruction for the South and pick the popular General Grant. The popular vote is close, but Grant easily wins the electoral vote.

1869

Transcontinental Railroad completed on May 10, 1869

They started building the railroad in 1863 during the war. The Central Pacific Railroad pushed from California eastward to Utah, run by a group of men known as "The Big Four"; Collis Huntington, Mark Hopkins, Charles Crocker, and Leland Stanford. These men have made their fortunes in the West and bankrolled the railroad to further their fortunes. The Union Pacific Railroad pushed westward from Omaha. The tracks meet at Promontory Summit, Utah. The country is finally connected, coast to coast. The trip from Omaha to Sacramento now takes only 12 days.

Grand Canyon explored

John Wesley Powell makes a wild trip down the Colorado River with four boats. After three months and 1,000 miles, he reaches open country, finishing the first known trip through the Grand Canyon. Powell had lost his right arm during the Civil War.

1870

> ### ★ 15ᵀᴴ AMENDMENT ★
> Protects the voting right of ex-slaves.

1870— **Southern states are slow to change**

The South uses a legal loophole to require literacy tests to vote, essentially prohibiting former slaves from voting. States that balk at approving the 14th amendment are threatened with military occupation, causing many to question whether the amendment is fairly passed. The Ku Klux Klan emerges to terrorize former slaves.

First black U.S. Senator

Hiram R. Revels, a Mississippi Republican, is elected U.S. Senator by the state legislature, which is the normal election procedure at this time, to fill a vacant seat. Southern Democrats oppose his election, arguing that no black man was a citizen before the 1868 passage of the 14th Amendment, and the Constitution requires nine years of citizenship to qualify for the Senate. His supporters claim that the *Dred Scott* decision applied only to blacks of pure African blood, and Revels is of mixed black and white ancestry, so he has always been a citizen. He wins his case and becomes the first black United States Senator on February 25.

The *Wild West* is settled

With the war over, thousands of ex-soldiers head west to become cowboys, ranchers, and drifters. This movement is facilitated by the new transcontinental railroad and homestead acts that encourage new settlements. New inventions like the steel plow, windmill (for pumping water), and barbed wire (to fence livestock) open vast areas for farming and ranching. The huge herds of 50 million buffalo will soon vanish.

The rise of the robber barons

The late 1800s give rise to the so-called "robber barons" of industry who take advantage of new technologies, inventions, and discoveries to amass vast fortunes. They often use monopolistic practices to corner markets and drive out competition. This leads to the passage of anti-trust laws, and the rise of unions across the country to protect workers.

- John D. Rockefeller starts the Standard Oil Company in 1870 after oil is discovered in 1859.
- Jay Gould tries to corner the gold market with the help of President Grant, but instead causes the Panic of 1869.
- J.P. Morgan owns half of the country's railroads by 1900.
- James Duke corners the tobacco market.

The robber barons give back

Andrew Carnegie makes a fortune in steel but starts the trend of helping society with his money, giving away more than $350 million and founding thousands of public libraries. The Rockefellers create Rockefeller Center in New York City. Leland Stanford founds Stanford University. James Duke helps found Duke University. Henry Frick funds the Frick Museum in New York City.

1871 **Georgia is the last state readmitted to the Union**
Georgia becomes the last state to ratify the Fifteenth Amendment in 1870. The following year, she is readmitted to the Union.

Great Chicago Fire
Mrs. O'Leary's cow starts a fire in her barn that quickly spreads and destroys $200 million of property and kills 300 people in Chicago.

Peshtigo Fire kills 1,000 on same day
On the same day as the Chicago Fire, the worst forest fire in American history sweeps northern Wisconsin and Michigan, destroying millions of dollars of property and timber.

1872 **Yellowstone becomes the first National Park**
The government makes Yellowstone, located mostly in present-day Wyoming, the world's first National Park. Since it is located in territory that has not yet become part of any state, the federal government has to assume control.

★**1872**★ Ulysses S. Grant re-elected

Candidate	Party	Electoral Vote	Popular Vote
Ulysses S. Grant Henry Wilson	Republican	286	3,598,235
Horace Greeley G. Gratz Brown	Liberal Republican	66	2,834,761

The Republicans pick Henry Wilson to be Grant's new running mate. Liberal Republicans and Democrats back Horace Greeley on a Liberal Republican ticket. Their party wants civil service reform and improvements in conditions in the South. After the election but before the electors meet to cast their votes, Greeley dies. This frees his electors who vote for other candidates.

Susan B. Anthony casts a vote
She breaks the law by casting a vote in the presidential election and is arrested 2 weeks later.

1875 **First Kentucky Derby run in Louisville**
The event will be held every year on the first Saturday in May as the first race in the coveted Triple Crown of horse racing—the Kentucky Derby, Preakness Stakes, and Belmont Stakes.

1876 — **Custer's Last Stand**

In 1868, Civil War hero General George Custer had killed Chief Black Kettle at the Battle of Washita along with a hundred other Indians. In 1876, Custer is ambushed by the Sioux at Little Big Horn in Montana. Custer and his 250 men are wiped out.

★1876★   RUTHERFORD B. HAYES   19

CANDIDATE	PARTY	ELECTORAL VOTE	POPULAR VOTE
Rutherford B. Hayes William Wheeler	Republican	185	4,036,572
Samuel Tilden Thomas Hendricks	Democratic	184	4,284,020

In one of the most disputed elections in our history, Tilden beats Hayes in the popular vote and leads by 19 electoral votes with 20 votes in dispute in three states. After a lengthy legal battle, Hayes is awarded the twenty votes and becomes president. In return for agreeing to this outcome, the Democrats get federal troops removed from southern states, effectively ending Reconstruction. This is a huge setback to the recovery in the South and to the welfare of the freed slaves.

1877 — **First telephone lines installed in Boston**
Alexander Graham Bell had patented the telephone a year earlier and tested it with his assistant Thomas Watson.

1878 — **Thomas Edison receives patent for phonograph**
He later receives a patent for the first practical incandescent light bulb that is finally bright enough and long-lasting.

★1880★   JAMES A. GARFIELD   20

CANDIDATE	PARTY	ELECTORAL VOTE	POPULAR VOTE
James A. Garfield Chester A. Arthur	Republican	214	4,446,158
Winfield S. Hancock William English	Democratic	155	4,444,260

Hayes does not seek reelection, honoring his earlier promises. Ulysses Grant tries for the Republican spot and is the early favorite at their convention. Garfield is there as a delegate giving a speech in support of John Sherman for president, but soon finds himself nominated. The delegates are stalemated for 35 ballots, but Garfield edges out Grant on the next vote. The Democrats nominate Civil War General Winfield S. Hancock. The popular vote difference is razor-thin at only 1,898 votes, but Garfield easily wins the electoral count.

★1881★   CHESTER A. ARTHUR   21

President Garfield is shot on July 2 by Charles J. Guiteau after less than a year in office. Guiteau shouts "I am a Stalwart. Arthur is now President." Arthur is a member of the Stalwart faction of the Republican Party, but there is no apparent conspiracy, and the deranged Guiteau is hanged a year later. Garfield lingers until dying on September 19, and Arthur becomes president. Arthur becomes a champion of civil service reform and leaves office 4 years later with high marks.

Shootout at the O.K. Corral in Tombstone, Arizona
The Earp brothers and Doc Holliday shoot it out with the Clinton gang, killing three of the gang.

1882 ### Chinese Exclusion Act signed

Chinese immigration exploded during the building of the Transcontinental Railroad. However, racism and the lack of jobs leads to calls to restrict their immigration. This law is supposed to last only ten years, but will be extended and stay in effect until 1943, and effectively bars all Chinese immigrants from entering the country.

1883 ### Pendleton Civil Service Reform Act passes
Pushed by Arthur, it stipulates that government jobs should be awarded based on merit, not on connections or politics.

Time zones are adopted in U.S.
Railroad improve service by adopting zones for timetables.

★1884★   GROVER CLEVELAND   22

CANDIDATE	PARTY	ELECTORAL VOTE	POPULAR VOTE
Grover Cleveland Thomas Hendricks	Democratic	219	4,874,621
James Blaine John Logan	Republican	182	4,848,936

This election is marred by a new level of personal attacks. Stories leak that Cleveland had fathered a child out of wedlock, while Blaine loses votes due to alleged anti-Catholic sentiments. Cleveland wins New York by the thinnest of margins, 1,047 votes, giving him the needed electoral votes. He becomes the first Democrat president since 1856. The Republican convention produces the famous *Sherman Pledge* made by General Sherman when he is pressured to run. He essentially states, "If drafted, I will not run; if nominated, I will not accept; if elected, I will not serve."

1884— **First roller coaster opens at Coney Island, NY**

1885— **Washington Monument is dedicated**
The 555-foot obelisk was started in 1848, but
work stopped during the Civil War. When re-
started in 1876, the same marble couldn't be
found, so the finished tower is of two distinct
colors. It is the tallest building in the world
until the Eiffel tower is finished in 1887.

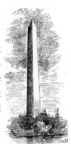

1886— **Apache Geronimo is arrested**

He has been fighting the government since
1850. His arrest ends major Indian resistance in the country. Almost 250,000 Native
Americans are now living on 187 reserva-
tions around the country.

An earthquake destroys Charleston, SC
The August 31 intraplate earthquake is one of most powerful ever to strike the eastern U.S. Two thousand buildings
are damaged and 100 lives are lost.

Statue of Liberty dedicated
The French gift now welcomes visitors and immigrants from her island perch in New York harbor. The torch is 305 feet from the ground.

2008	#95
2020	#120

American Federation of Labor (AFL) is founded
Samuel Gompers founds first major labor union.

1887— **Interstate Commerce Act of 1887**
The first federal law regulating private industry controls the
railroad industry and curtail its monopolistic practices. It
also creates the Interstate Commerce Commission.

★1888★   BENJAMIN HARRISON   *23*

CANDIDATE	PARTY	ELECTORAL VOTE	POPULAR VOTE
Benjamin Harrison Levi Morton	Republican	233	5,443,892
Grover Cleveland Allen Thurman	Democratic	168	5,534,488

Cleveland is running for a second term supporting a tariff
reduction, while Harrison opposes the reduction. Cleveland
wins the popular vote, but loses the election due to the loss
of his home state of New York by only 1% of the vote. This
is caused by dirty tricks by the Republicans who publish a
letter from the British ambassador supposedly recommending
Cleveland as the best candidate from the British point of view.
This enrages the Irish-American voters who then vote for Harrison. Harrison also backs a high tariff which gains him votes.

1889

Oklahoma Land Rush

At noon on April 22, a bugle sounds and 50,000 settlers rush into Oklahoma Territory to claim free land, resulting in more Indian relocation and eventual  statehood for Oklahoma. Each settler can claim 160 acres in exchange for living there and improving the land.

Johnstown Flood

A Pennsylvania dam collapses on May 31, sending twenty million tons of debris and water downstream to destroy the town of Johnstown, killing more than 2,000 people.

Kodak cameras go on sale

Photography is now available to everyone. The first camera takes round pictures on a 100-exposure roll of film.

1890

Yosemite Valley becomes a National Park

 Naturalist John Muir convinces the government to officially protect the park. The valley features majestic granite peaks carved by ancient glaciers, including the iconic Half Dome and El Capitan.

Sherman Antitrust Act

The government prohibits monopolies in order to stimulate competition and lower prices.

Massacre at Wounded Knee Creek

U.S. troops accidently kill the influential Chief Sitting Bull while trying to arrest him. Two weeks later, the army surrounds Indians under Chief Big Foot at Wounded Knee Creek, South Dakota. The Indians are not hostile and have almost no weapons.

Chief Sitting Bull

Something happens and the U.S. troops open fire and kill more than 150 men, women and children. Twenty-five U.S. troopers are also killed, mostly by their own fire.

Western frontier closes

Though there was never an official frontier nor any way to know when it is "closed", the push westward changes around this time. The railroad has been built, the Indian resistance has ended, most free land has been given away, the gold rush is over, and civilization has reached most towns. Many fear American drive and ingenuity will end along with the frontier...but they don't know what the next century has in store.

1892 **Ellis Island Immigration Station opens**

Until its closure in 1954, more than 12 million immigrants will come through this station, located on an island in New York Harbor. It can process up to 5,000 immigrants each day. Most immigrants spend less than a day on the island. Those found with health problems are held in the island's hospital. Around 2% are denied admission to the U.S. due to health problems or criminal background. (Today, almost 40% of American citizens are descendents of immigrants who came through Ellis Island.)

★1892★ GROVER CLEVELAND 24

CANDIDATE	PARTY	ELECTORAL VOTE	POPULAR VOTE
Grover Cleveland Adlai Stevenson	Democratic	277	5,556,918
Benjamin Harrison Whitelaw Reid	Republican	145	5,176,108
James Weaver James Field	Populist	22	1,041,028

Cleveland becomes the only president to serve two nonconsecutive terms, being the 22nd and 24th president. Currency policy is a major issue, and the new Populist Party makes a strong showing. Cleveland is against free coinage of silver, losing him support from western states. He also faces opposition from the New York Tammany organization. President Harrison's wife falls ill and dies two weeks before the election, putting a stop to further campaigning by all candidates.

1893 **Cherokee Strip Land Run**

The largest land rush in the history of the world takes place at Cherokee Strip in Oklahoma, on land purchased from the Cherokees for $8.5 million. More than 100,000 settlers wait at the starting line on September 16. When the gun fires at noon, they gallop out to claim their share of 7,000,000 acres. A smaller run in 1895 will be the last American land run.

1896 ***Plessy v. Ferguson***

Another bad Supreme Court decision holds that segregation in businesses is legal under a doctrine of "separate but equal." This is used to justify much of the future segregation in the South until it is essentially overturned by the 1954 *Brown v. Board of Education* ruling.

★1896★   WILLIAM McKINLEY   25

CANDIDATE	PARTY	ELECTORAL VOTE	POPULAR VOTE
William McKinley Garret Hobart	Republican	271	7,104,779
William Jennings Bryan Arthur Sewall	Democratic	176	6,502,925

The 1896 election heralds the disappearance of the old Democratic Party that favored small government and free trade. Bryan is strong in western and rural America, and among the Populist Party and silver backers. The Republicans spend five times what the Democrats spend, and hire speakers to canvas the country painting Bryan as a dangerous candidate. A big issue is whether to stay on the gold standard, or move to a silver standard pushed by Bryan, who feels it will expand the economy. McKinley's victory makes the gold standard and industrial growth important into the next century.

1897 — Yukon Gold Rush lures prospectors to Alaska
Gold is discovered along the Klondike River and thousands of Americans travel to Alaska to reach the goldfields.

1898 — Single-handed sail around the world in the *Spray*

Joshua Slocum becomes the first person to sail around the world single-handed when he returns to Rhode Island on his 36-foot sailboat *Spray*. He has spent three years sailing 46,000 miles westward around the world.

Spanish-American War starts

#72 **2008**
#91 **2020**

Hearst newspapers are accused of helping to incite unrest in Cuba in order to sell newspapers, so called "yellow journalism." The USS *Maine* blows up in Havana Harbor,

Cuba on February 15, killing 266. War is declared by both sides in April. Admiral Dewey attacks and destroys the Spanish fleet in Manila, Philippines. Troops land in Cuba, including Teddy Roosevelt and his Rough Riders, and defeat the Spanish at the critical battle of San Juan Hill. The *Buffalo Soldiers* also see action, earning 5 Medals of Honor. These are the black regiments that were formed in 1866.

Treaty of Paris ends Spanish-American War
The war ends four months later. Cuba gains her independence, but the U.S. reserves the right to a base at Guantanamo Bay. The U.S. also gets control of Puerto Rico, Guam, and the Philippines for $20 million, and annexes Hawaii.

1899 — **American Samoa acquired**
American gains control of Samoa in a treaty with Great Britain and Germany.

1 9 0 0

1900 — **Galveston hurricane kills 8,000 people**
The September 8th hurricane complete-
ly destroys Galveston, Texas, the "Jew-
el of Texas." The storm will remain the
worst natural disaster in U.S. history in
terms of lives lost.

★1900★ WILLIAM MCKINLEY RE-ELECTED

Candidate	Party	Electoral Vote	Popular Vote
William McKinley Theodore Roosevelt	Republican	292	7,228,864
William Jennings Bryan Adlai Stevenson	Democratic	155	6,370,932

In a rematch of the 1896 election, McKinley again defeats
Bryan. McKinley adds a new vice president, New York Governor Theodore Roosevelt. The current vice president, Garret
Hobart, had died in 1899, leaving the office vacant until the
election. The successful ending to the Spanish-American War
and a return to prosperity ensures McKinley's victory.

★1901★ TEDDY ROOSEVELT 26

Anarchist Leon Czolgosz shoots President McKinley at the
Pan-American Exposition in Buffalo, New York on September 6. McKinley appears to recover, but dies on September
14. His shooting leads to Secret Service protection being
assigned to all future presidents. At 42, Roosevelt becomes
the youngest U.S. President in history. He pushes a policy
of business regulation.

Oil is discovered in Texas
An oil well at Spindletop near Beaumont, Texas explodes in a 150-foot geyser that won't be
capped for 9 days. Texas enters the industrial
age, and oil prices drop to 3 cents a barrel.

1903 — **Panama Canal Zone is acquired by treaty**
Columbia refuses to ratify a proposed treaty cover-
ing the rights to a canal across Columbia, and President Roosevelt decides instead to help Panama set
up a new government in return for a signed treaty for
a canal across Panama.

1903— **Wright Brothers fly**
The Wright Brothers conduct the first heavier-than-air flight at Kill Devil Hill in North  Carolina. The flight lasts 12 seconds and covers 120 feet. By 1905, their flights will last more than 30 minutes.

★1904★ Teddy Roosevelt re-elected

Candidate	Party	Electoral Vote	Popular Vote
Theodore Roosevelt Charles Fairbanks	Republican	336	7,630,457
Alton Parker Henry Davis	Democratic	140	5,083,880

Roosevelt is easily picked as his party's candidate with the addition of the more conservative Fairbanks as running mate. The Republican platform calls for a protective tariff, a strong navy, and the gold standard. Both candidates have very similar campaign platforms, both believing in the gold standard and the importance of labor unions. In the end, Roosevelt's popularity gives him an enormous margin in his victory. He wins America's first Nobel Peace Prize in 1906 for helping to end the Russo-Japanese War.

1906— **San Francisco Earthquake**
A magnitude 7.9 earthquake strikes San Francisco at dawn. Most of the damage is done by fires started by the earthquake, fueled by breaks in natural gas lines, and with fighting hampered by breaks in water mains. Up to 3,000 die, and 4 square miles of the city are destroyed.

1907— **Monongah mine explosion in West Virginia**
A coal mine explosion in Monongah kills 362 miners, making it the worst mining disaster in U.S. history.

Great White Fleet circles the world
 Roosevelt sends a fleet of 16 battleships around the world to project American military and naval power.

1908— **FBI established as Bureau of Investigation**

First Model-T automobile produced
Henry Ford makes an affordable car and works on improving the assembly line which ends up cutting production time to make one car from twelve hours to only 90 minutes. He promises customers "a car painted any color that he wants so long as it is black."

1908 — **Grand Canyon becomes a National Monument**
President Roosevelt declares the Grand Canyon a national monument. The 277-mile long canyon has been carved by the Colorado River over the last 17 million years.

★1908★   WILLIAM HOWARD TAFT   **27**

CANDIDATE	PARTY	ELECTORAL VOTE	POPULAR VOTE
William Howard Taft James Sherman	Republican	321	7,678,395
William Jennings Bryan John Kern	Democratic	162	6,408,984

Roosevelt most likely would have won this election, but he has promised not to run again. His party picks his Secretary of War, Howard Taft, to make the run. The Democrats try again with William Bryan, though the silver issue is not as important now. Bryan ends up with the worst loss of his three attempts.

1909 — **NAACP founded on February 12**
The National Association for the Advancement of Colored People (NAACP) is founded on February 12, 1909, the 100th anniversary of the birth of Abraham Lincoln.

Robert Peary reaches the North Pole
The Navy Commander is first to reach the North Pole, accompanied by 4 Inuit guides, and his black assistant, Matthew Henson. There will be continual debate over the next century over whether he actually made it to the Pole.

1910 — **Boy Scouts of America founded**

Robert Baden-Powell had started Scouting in England in 1907. W.D. Boyce visits England in 1909 and learns of scouting. He returns to the U.S. and founds the Boy Scouts of America the next year. It will grow to host over 4.5 million members, and claim presidents, executives, teachers, police officers, and astronauts as members.

★1912★   Woodrow Wilson   28

Candidate	Party	Electoral Vote	Popular Vote
Woodrow Wilson Thomas Marshall	Democratic	435	6,296,284
Theodore Roosevelt Hiram Johnson	Progressive	88	4,122,721
William Howard Taft Nicholas Butler	Republican	8	3,486,242
Eugene V. Debs Emil Seidel	Socialist	0	901,551

The incumbent President Taft wins the Republican nomination, forcing Theodore Roosevelt to create his own Progressive Party. He tells the press he feels as strong as a "bull moose," earning his party the name, "Bull Moose Party." Wilson is nominated on the 46th ballot, thanks in part to the support of William Jennings Bryan. This is the first election where all 48 states cast votes, and the last election where the second place finisher is neither a Republican nor a Democrat. Taft's vice president, James Sherman, dies one week before the election, further dividing his party. Taft wins only eight electoral votes, the worst defeat ever for a sitting president and for the Republicans. Roosevelt has his own problems, surviving an assassination attempt on October 14 in Wisconsin, the bullet lodging in the 50-page speech in his pocket. Wilson wins the election in an electoral landslide.

Girl Scouts of America founded
Juliette Low meets Scout founder Robert Baden-Powell in England and returns to Savannah, Georgia to start the organization in the United States.

RMS *Titanic* sinks

The British passenger ship, *Titanic*, hits an iceberg and sinks, killing more than 1,400 people. The largest passenger ship in the world at 882 feet, she is on her maiden voyage from Southhampton, England with 2,223 people on board. She only has enough lifeboats for one-half of the passengers, and many are only half-filled leaving the sinking ship.

Wilson's early actions
Wilson had run on a progressive platform and promises to keep the U.S. out of any European war. He introduces a federal income tax and strengthens anti-trust laws. He also orders the Civil Service segregated, and nominates segregationists to cabinet posts.

1913 — **The Lincoln Highway connects the country**
The 3,389 mile route across the country connects Times Square in New York City with Lincoln Park in San Francisco, and is the first continuous road across the country. It will still take a motorist 20 to 30 days to drive across the country.

★ **16ᵀᴴ AMENDMENT** ★
Authorizes the collection of federal income tax.

★ **17ᵀᴴ AMENDMENT** ★
Changes the election of Senators from state legislatures to the voters of each state.

1914 — **World War I starts**
The June 28, 1914 assassination of Archduke Ferdinand in Sarajevo touches off a great world war. Austria-Hungary, Germany, Turkey, and Italy fight against the Allies consisting primarily of England, France, Belgium, Greece, and Russia. Italy eventually changes sides. Russia soon falls to Communism during the Bolshevik revolution and makes a separate peace with Germany. President Wilson declares American neutral. She will not enter the war until 1917. German forces sweep through Europe but stop at the Marne River, establishing a 4-year stalemate of trench warfare at its worst, including poison gas and the deaths of 200,000.

Panama Canal opens
George Goethals and over 50,000 men dig a canal across the 50-mile isthmus, fighting mud slides and yellow fever. An earlier French attempt had resulted in 22,000 worker deaths, while the American attempt loses 5,600 lives.

1915 — **Germans sink the *Lusitania***
A U-boat sinks the British RMS *Lusitania*, killing Americans on board and raising anti-German sentiment.

First phone service across the country
The first phone service is established between New York and San Francisco.

1916 — **Pancho Villa attacks the U.S.**
Pancho Villa is a Mexican Revolutionary General who has been robbing trains, and seizing Mexican haciendas to distribute to peasants. Upset at American support of his rivals, he leads 500 men in an attack on Columbus, New Mexico. Citizens and U.S. soldiers fight off the attack. President Wilson orders General Pershing to pursue Villa into Mexico. This *Pancho Villa Expedition* is unable to find Villa and returns home after nine months.

★1916★ Woodrow Wilson re-elected

Candidate	Party	Electoral Vote	Popular Vote
Woodrow Wilson Thomas Marshall	Democratic	277	9,126,868
Charles Hughes Charles Fairbanks	Republican	254	8,548,728

#79 2008

Europe is at war, but the U.S. is still not involved. The public is still neutral about entering the war, even though they support Britain and France. Wilson taps this sentiment with his slogan, "He kept us out of war." Republicans pull their party together and select moderate Supreme Court Justice Charles Hughes. The popular vote is close, but the electoral vote is razor-thin. Hughes will win if he carries California, but Wilson wins the state by only 0.4% to clinch the presidency.

First female member of Congress
Jeannette Rankin is elected a U.S. Representative from Montana. Montana had given women the vote in 1914.

1917
U.S. acquires Virgin Islands
U.S. buys what are now called the American Virgin Islands from Denmark for $25 million.

America enters World War I

#78 2008

#100 2020

U.S. tries to stay neutral, but German U-boats are sinking ships, including the *Housatonic*, resulting in the loss of American

#101 2020

life. The secret "Zimmerman" telegram is decoded by the British revealing German plans for an alliance with Mexico, giving them back American land at war's end. Wilson declares war on April 6, calling it a war to "make the world safe for democracy" and support England, France, Italy and Russia. The U.S. Army increases from 200,000 to 4 million men. In Europe, General Pershing keeps American troops under U.S. control. At home, Wilson clamps down on civil liberties and freedom of the press.

1918
U.S. Marines win the Battle of Belleau Wood
U.S. Marines fight one of their costliest battles ever at Belleau Wood, France, finally pushing back a German attack.

Sergeant Alvin York receives Medal of Honor
The Tennessee sharpshooter attacks a machine gun nest, single-handedly killing 28 German soldiers and capturing 132 others. He receives the Distinguished Service Cross and the French Croix de guerre.

1918

World War I ends

The armistice ending World War I is signed in a French rail car, taking effect at 11am on 11/11/1918. The Germans are finally convinced that the Americans have unlimited resources, and know how to fight. More than 10 million are killed in the war, including more than 110,000 Americans. This day will be commemorated in the U.S. as *Veterans Day*.

Spanish Flu epidemic devastates the world

The great Spanish Flu epidemic sweeps the world during the war, killing up to 50 million people worldwide, including more than 500,000 Americans.

1919

★ 18ᵀᴴ AMENDMENT ★

Prohibits the manufacture and sale of alcohol.

Wilson and the League of Nations

Wilson pushes his "14 points" for world peace and establishing the League of Nations. With little support from the opposition party, his plans are never confirmed by the Senate. The Treaty of Versailles ending the war imposes severe terms on Germany which will lead directly to World War II. They are prohibited from having subs and planes, lose a lot of territory, and are saddled with a debt they can't repay. The treaty also redraws the maps of Europe and Africa, sowing the seeds for future unrest and conflict. On November 19, the United States Congress refuses to approve the treaty. The U.S. never joins the League of Nations which is disbanded in 1946.

Red scare sweeps America

With the Communist takeover of Russia, a fear of Communism sweeps America with the Attorney General rounding up 6,000 suspected Communists.

Race riots kill 100's across country during 'Red Summer'

Violent riots spread from Chicago to more than 35 cities after a black swimmer was killed.

President Wilson suffers a stroke

He is left disabled until the end of his Presidency. The government essentially operates without a president for a year.

1920

★ 19ᵀᴴ AMENDMENT ★

Gives women the right to vote.

Women get the right to vote

The 19th amendment gives women the right to vote. Suffragettes have worked towards this goal for decades. Susan B. Anthony is critical in getting the amendment passed.

1920 ┤ **_KDKA_ first station to broadcast election results**

⋆1920⋆   Warren G. Harding   29

Candidate	Party	Electoral Vote	Popular Vote
Warren G. Harding Calvin Coolidge	Republican	404	16,144,093
James Cox Franklin D. Roosevelt	Democratic	127	9,139,661

The war is over, the post-war economy is not doing well, and the League of Nations is still a contentious issue. Wilson is unpopular, and incapacitated after a stroke. Irish and German communities in America are upset at Wilson's policies. Women in all states can now vote for president. The Republicans consider running Teddy Roosevelt, but he dies in 1919 so they run the relatively unknown Senator Harding. The Democrats pick Ohio Governor Cox, and Franklin Roosevelt for the second spot. Harding campaigns against Wilson's policies and wins an enormous landslide victory and one of the largest popular vote margins in history. The Socialist candidate, Eugene V. Debs, receives almost one million votes even though he is in prison.

Roaring '20s
Helped by the prohibition of alcohol, the Twenties become a lawless decade since almost everyone violates prohibition. Speakeasies spring up serving illegal alcohol. Corruption exists at every level of government. Organized crimes takes over with leaders like Al Capone and John Dillinger. President Harding implements a "hands-off" policy with the economy and the stock market booms. His successor, Coolidge, will continue this hands-off approach. Jazz music takes off with singers like Louis Armstrong, and New York's Broadway offers great plays by playwrights like Eugene O'Neill and Noel Coward.

1921 ┤ ### Sales tax
West Virginia becomes the first state with a sales tax.

1922 ┤ ### Lincoln Memorial is dedicated in D.C.
The inside is inscribed with the words of his Gettysburg Address and Second Inaugural Speech, and contains a massive statue by Daniel Chester French.

Teapot Dome Scandal rocks the country
Secretary of the Interior Albert Fall is convicted of taking bribes from oil companies to secure lucrative government leases of petroleum reserves at Teapot Dome, Wyoming.

1922— **First female U.S. Senator**

Rebecca Felton is appointed by the governor of Georgia to fill a vacant U.S. Senate seat, becoming the first female member of the Senate.

★1923★ CALVIN COOLIDGE 30

Harding dies suddenly from a heart attack and his vice president, Calvin Coolidge, takes over the presidency.

Hollywood arrives

A real estate developer erects a huge *Hollywoodland* sign in the hills of Los Angeles. The *"land"* is removed in 1949.

1924— **Immigration Act of 1924**

Limits immigration to 2% of each nationality in America in 1880, discriminating against Far Eastern and East European immigrants. It will be in effect until the Immigration Act of 1965 which will focus on individuals more than quotas.

Indian Citizenship Act

The government gives U.S. citizenship and voting rights to all Native Americans born in the United States.

★1924★ CALVIN COOLIDGE RE-ELECTED

CANDIDATE	PARTY	ELECTORAL VOTE	POPULAR VOTE
Calvin Coolidge Charles Dawes	Republican	382	15,723,789
John Davis Charles Bryan	Democratic	136	8,386,242
Robert La Follette, Sr. Burton Wheeler	Progressive	13	4,831,706

The economy is booming, the war is long since over, and the voters are happy with the current administration. The Democratic Party is in disarray, needing 100 ballots to nominate the unknown but conservative Davis as their candidate. Liberal Democrats leave their party to back the Progressive Party candidate. This is the first national election in which Native-Americans can vote. Both major parties push a conservative agenda of smaller government, less regulation, and reduced taxes, but Coolidge wins in another landslide.

First elected female governor

Nellie Ross is elected governor of Wyoming, becoming the first elected female governor in the country. Wyoming had given women the right to vote in 1869.

1924 First Macy's Thanksgiving Day parade in New York City

1925 Deadly Tri-State Tornado kills 695

HERALD EXAMINER

1,000 DEAD, 3,000 HURT LATEST TOLL OF TORNADO

In the Twinkling of an Eye, Murphysboro Was No More

The deadliest tornado in our history (though this is unofficial) kills 695 in Missouri, Illinois, and Indiana. Its continuous path is the longest ever recorded, at more than 200 miles and lasting more than 3 hours.

Scopes Monkey Trial
A high school teacher, John Scopes, is accused of violating Tennessee law prohibiting the teaching of evolution. Scopes is represented by the ACLU and Clarence Darrow, and prosecuted by William Jennings Bryan. Scopes is found guilty, but the verdict is later overturned.

1926 First liquid fuel rocket
Robert Goddard, the "father of rocketry", launches the world's first liquid-fuel rocket in Massachusetts.

1927 Charles Lindbergh flies the Atlantic

He makes the first non-stop solo flight across the Atlantic, flying 3,600 miles from New York to Paris in the *Spirit of St. Louis*. The plane is on display now in the Space Museum in Washington, D.C.

***The Jazz Singer* opens in New York City**
It is the first full-length "talking" movie, starring Al Jolson. The audience loves it. The days of silent film are numbered.

★1928★   HERBERT HOOVER   31

Candidate	Party	Electoral Vote	Popular Vote
Herbert Hoover Charles Curtis	Republican	444	21,427,123
Al Smith Joseph Robinson	Democratic	87	15,015,464

Coolidge decides not to run again as the economy continues to boom. Many influential Democrats decide not to run in an obvious losing cause, so their party picks New York Governor Al Smith as their candidate. He is hampered by his anti-prohibition stance, the well-known corruption of his home state, and the fact that he is a Roman Catholic. Many fear that the Pope would control any Catholic president. Hoover wins in a third consecutive Republican landslide.

1929

St. Valentine's Day Massacre
Al Capone's gang massacres seven members of the rival Moran Gang on Valentine's Day in Chicago.

Stock market crashes on *Black Thursday*
The decade of speculation and buying stock on margin comes to a screeching halt on October 24, 1929. Collapsing prices mark the start of the decade-long Great Depression, the longest economic recession in modern history. Many lose their life savings as 5,000 banks will soon fail.

2020 #103,104

1930

Ninth planet Pluto is discovered
Clyde Tombaugh discovers the new planet at Lowell Observatory in Arizona after a year of carefully comparing photographs of the night sky. Venetia Burney, an eleven-year-old English schoolgirl, is credited with suggesting the name for the new planet, Pluto. In 2006, astronomers will reclassify Pluto as a minor planet, reducing the official number of planets back to eight.

Smoot-Hawley Tariff Act
Though it is supposed to help Americans by increasing tariffs on imports, it only worsens the depression.

1931

Star Spangled Banner picked as anthem
President Hoover signs a congressional resolution naming it the national anthem.

Empire State Building complete
Built in only 410 days, the 1250-foot tall Empire State Building edges out the Chrysler Building to become the world's tallest. It remains the world's tallest for forty years.

1932

"Bonus March" heads to Washington
Twelve million people are out of work by 1932. Thousands of World War I vets march on Washington demanding their promised bonus pay from the war.

Amelia Earhart is first woman to fly the Atlantic nonstop
She had made an earlier flight as a passenger with two others. This flight was solo, going from Newfoundland to Northern Ireland in 15 hours.

Hoovervilles spring up all over the country
These homeless camps are named after the president many blame for their problems. Hoover resists using federal money to help the states, but his policies like the Smoot-Hawley Tariff only make things worse.

First elected female U.S. Senator
Hattie Caraway is the first woman actually elected, not appointed, to the Senate.

★1932★   Franklin D. Roosevelt   32

CANDIDATE	PARTY	ELECTORAL VOTE	POPULAR VOTE
Franklin D. Roosevelt John Garner	Democratic	472	22,821,277
Herbert Hoover Charles Curtis	Republican	59	15,761,254

#105 **2020**

The depression hits the country hard. Voters blame Hoover for the crisis, or at least feel that he is unable to fix the problems. Roosevelt takes advantage of the crisis and promises that his "New Deal" will put the country back on its feet. Hoover warns that Roosevelt will increase taxes and the federal debt to pay for his social programs. But an unemployment rate over 20% makes voters willing to take the chance. Roosevelt picks "Happy Days are Here Again" as a campaign song. Ironically, those happy days won't show up for fifteen years. This is the first election in 56 years in which a Democratic candidate wins a majority of the popular vote. The pre-TV American public will almost never see the braces and wheelchair Roosevelt needs after contracting polio in 1921.

1933

★ 20ᵀᴴ Amendment ★
Sets the dates for the commencement of terms for newly elected members of Congress and the President.

★ 21ˢᵀ Amendment ★
Repeals prohibition and nullifies the 18th amendment.

Albert Einstein flees Europe
The world-renown physicist arrives in the U.S. after fleeing Nazi Germany's persecution of Jews and intellectuals. He learns that the German government has banned Jews from teaching and has burned his books.

Assassination attempt on FDR
The president-elect is giving a speech in Miami when Guiseppe Zangara, an Italian anarchist, fires 5 shots at close range. All miss Roosevelt, but Chicago Mayor Anton Cermak is struck and later dies.

Wiley Post flies alone around the world
He becomes the first to make a solo round-the-world airplane trip, landing back in New York after almost eight days. He will die in 1935 in a plane crash in Alaska that will also kill humorist Will Rogers.

1935 **Dust storm strikes Washington, D.C.**

The Great Plains becomes a Dust Bowl due to severe drought, single crop-farming, and bad farming practices and policies. Farmers have plowed up grass lands to plant cash crops, exposing the soil to the sun and wind. Dust storms darken the skies for hours and leak into every house through the tiniest crack. More than 100 million acres lose most or all of their topsoil. During legislation in Washington on the need for a Soil Conservation Act, a dust storm from the Great Plains hits the city. The act passes later the same year.

Bad times breed Fascism and Communism

The world-wide depression creates a ripe breeding ground for the rise of the Nazis in Germany, Fascists in Spain and Italy, and the Communists in Russia and France.

FDR pushes his New Deal

FDR creates an astounding number of new government acts using his executive powers and the Democrat control of both houses of Congress. Many have unintended consequences that will prolong the depression instead of ending it, and make citizens dependent on the government. Many government projects take work away from the private sector and actually discourage new job formation. Social Security benefits are set to begin at age 65, which is just two years greater than the average life span in 1936 of 63 years. In 2011, the average life span will increase to 78 years.

- FHA: Federal Housing Administration guarantees home loans.
- FSA: Farm Security Administration helps poor farmers.
- CCC: Civilian Conservation Corps puts men to work building public structures.
- FCC: Federal Communication Commission monitors airwaves.
- WPA: Works Progress Administration puts people to work and funds the arts.
- SSA: Social Security Act provides benefits to retirees and the unemployed, and a lump-sum benefit at death.
- FLSA: Fair Labor Standards Act sets maximum work hours and minimum wages.
- FDIC: Federal Deposit Insurance Corporation guarantees deposits in banks.
- TVA: Tennessee Valley Authority builds dams to provide power and control floods.
- SEC: Securities and Exchange Commission monitors the securities market.
- Revenue Wealth Tax Act: Increases taxes on the rich up to 75% and increases estate taxes.

1935 — ### The New Deal reaches too far

The National Industrial Recovery Act is declared unconstitutional. It was designed to stimulate recovery by permitting monopolies, setting minimum wages, and allowing collective bargaining.

The Agricultural Adjustment Act paid farmers to not grow crops, produce milk, or raise animals. This was paid for by taxing the producers. The Supreme Court declares the Act unconstitutional since it is illegal to tax one group and give that money to another.

Labor Day Hurricane

Devastating storm hits the Florida Keys, killing 400 people and destroying the Key West railroad. Its 892 mbar pressure reading when it touches land will remain the lowest in American history.

Huey "The Kingfish" Long killed by gunman

The U.S. Senator and former Louisiana Governor pushed a Share-Our-Wealth program to spread the wealth around.

Hoover Dam built

President Roosevelt dedicates Hoover Dam in Nevada (known as Boulder Dam at the time). The dam plays a vital part in the upcoming war by providing electricity to make aluminum needed for the airplanes that help win the war.

Italy invades Ethiopia

The attack highlights the weakness of the League of Nations. Italy and Ethiopia both belong, but that does nothing to stop the invasion or protect Ethiopia.

1936 — ### Spanish Civil War

The liberal, Communist-leaning government is attacked by right-wind fascists, led by General Franco who is aided by Hitler and Mussolini. Hitler uses Spain as a testing ground for his new weapons and tactics. Russia backs the government, but the U.S. stays neutral during the 3-year war.

Jesse Owens humiliates Hitler

The black runner shatters Hitler's claims of Aryan superiority at the Berlin Olympics by winning 4 gold medals.

★1936★ FRANKLIN ROOSEVELT RE-ELECTED

CANDIDATE	PARTY	ELECTORAL VOTE	POPULAR VOTE
Franklin Roosevelt John Garner	Democratic	523	27,752,648
Alf Landon Frank Knox	Republican	8	16,681,862

The Great Depression continues and FDR is still pushing his New Deal programs. The voters are willing to give him more time, even though unemployment is still above 16%. Roosevelt wins a lopsided victory, earning more electoral votes than any president except for Reagan in 1984.

1937 — Graf Zeppelin *Hindenburg* explodes upon landing

The German airship blows up and burns in New Jersey, killing 35 people, and effectively ending airship travel. The live coverage by Herbert Morrison will become famous.

Golden Gate Bridge opens in San Francisco

The new suspension bridge is the world's longest and will remain the longest until the 1964 construction of the Verrazano-Narrows Bridge in New York.

FDR threatens to pack the Supreme Court

The Supreme Court thwarts some of his policies so he threatens to add extra judges that will approve them. Fortunately, Congress does not approve of his plan.

Amelia Earhart disappears in the South Pacific

Her world circumnavigation attempt ends in tragedy. Her plane will never be found.

1938 — Chamberlin's "Peace for our Time"

In misguided appeasement, British Prime Minister Neville Chamberlin signs a treaty with Hitler, saying it will guarantee "Peace for our time." It gives Hitler control of the Sudetenland area of Czechoslovakia, which he then immediately occupies, burning synagogues, and sending Jews to concentration camps. A year later, Europe is at war.

War of the Worlds radio show scares the nation

Orson Welles plays a Halloween stunt on national radio by presenting H.G. Wells' novel, *The War of the Worlds*, as if it is real. He broadcasts simulated news flashes reporting aliens landing and using death rays to kill Americans. Hundreds of listeners panic, believing the alien attack is real.

1939 — **Spanish Civil War ends with General Franco victorious**
He keeps Spain essentially neutral during World War II.

The movie *Wizard of Oz* opens in Hollywood
Judy Garland achieves immortality with her rendition of "Over the Rainbow." The film will become an American classic.

Hitler signs a non-aggression treaty with Russia
Hitler buys time, but makes secret plans with Russia to divide European countries between them, including Poland, Romania, Lithuania, Estonia, Latvia and Finland.

Hitler invades Poland to start World War II
In response, France and Britain declare war on Germany. America remains neutral though Roosevelt helps supply Britain under the authority of the Lend-Lease Act.

1940 — **Hitler occupies France**

Hitler defeats France in a month, outflanking her vaunted Maginot Line. He divides France into a German-occupied North, and a free-French Vichy government in the South. On June 22, France is forced to sign the surrender documents in the same railcar used when Germany surrendered at the end of the first World War.

Mass evacuation at Dunkirk, France
The Nazis trap the British Army against the sea in Dunkirk and only a miraculous evacuation by small boats saves more than 300,000 soldiers.

The Battle of Britain saves England and the world

Hitler prepares to invade across the English Channel, but needs air superiority first. He spends the summer relentlessly bombing England, which is saved only by the valiant defense of the British RAF. Hitler postpones his invasion and turns his attention toward Russia. Churchill thanks those pilots with his famous saying, "Never was so much owed by so many to so few."

America First Committee tries to keep U.S. out of war
Charles Lindbergh leads isolationist, anti-war groups demanding all aid to Europe stopped and the U.S. kept out of the war.

★1940★ Franklin Roosevelt re-elected

Candidate	Party	Electoral Vote	Popular Vote
Franklin Roosevelt Henry Wallace	Democratic	449	27,313,945
Wendell Willkie Charles McNary	Republican	82	22,347,744

The war has started in Europe and is a major issue in the election. Unemployment is still high. Roosevelt becomes the first president to run for a third term, breaking with tradition, as he feels that only he has the necessary experience to handle the upcoming war, though he promises he will not involve the country in the war. The Republicans pick a businessman, Wendell Willkie, who is strongly in favor of giving Britain all the aid possible short of declaring war. Roosevelt's current vice president, John Garner, differs with FDR over his liberal policies, and Roosevelt picks Henry Wallace as a new running mate. Wallace is a liberal socialist who favors the USSR, but will fortunately be replaced before Roosevelt dies.

1941 — Mount Rushmore is finished

Started in South Dakota in 1927 by Gutzon Borglum, it is finally finished by his son, Lincoln Borglum. Sixty-foot-high faces of George Washington, Thomas Jefferson, Theodore Roosevelt, and Abraham Lincoln are carved on the granite cliffs. The initial plans had called for each president to be carved from head to waist, but lack of funding stopped further carving. Thomas Jefferson was started on the other side of Washington, but unstable rock there forced the workers to move him to the other side.

Pearl Harbor - December 7

Carrier-launched Japanese aircraft attack the U.S. fleet at Pearl Harbor on the island of Oahu. The surprise attack sinks a number of ships and kills 2400 Americans. On the same day, the Japanese also occupy Wake Island, Guam, Singapore, the Philippines, and Hong Kong. FDR declares war on Japan. Germany and Italy then declare war on America. The "*Allies*" consist primarily of England, America, France, China, and the Soviet Union. They face the "*Axis*" forces of Germany, Italy, and Japan, although Hungary, Romania, Slovakia, and Bulgaria also join. World War II starts for America.

2008 #78

2020 #100,106

2008 #81

1942 **Japanese internment camps ordered by FDR**
The U.S. government relocates Pacific coast Japanese-Americans to internment camps to protect them from anti-Japanese actions, and reduce chances for espionage.

Bataan Death March

Over 75,000 American and Filipino troops surrender at Bataan and Corregidor in the largest mass surrender in American history. The Japanese force the prisoners on a brutal march to POW camps that kills 7,000 prisoners. MacArthur escapes to Australia.

30 Seconds over Tokyo

Captain Jimmy Doolittle leads a flight of sixteen specially outfitted B-25's launched from the aircraft carrier USS *Hornet*. They drop bombs on Tokyo in a symbolic move that improves morale at home, and undermines Japanese leadership. The Japanese government had promised their people they would never be attacked. In retaliation, the Japanese massacre more than 250,000 Chinese civilians they accuse of helping the downed aviators.

Battle of the Coral Sea on May 4-8
Japanese and American naval forces fight the first naval battle between aircraft carriers, and the first naval battle where the ships of each side never see each other.

Battle of Midway on June 4-6

Trying to lure American carriers into a trap, the Japanese Navy attacks Midway, a small but strategic island in the middle of the Pacific. Americans have broken Japan's secret code and know the attack is coming. In one of the most decisive naval battles in history, the U.S. sinks four Japanese carriers and a heavy cruiser, while losing only one carrier and a destroyer. This defeat starts Japan on their slow retreat back to their mainland.

Battle of Stalingrad
In one of the bloodiest battles in history, the Germans fail to take Stalingrad, marking the end of their eastern advance into Russia. Two million die on both sides and the city is reduced to rubble. The Russian-German animosity pervades the war. Later, thousands of Germans flee toward advancing Americans rather than risk surrendering to the Russians.

1942 — **Battle of Guadacanal**
Allied forces land on the island of Guadacanal to deny its use to the Japanese threatening Allied supply routes.

1943 — **Germans surrender in North Africa**
The Allies surround the Axis forces in Tunisia and force the surrender of over 275,000 enemy troops. This enables the Allies to begin preparing for the invasion of Italy.

Allies land in Sicily, Italy
A large Allied assault takes the island and moves onto mainland Italy. Italy surrenders but the Germans keep fighting in Italy. Rome is not liberated until June 5, 1944. Mussolini is imprisoned but rescued by the Germans who need him to head the government. When Rome finally falls, Mussolini and his mistress are captured, shot, and hung upside down on meat hooks in a public square, before being stoned.

John F. Kennedy's PT-109 sinks
A Japanese destroyer rams and sinks the future president's torpedo boat in the Solomon Islands. Kennedy leads his men to safety and rescue six days later.

General Eisenhower picked to head invasion
Roosevelt names Dwight Eisenhower Supreme Allied Commander in Europe. He is responsible for the upcoming invasion and liberation of Europe.

1944 — **D-Day at Normandy, France on June 6**

The largest invasion force in history, with 7,000 ships supported by 11,000 planes, lands 150,000 troops at Utah, Omaha, Juno, Sword, and Gold beaches. The Germans still think the invasion will be at Calais. Months of fighting lie ahead as the Allies move eastward.

GI Bill passed by government
This pays for the education of returning servicemen.

America retakes Guam on July 21
After ending the Japanese carrier threat at the Battle of the Philippine Sea, Allied forces retake Guam, an American possession the Japanese captured after Pearl Harbor. During occupation, they had tortured and raped the locals. Guam celebrates Liberation Day every year on July 21.

Pilot George H.W. Bush shot down in the South Pacific
George H.W. Bush, the future 41st President, is shot down and survives in a raft until picked up by an American sub.

MacArthur returns to the Philippines

Fulfilling his earlier vow to the Filipino people that "I shall return," MacArthur wades ashore at Leyte Island to start the long battle to retake the islands.

1944 Battle of Leyte Gulf
One of the biggest naval battles ever results in Japan's largest loss of ships and crew, and the use of kamikaze planes.

★1944★ Franklin Roosevelt re-elected

Candidate	Party	Electoral Vote	Popular Vote
Franklin Roosevelt Harry S. Truman	Democratic	432	25,612,916
Thomas Dewey John Bricker	Republican	99	22,017,929

The war is beginning to wind down and Roosevelt remains popular, although many in his party are skeptical of his economic policies. There is stiff opposition to his current vice president and the party forces FDR to select Senator Truman as his new running mate. It is a fortunate pick, as events will soon reveal. New York Governor Dewey becomes his opponent. Roosevelt easily wins a record 4th term.

Battle of the Bulge
As Allies push the Germans back towards their homeland, the Germans stage a massive counterattack, resulting in one of the largest U.S. losses in the war. The Germans  surround the town of Bastogne and demand surrender. The American Commander McAuliffe replies, "Nuts." The Americans hold the town until they are relieved.

Allies discover Nazi death camps throughout Europe
The extent of the Nazi systematic extermination of Jews and others considered "undesirable" is revealed as concentration camps are discovered by the advancing Allies. The *Holocaust* kills more than 11 million men, women, and children.

1945 Yalta Conference in Ukraine
Stalin, Roosevelt, and Churchill meet to discuss the future of postwar Europe.

Iwo Jima
U.S. Marines take Iwo Jima in a bloody battle costing 6,800 American lives, and the lives of 20,000 Japanese defenders. It is the first invasion of a Japanese home island.

Battle of Okinawa
The largest Pacific amphibious assault secures Okinawa as an airbase for the upcoming invasion of Japan. The battle lasts 3 months and results in an enormous loss of life. Over 100,000 Japanese troops are killed or captured, and thousands of civilians are killed or commit suicide. This is a harbinger of what the invasion of the Japanese mainland will be like.

★1945★   HARRY S. TRUMAN   33

President Roosevelt dies on April 12 and Truman becomes president. He has a full plate, as he must end the war in Europe, and decide whether to use the atomic bomb on Japan. Then, he has a post-war world to handle along with the start of the Cold War. Fortunately for the country, Truman assumes the job and not Roosevelt's previous vice president, Wallace, who was taken off the ticket just the year before. Wallace is opposed to the Truman Doctrine and the Marshall Plan.

The Soviets take Berlin and Germany surrenders
Eisenhower decides to let the Russians take Berlin, saving tens of thousands of American lives. The bloody final battle results in 100,000 killed on each side. On April 30, Hitler and his wife, Eva Braun, commit suicide in their Berlin bunker and their bodies are cremated. Germans continue fighting westward to surrender to the Western Allies instead of the Soviets. Germany finally surrenders on May 8, 1945. Europe is finally at peace. The war with Japan continues.

Manhattan Project develops the A-Bomb
Working in secret, scientists in the U.S. develop the atomic bomb, employing up to 130,000 people in the process. It is successfully tested in New Mexico on July 16. Now, President Truman must decide how to use the weapon. America has only two working atomic bombs by August of this year. Based on fierce fighting seen in recent battles like Iwo Jima and Okinawa, it is felt that an invasion of the Japanese homeland will result in more than one million American casualties. After discussions on where and how to drop the bombs, Truman decides that with only two working bombs available, they must bomb the Japanese homeland.

Atomic bombs blast Hiroshima and Nagasaki

The *Enola Gay* drops the first atomic bomb on Hiroshima on August 6. The Japanese government still will not agree to the Allied terms of surrender, so the second atomic bomb is dropped on Nagasaki three days later. Together, they kill around 200,000 people.

Japan finally surrenders on August 15

The formal surrender is signed on the deck of the USS *Missouri* on September 2 in the presence of 250 Allied ships, and 2,000 planes overhead. World War II is finally over. General MacArthur takes over as Military Governor of Japan and wisely allows the Emperor to retain his throne. He drafts a new constitution that remains in effect to this day.

1945 — Germany is divided

As pre-arranged, the Allies divide Germany into sectors—the Soviets control the Eastern half, and the Allies control the western portion. Berlin is stuck deep inside the Soviet sector and is itself divided into four parts—Soviet, French, American, and British.

War crime trials start in Nuremberg, Germany

The Allies hold a series of tribunals to try Nazi leaders as war criminals. Some of the worst villains have already committed suicide, including Hitler, Heinrich Himmler, and Joseph Goebbels. Twelve defendants are sentenced to hang. Two of them escape hanging by committing suicide, including Hermann Göring the night before his hanging.

United Nations is established

The new organization is ratified in San Francisco by the five permanent members of the new Security Council—the United States, France, the Republic of China, the Soviet Union, and the United Kingdom.

1946 — Philippines becomes an independent nation

On July 4, 1946, the American government signs a treaty with the Philippines that grants her independence. The U.S. retains a number of military bases, and pledges continued economic assistance.

First computer (ENIAC) unveiled

It has 17,000 vacuum tubes, 70,000 resistors, and 6,000 switches. Weighing 30 tons, it occupies 1800 square feet of space. Today, your laptop computer is probably 100 times more powerful.

First U.S. rocket to fly 50 miles into space

The United States launches a captured German V-2 rocket to an altitude of 69 miles.

1947 — Jackie Robinson breaks race barrier

He becomes the first black major league baseball player, plays in six World Series, and is named MVP in 1949.

Truman forms the U.S. Air Force

The new force is created from the old Army Air Corps.

CIA established

Truman forms the National Security Council, the CIA (from the World War II OSS), and the Department of Defense (from the old Department of War).

1947 **Chuck Yeager breaks the sound barrier**
He becomes the first man to break
the sound barrier in the experimen-
tal jet *X-1*, topping 807 mph.

1948 **Truman desegregates the military**
His Executive Order 9981 orders all armed forces integrated. He resorts to using an executive order because the
southern Democrats would have blocked integration.

"Iron Curtain" falls over Europe
Germany and Berlin have been split
since the war and the Allies rely
on rail and highway lines across the
Soviet sectors of Germany to supply Berlin. The Soviets still greatly
outnumber the American forces in
Europe. The 22,000 Allied troops in
Berlin are surrounded by 1,500,000 Soviet troops. In 1948, the Soviets close

rail and highway access to Berlin to starve the civilians and
force the Allies out of Germany. Their military assures the
Kremlin that the Americans can never supply Berlin from the
air. The U.S. responds with a year-long airlift to supply Berlin
by flying more than 250,000 flights, often only minutes apart.
They land more than 1.7 million tons of food, coal, and supplies. A year later, the Soviets lift the blockade.

Truman Doctrine
Truman warns the USSR that we will do whatever it takes to
stop the spread of Communism. The Cold War starts, pitting
Western democracies against the Communist Soviet Union
and spread of communism.

 *#*83
*#*108,109

Marshall Plan rebuilds Europe
America spends more than $13 billion to rebuild war-torn
Europe and keep countries out of Communist control.

★1948★ HARRY S. TRUMAN RE-ELECTED

CANDIDATE	PARTY	ELECTORAL VOTE	POPULAR VOTE
Harry S. Truman Alben Barkley	Democratic	303	24,179,347
Thomas Dewey Earl Warren	Republican	189	21,991,292
Strom Thurmond Fielding Wright	Dixiecrat	39	1,175,930

The Republicans want Eisenhower, but he refuses. Southern
Democrats form the Dixiecrats to push policies of racial segregation. Everyone picks Dewey to defeat the incumbent Truman, but Truman wins in one of our greatest upsets.

1949 — **NATO established to counter the Soviet threat**
The North American Treaty Organization is established, stating that an attack on a member will be considered an attack on them all. The Soviets get the atom bomb in 1949.

Chinese Nationalist Government is exiled to Taiwan
The communists under Mao Zedong force the Chinese Nationalist government to flee to the island of Taiwan where they form a new government under Chiang Kai-shek. The government in Taiwan continues to represent China in the United Nations until 1971 when the Communist government of mainland China takes her seat.

1950 | **Korean War starts**

#78 2008
#100 2020

The Russians had declared war on Japan days before World War II ended in order to take over countries that Japan occupied during the war. When

Japan surrendered to the Soviet Union, the Russians took over North Korea. In 1950, North Korean Communists invade South Korea, intent on taking over the entire country. American and United Nations troops are sent in, commanded by General MacArthur. The North Koreans capture almost the entire South. General MacArthur lands forces behind the enemy lines at Inchon, catching the North Koreans off guard and they are pushed back almost all the way to China. This leads to the entry of 500,000 Chinese Communists into the war, and

#110 2020

the Southern forces are forced to retreat south of Seoul. The United States also wants to stop the spread of communism.

Assassination attempt on President Truman
Two Puerto Rican Nationalists attempt to assassinate the President while he is living at the Blair House during White House renovation. They kill a White House policeman before the police kill one and wound the other.

1951 —

★ **22ND AMENDMENT** ★
Limits presidents to two terms, or 10 years if serving a partial term.

General MacArthur removed from command
President Truman relieves MacArthur of command in Korea due to a number of public disagreements, primarily because of MacArthur's aggressive approach to the war.

1952 — **First thermonuclear bomb**
America explodes a hydrogen bomb 500 times more powerful than the Hiroshima blast.

Puerto Rico becomes a U.S. Commonwealth
Puerto Rico approves a new Constitution which is ratified by the U.S. Congress and signed by President Truman.

★1952★   DWIGHT D. EISENHOWER   34

CANDIDATE	PARTY	ELECTORAL VOTE	POPULAR VOTE
Dwight D. Eisenhower Richard Nixon	Republican	442	34,075,529
Adlai Stevenson John Sparkman	Democratic	89	27,375,090

This election takes place amidst the stalemated Korean War, increasing Cold War tensions, and anti-Communist investigations led by Senator McCarthy. The recently passed 22nd Amendment does not apply to the sitting president, so Truman is able to run again, but his sinking popularity and early primary losses cause him to drop out. Governor Stevenson of Illinois, grandson of the 1892 vice president, is selected by the Democrats. The Republicans favor the more conservative Robert Taft who wants to overturn many of Roosevelt's New Deal programs, but they select the war hero General Eisenhower as having the best chance to win. Ike campaigns with the popular slogan, "I Like Ike." Ike's running mate, Richard Nixon of California, is accused of accepting illegal gifts. In a televised speech known as the "Checkers" speech, he denies the charges and states that he will not return the dog Checkers that a supporter had given him because his children are so attached to it. Eisenhower wins in a landslide, ending 20 years of a Democratic White House.

1953

Soviet leader Joseph Stalin dies
Nikita Khruschev takes over control of the USSR.

Soviet spies executed
The Rosenbergs are convicted of being Soviet spies and are executed.

Korean War ends
An armistice ends the war without a peace treaty ever being signed. The Communists don't want their freed POW's to stay in the South but rather be forcibly sent to the North. America pledges long-term aid and security, and our forces are still in South Korea today. More than 36,000 American lose their lives in this war, but millions of Chinese and North Korean soldiers, and Korean civilians die.

Dr. Jonas Salk invents polio vaccine
The vaccine ends a dreadful scourge that had even crippled Franklin Roosevelt. Polio will be essentially eradicated worldwide by the end of the century.

1954 — McCarthy Hearings

Senator Joseph McCarthy holds hearings about communism in America. Anti-communist sentiment sweeps America and many careers are affected by the hysteria. Documents released later show that there were indeed Communists in the government, but many innocent people will have their lives destroyed.

Brown v. Board of Education

A Supreme Court decision declares that segregation in public schools is illegal.

Elvis Presley is aired for the first time

A Memphis, Tennessee radio station broadcasts "That's All Right" which some say is the first rock and roll hit.

Pledge of Allegiance changed

President Eisenhower officially adds "under God" to the Pledge of Allegiance.

1955 — McDonald's restaurant opens

The first *McDonald's* opens in Des Plaines, Illinois.

Disneyland opens in Anaheim, California

Rock and Roll music takes off

The new music genre explodes with *Bill Haley and the Comets* release of "Rock Around the Clock" making it to Number 1 on the charts.

"In God We Trust" added to money

Congress orders the motto "In God We Trust" put on all U.S. currency, and makes it the official national motto.

Rosa Parks keeps her seat on the bus

The black woman is arrested for refusing to give up her seat to a white man, touching off a boycott and the civil rights movement that ultimately results in the Civil Rights Act that ends racial discrimination.

#84 **2008**
#112 **2020**

1956 — Interstate Highway Act

The U.S. starts large-scale construction of interstate highways. Side effects include loss of railroads and right-of-ways that would be useful in the future, and the explosion of suburbs.

Andrea Doria sinks

The liner *Andrea Doria* sinks off Nantucket after colliding with the Swedish liner *Stockholm*. Forty-six passengers die.

★1956★ DWIGHT EISENHOWER RE-ELECTED

CANDIDATE	PARTY	ELECTORAL VOTE	POPULAR VOTE
Dwight D. Eisenhower Richard Nixon	Republican	457	35,579,180
Adlai Stevenson Estes Kefauver	Democratic	73	26,028,028

Eisenhower and Nixon are picked to run again, and the Democrats pick Stevenson again. However, Stevenson lets the convention select his running mate, setting off a scramble to fill that spot. Stevenson's running mate in 1952, John Sparkman, is ignored due to his stance against racial integration. Senator Kennedy almost wins the nomination on the second ballot before the delegates pick Kefauver. There are concerns about Eisenhower's health, but his doctors clear him for running again. The country is prosperous and Ike has ended the Korean War, so he wins again in a landslide.

1957 — Eisenhower signs Civil Rights Act of 1957

The first civil rights act since Reconstruction focuses on voting rights for blacks. The Democrat Senator from South Carolina, Strom Thurmond, sustains the longest one-person filibuster in history (24 hours) to try to block the bill. The act sets the scene for later civil rights legislation.

Integration enforced in the South

Federal troops are sent to Central High School in Little Rock, Arkansas to enforce integration.

Space Race begins

The Soviets launch the first satellite, *Sputnik*. Americans launch their first satellite a year later.

1958 — NASA is formed to send America into space

The National Aeronautics and Space Administration selects the first seven Astronauts—Alan Shepard, Virgil Grissom, John Glenn, Scott Carpenter, Walter Schirra, Gordon Cooper, and Donald Slayton.

USS *Nautilus* reaches the North Pole

The first nuclear submarine travels under Arctic ice to become the first vessel to reach the North Pole on August 3.

1959 — Castro takes over Cuba

Fidel Castro and his gang of rebels oust President Batista and make Cuba a Communist state propped up by the Soviet Union. He will rule Cuba into the next century.

1959 — **Saint Lawrence Seaway opens**
The seaway connects the Atlantic Ocean to Lake Superior, using locks, canals, and the Saint Lawrence River.

Alaska and Hawaii become states
Alaska becomes the 49th state, and Hawaii follows soon thereafter as the 50th.

"The day the music died"
An airplane crash kills rock stars Buddy Holly, Ritchie Valens, and "Big Bopper" J.P. Richardson.

1960 — **First weather satellite Tiros I launched**

★1960★   JOHN F. KENNEDY   35

CANDIDATE	PARTY	ELECTORAL VOTE	POPULAR VOTE
John F. Kennedy Lyndon Johnson	Democratic	303	34,220,911
Richard Nixon Henry Cabot Lodge, Jr.	Republican	219	34,108,157
Harry Byrd Strom Thurmond	Democratic	15	not on the ballot

Eisenhower cannot run again due to the terms of the 22nd amendment, so the Republicans pick his vice president, Richard Nixon, as their candidate, and Henry Cabot Lodge as his running mate for his foreign policy experience. Kennedy competes with Senate Majority Leader Johnson for the Democratic nomination. When Kennedy wins the nomination, he selects Johnson as his vice president to gain support from southern states. Nixon wastes time honoring his pledge to campaign in all 50 states—Hawaii and Alaska were just admitted as states. Kennedy's campaign is well-funded and well-run, and he directly addresses concerns about his Roman Catholic faith. His faith probably wins him more votes than it loses. Seventy million viewers watch the first televised presidential debate, in which a well-prepared and healthy-looking Kennedy bests the tired and pale-looking Nixon. Nixon does much better in the next three debates, but fewer people watch them. Kennedy wins the election with a popular margin of only 0.1%, but a wider margin in the Electoral College. However, ten states are decided by 2% or less of the vote, and there are charges that fraud in Illinois and Texas gave those states to Kennedy. If Nixon had won those two states, he would be president. Kennedy becomes the youngest elected president and ushers in a new generation of leaders.

1961

★ 23RD AMENDMENT ★
Grants Washington, D.C. representation in the Electoral College.

1961 — **Bay of Pigs disaster in Cuba**
U.S.-backed exiles invade Cuba but are killed or captured in a failed attempt to topple Castro.

First U.S. advisors arrive in South Vietnam

First American in space
Alan Shepard becomes the first American in space. The Russian Yuri Gagarin had become the first human in space the month before.

Freedom Riders
Thirteen men and women, both white and black, ride together on a bus from Washington, D.C. to New Orleans. They oppose southern laws that prevent whites and blacks from sitting together on buses. In Alabama, their bus is attacked and the riders beaten. In Mississippi, they are arrested and thrown into jail.

Berlin Wall divides the city
The Soviets build a solid wall to keep East Germans from escaping to the West, though the Soviets are brazen enough to call it an "Anti-Fascist Protection Rampart" supposedly to keep outside influences away from East Germany. Almost 200 people will die trying to escape to West Germany until the wall is torn down in 1989. The last time an escapee will be shot by a guard is in February of 1989.

1962 — **John Glenn orbits the Earth in *Friendship 7***
Kennedy's 1961 speech had challenged the U.S. to put a man on the moon, and this is the first step.

Cuban Missile Crisis
The USSR places nuclear missiles in Cuba but are spotted by American U-2 spy planes. The U.S. blockades Cuba and Kennedy forces the Soviets to back down. In exchange for removing the missiles, Kennedy agrees to remove missiles from Turkey, and never invade Cuba.

1963 — **"I Have a Dream" speech on August 28**
Martin Luther King delivers his famous "I Have a Dream" speech on the steps of the Lincoln Memorial in Washington, D.C. to over 200,000 civil rights supporters.

JFK assassinated on November 22

Lee Harvey Oswald shoots the president while he is riding in a Dallas motorcade, and Kennedy dies 30 minutes later. Oswald is arrested, but is killed days later by Jack Ruby.

★1963★   Lyndon B. Johnson   36

After Kennedy is shot in Dallas, his vice president, Lyndon Johnson, becomes president. Johnson is driven to the airport in an unmarked car and waits on board Air Force One for the arrival of Jackie Kennedy and her husband's casket. Upon her arrival, Johnson is administered the oath of office by federal judge Sarah Hughes. It is the only time a woman has administered the oath, and the only time it has been done in an airplane. Nine minutes later, the plane departs for Washington, D.C.

1964

★ 24ᵀᴴ Amendment ★

Prohibits the use of poll taxes to restrict voting rights.

Vietnam crisis heats up

Vietnam was divided in two in 1954 with the Communist Ho Chi Minh controlling the North, and Ngo Dinh Diem governing the South. The South is supported first by the French, and then by the United States. The North is propped up and supplied by China and the USSR.

Alaska Good Friday Earthquake

A devastating 9.2 earthquake hits Alaska on Good Friday, lasting for four minutes. It is the most powerful earthquake in North American history. The immediate shaking and resulting tsunami cause 130 deaths.

Civil Rights Act of 1964

President Johnson signs the Civil Rights Act that outlaws discrimination against blacks and women, ending segregation in schools and public places. It also protects voter registration. Martin Luther King receives the Nobel Peace Prize later this year.

Gulf of Tonkin incident

U.S. advisors are already in Vietnam. The North Vietnamese attack the USS *Maddox,* leading President Johnson to commit troops and resources. The U.S. bases its policies on the Domino Principle—the fear that if one nation falls to Communism, other nations will also fall like dominoes.

★1964★ LYNDON JOHNSON RE-ELECTED

CANDIDATE	PARTY	ELECTORAL VOTE	POPULAR VOTE
Lyndon Johnson Hubert Humphrey	Democratic	486	43,127,041
Barry Goldwater William Miller	Republican	52	27,175,754

Johnson is picked by his party, but has problems with Attorney General Robert Kennedy. The two have disliked each other ever since Kennedy tried to keep Johnson from being his brother's running mate in 1960. Kennedy wants the vice president spot, but Johnson announces that no cabinet member will be considered, and schedules Kennedy's speech on the last day of the convention to further diminish his influence. Johnson picks the liberal Hubert Humphrey as his running mate. The Republican Party is split, with conservatives favoring Barry Goldwater, a Senator from Arizona, and the moderates Nelson Rockefeller of New York. The conservatives support a low-tax, small government platform and oppose the social welfare programs of Johnson. Rockefeller is the front-runner for the Republican nomination until he remarries a new wife, 15 years younger, with four children, and who has just divorced her husband, leading to accusations of adultery. The scandal dies down, only to reemerge three days before the California primary when his new wife gives birth. He never recovers and Goldwater wins the nomination. Johnson wins in a landslide with a large popular vote margin. The election marks the first participation of the District of Columbia after the passage of the 23rd Amendment. It also is the first time Republicans win Georgia, and the first time they win three other southern states since Reconstruction. The election marks the emergence of the modern conservative movement, punctuated by Ronald Reagan's landslide victory in the California governor's race two years later.

1965 — Selma civil rights march

Troopers meet a civil rights march in Selma, Alabama with tear gas and billy clubs. Reverend Martin Luther King, Jr. leads thousands on a march from Selma to Montgomery.

Dominican Republic military action

President Johnson sends 42,000 soldiers to the Dominican Republic against the advice of his civilian advisers. He fears a Communist takeover of that country due to civil unrest. U.S. forces leave a year later. Forty-four American soldiers are killed during the occupation.

1965

The Great Society
President Johnson proposes the *Great Society*, involving a massive government commitment to Social Security, Medicaid, and Medicare.

President Johnson signs the Voting Rights Act
The Act bans literacy tests and similar barriers to voting, ensuring blacks will not be denied the right to vote.

Watts race riots
A routine arrest of a black driver by a white police officer touches off race riots in Los Angeles that kill 35 people.

1966

Miranda ruling
A Supreme Court ruling protects the rights of arrested citizens, resulting in the well-known Miranda Rights that must be read to all suspects.

First black Cabinet member
Robert Weaver becomes the first black cabinet member as head of Housing and Urban Development.

1967

First Super Bowl
Led by Bart Starr, the NFL Green Bay Packers defeat the AFL Kansas City Chiefs. The 2011 Super Bowl will be the most watched TV show in history.

Spacecraft fire kills three astronauts
Three NASA astronauts die in a spacecraft fire at Cape Canaveral; Gus Grissom, Edward White II, and Roger Chaffee.

★ 25ᵀᴴ Amendment ★
Defines the order and process of presidential succession.

First black Supreme Court Judge
Thurgood Marshall becomes the first black Supreme Court Justice.

Summer of Love
The Sixties see sexual freedom, the birth control pill, protest marches, drugs, and hippies.

1968

More troops in Vietnam
U.S. Troop strength in Vietnam rises to 500,000 troops. The U.S. wants to stop the spread of communism.

Tet offensive in Vietnam
Though technically a victory for the U.S., this offensive by the North Vietnamese helps drive sentiment against the war. Up to 1,000 soldiers are dying each month.

#78 2008

#100,111 2020

1968 — My Lai shooting
American troops kill innocent civilians in Vietnam.

Martin Luther King assassinated
Escaped convict James Earl Ray shoots King at a hotel in Memphis, Tennessee.

Robert Kennedy assassinated
An Arab nationalist, Sirhan Sirhan, shoots and kills presidential candidate Robert Kennedy as he campaigns in Los Angeles.

Intel Corporation starts

It soon becomes the leading developer of the microchip and the world's largest semiconductor chip maker.

Democratic National Convention riots
The Chicago convention is marked by huge anti-war demonstrations.

★1968★ RICHARD M. NIXON 37

CANDIDATE	PARTY	ELECTORAL VOTE	POPULAR VOTE
Richard M. Nixon Spiro Agnew	Republican	301	31,783,783
Hubert Humphrey Edmund Muskie	Democratic	191	31,271,839
George Wallace Curtis LeMay	American Independent	46	9,901,118

The 1968 election happens at a tumultuous time in our history. Civil Rights leader Martin Luther King, Jr. and presidential candidate Robert Kennedy have both been assassinated, and anti-war and race riots break out all over the country. Johnson announces he is suspending bombing in North Vietnam, and then withdraws from the race. His health is bad and he dies in 1973, two days after a new term would have ended. His popularity has also plummeted due to the ongoing war in Vietnam. Hubert Humphrey is picked as the Democratic candidate and runs on an anti-war platform. Nixon runs on a promise to restore law and order. Alabama Governor George Wallace also runs a strong campaign based on maintaining racial segregation. He picks retired General Curtis LeMay as his running mate, but LeMay makes a gaffe when he suggests we use nuclear weapons in Vietnam. The Democratic National Convention in Chicago is beset by violent anti-war protests. Nixon wins the election with a narrow popular vote margin, but wider electoral margin.

1968

Astronauts circle the Moon

On Christmas Eve, the astronauts onboard Apollo 8 beam back a message of hope to Earth as they prepare to circle the moon several times before returning to Earth.

1969

Apollo 11 lands on the Moon—July 20, 1969

Neil Armstrong and Edwin Aldrin walk on the moon, fulfilling President Kennedy's 1961 pledge. They leave a plaque that reads, "HERE MEN FROM THE PLANET EARTH FIRST SET FOOT UPON THE MOON JULY 1969 A.D. WE CAME IN PEACE FOR ALL MANKIND." 600 million people worldwide watch the event live on TV.

Woodstock Music Festival

Max Yasgur's farm in New York is the scene of a huge outdoor music festival attended by 400,000.

First messages sent on ARPANET

A UCLA programmer sends the first message on the Department of Defense network that will become the Internet.

1970

Apollo 13 mission aborted

An explosion cripples the moon-bound spacecraft. Aided by radio instructions from Houston, the astronauts' ingenuity and endurance help them reach home safely.

Earth Day is first observed in the U.S.

U.S. Environmental Protection Agency (EPA) founded.

Cambodia invaded by U.S.

The invasion sparks huge student protests resulting in an accidental National Guard shooting resulting in the deaths of four Kent State students in Pennsylvania.

1971

Texas Instruments introduces first pocket calculator

★ 26ᵀᴴ AMENDMENT ★

Changes the national voting age from 21 to 18.

"Pentagon Papers" are released

A former Marine releases confidential documents concerning the Vietnam War to the New York Times, further eroding public support for the war.

1972

President Nixon visits Communist China

He opens trade relations on the first visit of an American president since the Communists took over.

1972— **Watergate break-in**

Nixon operatives break into the Democratic National Committee office at the Watergate building in Washington, D.C. This eventually leads to Nixon's resignation in two years. "Watergate" enters the national language, helping to name future scandals from Travelgate to Monicagate. The irony is that the break-in is completely unnecessary as Nixon easily wins reelection.

Munich Summer Olympics end in tragedy

American Mark Spitz wins 7 Olympic swimming medals. An Arab terrorist group kidnaps and murders 11 Israeli Olympians.

★1972★ RICHARD NIXON RE-ELECTED

CANDIDATE	PARTY	ELECTORAL VOTE	POPULAR VOTE
Richard Nixon Spiro Agnew	Republican	520	47,168,710
George McGovern Sargent Shriver	Democratic	17	29,173,222

The Democrats think that Ted Kennedy will be their candidate, but his role in the fatal accident at Chappaquiddick in 1969 ends his chances. Ed Muskie is another favorite, but George McGovern wins the nomination. McGovern's first pick for his running mate is Senator Thomas Eagleton. After the convention, he discovers that Eagleton had undergone electroshock therapy for depression and withheld this information. McGovern initially backs Eagleton completely, but doctors advise him that the condition could reoccur and endanger the country. Three days later, McGovern asks Eagleton to withdraw, and picks Shriver instead. However, his apparent indecision sinks his campaign. McGovern runs an anti-war campaign against incumbent Republican President Richard Nixon. Nixon wins in a landslide with one of the largest margins in history in the first election where the Republicans capture every Southern state.

Apollo 17 moon landing is America's last

Eugene Cernan, Ronald Evans, and Harrison Schmitt make the sixth lunar landing.

1973— **Paris Peace Treaty**

A treaty is signed to end the Vietnam War, but fighting continues and the U.S. resumes bombing in Cambodia.

***Roe v. Wade* legalizes abortion**

This Supreme Court decision legalizes abortions in the first trimester. Texas District Attorney Henry Wade had defended Texas against Jane Roe's lawsuit about abortion.

1973 — **OPEC oil embargo**
To punish countries that supported Israel in their recent war, the oil producing nations restrict oil exports. The cost of gasoline in the U.S. rises from 40 cents to above 55 cents a gallon, resulting in widespread shortages and conservation efforts such as reducing speed limits. Inflation continues throughout the decade with gold and gas prices soaring, and interest rates topping 12%.

Vice President Spiro Agnew resigns
Corruption charges force him from office. President Nixon picks Gerald Ford as the new vice president.

Endangered Species Act
President Nixon signs an environmental law to protect species identified as endangered by mankind's actions.

1974 — **New home run record on April 8, 1974**
Atlanta Brave Henry Aaron breaks Babe Ruth's home run record when he hits his 715th home run.

President Richard Nixon resigns
He becomes the first president in history to resign. Investigations uncover his involvement in the Watergate scandal and his attempts to hamper the investigation. He admits to taping Oval Office conversations, but one of  the critical tapes has an unexplained 18½ minute gap.

★**1974**★　　　　　GERALD FORD　　　　　**38**

Vice President Ford becomes president when Nixon resigns. He is the only president never to have been elected, since he was picked by Nixon to be vice president after Spiro Agnew resigned. Ford names Nelson Rockefeller as the new vice president.

President Ford pardons Nixon amid much criticism
He feels that the nation must leave the scandal behind.

1975 — **South Vietnam surrenders**
The last U.S. civilians are evacuated from Saigon. Khmer Rouge forces take over Cambodia and embark on four years of terror, resulting in 1.5 million deaths. Saigon is eventually renamed Ho Chi Minh City.

1975 — **President Ford survives 2 assassination attempts**
Lynette "Squeaky" Fromme botches an attempt in Sacramento, California, and Sara Jane Moore's shot misses two weeks later in San Francisco.

1976 — **Viking 1 and 2 land on Mars**
They are the first landers to successfully complete their mission and transmit information back to Earth. Of 38 Soviet and U.S. launches of spacecraft for Mars, only 19 succeeded. Most of the failures were Soviet.

Woman admitted to military academies
The U.S. Naval Academy and West Point admit women for the first time.

⋆1976⋆   JIMMY CARTER   39

CANDIDATE	PARTY	ELECTORAL VOTE	POPULAR VOTE
Jimmy Carter Walter Mondale	Democratic	297	40,831,881
Gerald Ford Bob Dole	Republican	240	39,148,634

Gerald Ford narrowly beats out fellow Republican Ronald Reagan for the Republican nomination. After Reagan's stirring final speech, many delegates wish they had nominated him instead. Ford is still saddled with the effects of the Watergate scandal, and his subsequent pardoning of Nixon. Ford also misspeaks in the debate when he says that there is no Soviet domination of Europe. The Democrats select the relatively unknown former Georgia Governor Carter. He runs as an outsider and reformer. Carter wins a very close election, taking Wisconsin and Ohio by very slim margins. Winning those states would have given Ford the election. The 27 states won by Ford are the most ever won by a losing candidate.

1977 — **Apple jump-starts the computer age**
Steve Wozniak and Steve Jobs release the Apple computer that really starts the computer age as business and homes start adopting computers. Earlier minicomputers like the Altair were mainly for hobbyists. The release of the Apple Macintosh and the IBM PC further advance home computers. Bill Gates forms Microsoft which becomes one of the largest companies in the world, and he becomes the world's richest man selling MS-DOS and Windows platforms, and applications like Word and Excel.

1977 — **George Lucas' movie *Star Wars* debuts**
The ground-breaking epic cost only $11 million and will earn over $800 million and receive six Academy Awards.

Elvis Presley dies suddenly in Memphis
However, many people will still report seeing him alive.

Trans-Alaska pipeline is finished stretching 800 miles
It will carry almost 16 billion barrels of oil by 2010.

Carter turns over the Panama Canal
Carter agrees to turn over the canal to Panama at a future date. He also pardons most Vietnam War draft evaders.

1978 — **Camp David Accords**
Anwar El Sadat of Egypt and Menachem Begin of Israel sign an historic peace agreement at the White House, arranged by Jimmy Carter.

Jonestown mass suicide one of largest in history
Politicians investigate Reverend Jim Jones' People's Temple in Guyana. The paranoid Jones convinces his entire following to drink poisoned kool-aid. More than 900 men, women, and children die.

1979 — **U.S. establishes diplomatic ties with Communist China**

Ross Perot rescues EDS employees held captive in Iran
Retired Colonel Simons leads volunteer team on daring mission to rescue 2 employees from Iranian prison and get them out of the country as the Iranian revolution takes hold.

Three Mile Island nuclear reactor accident in Pennsylvania
A partial core meltdown is the worst accident in the U.S. nuclear industry's history. Radioactive gases are released but no one is killed or injured. The worst effect is turning public opinion against nuclear energy. The building of new reactors in the U.S. grinds to a halt.

Iranian hostages taken November 4
Radical Iranian students take sixty-six Americans hostage at our Embassy in Tehran. The U.S. had backed the Shah of Iran who was modernizing the country but was overthrown by the religious Ayatollah Khomeni. The hostages are held until January 20, 1981 when Reagan is inaugurated.

U.S.S.R. invades Afghanistan
The Soviets will occupy Afghanistan for ten years but fail to subdue the country and will be forced to retreat.

1980

Iranian rescue mission ends in disaster

Carter authorizes a daring helicopter mission into Iran to rescue the hostages but it ends in failure when a helicopter crashes in a desert storm, killing 8 soldiers.

Mount St. Helens explodes

The Washington volcano causes billions of dollars in damage and kills fifty-seven people. It is the deadliest volcano in American history. Its height is reduced by 1,312 feet.

The day before   **After the eruption**

U.S. boycotts Moscow Summer Olympics

 In a response to the Soviet occupation of Afghanistan, the U.S. withdraws from the Moscow games. However, in the winter games at Lake Placid, NY, the U.S. hockey team defeats the superior Soviet squad, 4-3, giving the country a huge morale boost.

★1980★   RONALD REAGAN   40

CANDIDATE	PARTY	ELECTORAL VOTE	POPULAR VOTE
Ronald Reagan George H.W. Bush	Republican	489	43,903,230
Jimmy Carter Walter Mondale	Democratic	49	35,480,115
John Anderson Patrick Lucey	Independent	0	5,719,850

Incumbent Jimmy Carter fends off a challenge from Ted Kennedy, but is dogged by a bad economy, high inflation, and the ongoing Iranian hostage crisis. The Republicans pick Reagan, a former Hollywood actor of 53 films and two-term California governor, who almost was picked four years earlier. He believes in states' rights, lower taxes, and small government. Carter attacks Reagan as a right-wing radical who poses a threat to world peace and social welfare programs. The second presidential debate, held one week before the election, is a turning point. After the debate, the tight race opens up in Reagan's favor. Carter makes a few gaffes in the debate, at one point saying he relies on his 12-year old daughter for advice on nuclear arms policy. Republicans win control of the Senate for the first time in 28 years and begin the Reagan Revolution. His electoral college victory is the most lopsided ever for a non-incumbent.

1981

President Reagan revitalizes America
He is named "The Great Communicator" as he works to reduce the size of government. He lowers the top tax rates from 70% to 28%. His economic policies help produce a decade of reduced inflation, interest rates, and unemployment rates. His beliefs and speeches lead to a surge in patriotism.

President Reagan shot

John Hinckley almost kills the president in a shooting that severely wounds James Brady. Reagan survives the attempt, feeling God now has a specific purpose for him. He teams with Britain's Margaret Thatcher and Pope John Paul II, both of whom also survived assassination attempts, to help defeat Communism in Europe and bring down the Iron Curtain.

First space shuttle blasts off on April 12
Columbia blasts off from Cape Canaveral and returns to Earth two days later.

First female Supreme Court Justice
Sandra Day O'Conner becomes the first female Supreme Court Justice.

HIV and AIDS
The new scourge kills tens of thousands in the next decade. Reagan is accused of ignoring the problem, but both Democrat and Republican politicians avoid the issue. Annual federal spending on AIDS programs increases from $8,000,000 to $2,300,000,000. By 2010, more than 25 million worldwide will die from this disease, 500,000 in the U.S.

1982

Vietnam Veterans Memorial
A new polished black granite wall, designed by U.S. architect Maya Lin, is finished in Washington, D.C. containing the names of the 58,000 Americans who died in the war.

1983

Evil Empire speech
President Reagan delivers his famous speech calling the Soviet Union an "evil empire."

Pioneer 10 leaves the solar system
Launched in 1972, the satellite becomes the first spacecraft to leave our solar system. It will communicate until 2003.

Reagan announces SDI program
Reagan's push for the Strategic Defense Initiative (SDI) for space-based defense convinces the USSR that they cannot afford to compete against such a system and eventually leads to the Soviet collapse.

1983 — **First American woman in space**

Sally Ride becomes the first American woman in space on board the shuttle *Challenger.*

Marines die in Lebanon blast

A terrorist explosion at a Marine barracks in Beirut, Lebanon kills 241 Marines. Islamic Jihad claims responsibility.

America invades Grenada

After a Marxist takeover of this Caribbean island, Reagan sends 8,000 troops to take control and rescue American students held there. Many debate whether the invasion is necessary, but it is a case of acting early to deter this and future Communist incursions into this part of the world.

1984 — **First woman on presidential ticket**

Geraldine Ferraro becomes the first woman on a major presidential ticket in history, being named the vice presidential candidate for Walter Mondale. Their ticket is defeated by Ronald Reagan in a landslide.

★1984★ RONALD REAGAN RE-ELECTED

CANDIDATE	PARTY	ELECTORAL VOTE	POPULAR VOTE
Ronald Reagan George H. W. Bush	*Republican*	525	54,455,472
Walter Mondale Geraldine Ferraro	*Democratic*	13	37,577,352

The incumbent Reagan runs again with the same vice president, George H.W. Bush. The Democrats have more trouble. Walter Mondale, Jesse Jackson, and Gary Hart all vie for the nomination. Ted Kennedy decides not to run again, but not before making secret advances to Soviet Secretary Andropov in an attempt to discredit Reagan and his policies. Jackson makes racist remarks about Jews and loses backing. Hart lacks financing and stumbles in the televised debates. Mondale wins the nomination and picks Representative Geraldine Ferraro as his running mate, the first woman named on a major party's presidential ticket. He hopes to appeal to women voters. He runs a liberal campaign pushing for a nuclear freeze and calls Reagan's economic policies unfair. The election is never really in doubt. Reagan carries every state except Mondale's home state of Minnesota. He receives the highest number of electoral votes in history.

1986 — **Space shuttle *Challenger* explodes on takeoff**

A faulty o-ring leads to an explosion that kills all seven astronauts, including teacher Christa McAuliffe.

1986 — U.S. bombs Libya

Reagan determines Libya is behind a deadly Berlin disco bombing and orders American aircraft to bomb sites in Libya, almost killing leader Qaddafi in the process. Qaddafi's government has been financing and conducting anti-Western acts around the world for 2 decades, ignoring U.S. sanctions.

Reykjavik summit

Reagan and Gorbachev meet in Iceland to discuss disarmament. Reagan stands firm against the Soviet request to dismantle the Strategic Defense Initiative and the meeting is terminated.

Iran Contra scandal harms Reagan's legacy

In a scandal that almost destroys his presidency, information is released that details an American deal to give arms to Iran in return for the release of hostages held in Lebanon.

1987 — "Mr. Gorbachev, tear down this wall!"

Reagan bluntly confronts the Soviets in a speech in front of the Berlin Wall. To the deafening cheers of Berliners, he implores Gorbachev to tear down the Berlin Wall.

Black Monday

The stock market falls 508 points in the largest percentage drop in history. It is caused by a number of factors, including program trading and speculation.

★1988★   GEORGE H. W. BUSH   41

Candidate	Party	Electoral Vote	Popular Vote
George H.W. Bush Dan Quayle	Republican	426	48,886,597
Michael Dukakis Lloyd Bentsen	Democratic	111	41,809,476

Ronald Reagan can't run again, so Vice President Bush becomes the Republican nominee. Democrats pick Massachusetts Governor Michael Dukakis. Democratic contender Gary Hart drops out after an affair with Donna Rice is revealed. Senator Kennedy declines to run, and Senator Joe Biden, accused of plagiarism in a speech, also drops out. Dukakis picks Texan Lloyd Bentsen as his running mate for his experience and to help in winning southern votes. Bush picks Dan Quayle of Indiana who becomes known for his verbal gaffes. Dukakis stages a disastrous photo-op wearing a tank commander's helmet, and is also hurt by the "Willie Horton" ads blaming him for releasing a convicted murderer who then commits rape. Bush benefits from a good economy, stability abroad, and Reagan's legacy, to easily win.

1988 — **First Hispanic Cabinet Member**
President Reagan nominates the first Hispanic to serve in the cabinet, Lauro Cavazos, as Secretary of Education.

Pan Am Flight 103 destroyed
Libyan terrorists blow up Pan Am Flight 103 over Scotland, killing 270 people.

1989 — ***Exxon Valdez* runs aground**

The tanker hits a reef in Prince William Sound, Alaska, and spills ten million gallons of crude oil causing great environmental damage.

First black governor elected in Virginia
Douglas Wilder is the nation's first elected black governor.

Berlin Wall and Iron Curtain fall

Helped by Reagan's policies, and Soviet leader Gorbachev's *glasnost* and *perestroika*, the Soviets relax their iron grip on Europe and jubilant Berliners tear down the Berlin Wall on November 9. This picture shows them on top of the wall in front of the Brandenburg Gate where Reagan spoke 2 years earlier. Over the next two years, the U.S.S.R. is dissolved into separate nation states.

U.S. invades Panama to capture fugitive General Noriega
The military dictator is accused by the U.S. of drug trafficking and racketeering, is tried in U.S. courts, and imprisoned.

1990 — **Hubble space telescope**

The space shuttle deploys the most powerful telescope in history to help unlock secrets of the universe. It will be serviced 5 times by space shuttle missions and will still be working in 2011.

Picture from shuttle *Discovery*

Iraq invades Kuwait
Hoping to expand his oil resources, Saddam Hussein invades neighboring Kuwait and incites fears he could advance on Saudi Arabia. President Bush builds an international coalition to remove him from Kuwait.

1991 — **Operation Desert Storm**
Congress approves war and President Bush orders Operation Desert Storm to retake Kuwait. A month of aerial bombing, including American stealth airplanes, leads to a short ground war lasting 100 hours. Iraq launches 39 missiles into Israel, killing 74 people. The U.S. deploys Patriot missiles to help shoot down these incoming missiles.

2008 #78

2020 #100,114

1991 — **Iraq war ends**
The coalition forces drive Iraq from Kuwait, but President Bush stops short of destroying the entire Iraqi army. American losses are around 150 killed while Sadaam loses anywhere from 25,000 to 35,000 troops.

1992 — **Formal end to the cold war**
President Bush and Russian President Yeltsin formally declare an end to the cold war.

Rodney King verdict sparks riots
Police officers accused of beating King in a year-earlier arrest are acquitted, touching off violent riots in Los Angeles that kill 54 people and damage $500 million of property.

Bosnia secedes from Yugoslavia
Years of war ensue with U.N. and U.S. involvement.

★ **27ᵀᴴ AMENDMENT** ★
Prevents any laws that affect Congressional salaries from taking effect until the next Congressional session.

1992   BILL CLINTON   42

CANDIDATE	PARTY	ELECTORAL VOTE	POPULAR VOTE
Bill Clinton Al Gore	Democratic	370	44,909,806
George H. W. Bush Dan Quayle	Republican	168	39,104,550
Ross Perot James Stockdale	Independent	0	19,743,821

This three-way race has the strongest independent candidate since Teddy Roosevelt. Bush had 89% approval ratings after the Gulf War, but they are steadily falling. He raised taxes after promising he would not. His foreign policy experience is less important after the end of the Cold War. Several Democrats run for office, including Jerry Brown of California. His bid ends shortly after announcing in New York that he might pick Jesse Jackson as a running mate. The Jewish community still distrusts Jackson after earlier anti-Semitic remarks. Clinton wins the nomination and picks Al Gore of Tennessee as his running mate, bringing stronger family values and environmental experience to the race. Independent Texas billionaire Ross Perot promises to reduce debt and stop the NAFTA agreement. He gains support across the country and leads the race for two months. Clinton is accused of dodging the draft during the Vietnam War, using marijuana, which he famously says he "didn't inhale," and engaging in extramarital affairs. Clinton comfortably wins the election and, more importantly, the Democrats regain control of both houses of Congress.

1993

World Trade Center explosion
Islamic extremists explode bombs in the basement of the World Trade Center in an attempt to destroy the building.

Branch Davidian standoff
A religious sect holds off the federal government at their compound near Waco, Texas. A government attack results in the death of 84 cult members and 4 agents.

Missile strike on Iraq
Clinton launches cruise missiles at several sites in Iraq in retaliation for an Iraqi assassination attempt on former President Bush.

American soldiers killed in Somalia
Islamic militia members ambush and kill 18 members of Task Force Ranger in Mogadishu, leading to a U.S. withdrawal from Somalia.

1994

North American Free Trade Agreement takes effect
Canada, Mexico, and the United States sign the NAFTA agreement to improve trade between the nations.

Contract with America pays off for Republicans
Republicans devise a "Contract with America" of pledges and promises, and gain control of both Senate and House for the first time in 40 years.

1995

Oklahoma City bombing
U.S. extremist Timothy McVeigh explodes a home-made bomb by the federal building, killing 168 people. He will be executed on June 11, 2001.

U.S. establishes diplomatic ties with Vietnam

O.J. Simpson trial
The circus trial of former football star and actor O.J. Simpson for the murders of his ex-wife and her friend comes to an end. The jury acquits Simpson of the crime.

1996

Welfare Reform
Pushed by a Republican Congress, President Clinton signs a Welfare Work bill that ends lifetime welfare benefits and requires work to continue benefits.

Pipe bomb explodes at the Atlanta Olympics
A domestic terrorist, Eric Rudolph, detonates the largest pipe bomb in our history at Centennial Olympic Park in Atlanta, killing two people and injuring 111.

★1996★ Bill Clinton re-elected

Candidate	Party	Electoral Vote	Popular Vote
Bill Clinton Al Gore	Democratic	379	47,401,185
Bob Dole Jack Kemp	Republican	159	39,197,469
Ross Perot Patrick Choate	Reform	0	8.085,294

As an incumbent without competition, Clinton can focus on the election. The Republican Party is on a high after regaining control of Congress in the 1994 elections, but do not have an obvious candidate. They finally pick Bob Dole, whom Clinton depicts as an aged conservative—Dole is 73 compared to the 50-year-old Clinton. Dole highlights the perception by falling off a stage during an event, and forgetting that a baseball team has changed towns. He runs on a platform of reduced taxes and supply-side economics. Perot runs again, but garners only half the votes he got four years earlier. Clinton easily wins reelection in a manner almost identical to the 1992 election.

1998 — African embassy bombings
Al-Qaeda terrorists explode bombs at U.S. embassies in Africa, killing more than 200.

Clinton caught in scandal
President Clinton is accused of having sex with intern Monica Lewinsky and then attempting to cover up the act. The House votes to impeach Clinton on charges of perjury and obstruction of justice.

1999 — President Clinton acquitted of impeachment charges
Clinton is impeached by the House but acquitted by the Senate. President Andrew Johnson was also impeached and acquitted.

NATO attacks Yugoslavia
NATO forces attack Yugoslavia over ethnic cleansing charges during the Kosovo War.

Columbine High School shooting
Two Colorado high school seniors use an arsenal of weapons to kill 12 students, a teacher, and then themselves.

Slovenia
Croatia
Bosnia Herzegovina
Serbia
Macedonia
FORMER YUGOSLAVIA

Panama Canal transferred
Complete control of the Panama Canal is transferred to Panama following terms of the treaty signed by Carter in 1977.

2 0 0 0

2000 **Y2K disaster fizzles**
Experts predict a disaster when clocks roll over from 1999 to 2000. This Y2K, or Millennium, bug would affect computer programs that represent the year with only two digits, thus possibly treating the new year '00' as 1900 and not 2000. However, no major problems occur.

Terrorists attack USS *Cole*
Al-Qaeda terrorists ram the USS *Cole* in Yemen with a small boat of explosives, killing 17 sailors and injuring 39. The Navy's rules of engagement prevent them from firing on the approaching vessel.

Damage to USS *Cole*

★2000★　　　　GEORGE W. BUSH　　　43

Candidate	Party	Electoral Vote	Popular Vote
George W. Bush Dick Cheney	*Republican*	271	50,456,002
Al Gore Joe Lieberman	*Democratic*	266	50,999,897

The Republicans pick the 41ˢᵗ President's son, Texas Governor George W. Bush, as their candidate. Bill Clinton has served his maximum two terms, so his vice president, Al Gore, runs for the Democrats. Gore picks Joe Lieberman, the first Jewish-American chosen by a major party. Bush initially asks Secretary of Defense Dick Cheney to help him pick a vice president, but ends up selecting Cheney as his running mate. Cheney is also from Texas and electors can't cast both their votes to candidates from the same state, so Cheney changes his registration back to Wyoming. Bush's campaign is well-funded and he has obvious name recognition because of his father. Republicans run against the Clinton scandals, which Gore tries to ignore. Ralph Nader enters the race and eventually wins 2.7% of the popular vote, potentially affecting the outcome. The vote is extremely close but Gore concedes the race late in the night. He later recants as he learns that Florida, New Mexico, and Oregon are too close to call. Gore requests a hand recount of several Florida counties reporting voting irregularities. Both the Florida Supreme Court and the U.S. Supreme Court get involved. When the dust settles, Bush is declared winner on December 12. Bush wins all southern states, including Gore's home state of Tennessee, and Bill Clinton's home of Arkansas. Bush is the 4th president to receive fewer popular votes than the losing candidate.

2001

China illegally grounds U.S. plane
China intercepts and illegally detains a U.S. reconnaissance plane over international waters.

World Trade Centers destroyed—September 11, 2001

#86 **2008**

#115 **2020**

Islamic extremists hijack airplanes and fly them fully loaded into both World Trade Center towers in New York City, and the Pentagon in Washington, D.C. The Trade Center towers are both destroyed, but the Pentagon is only damaged. Heroic passengers attack the terrorists on a fourth plane causing it to crash in a Pennsylvania field, most likely sparing the White House. More than 3000 people are killed, and a world-wide war on terror is launched.

United States attacks Afghanistan

#116 **2020**

Intelligence identifies extremist Osama bin Laden as the mastermind of the 9/11 attack. After Afghanistan refuses to hand him over, the U.S. attacks in October and achieves victory two months later. Unfortunately, bin Laden escapes.

Patriot Act signed
President Bush signs the widely supported Patriot Act to remove restrictions on the law enforcement and intelligence services to allow them to better fight terrorism. Opposition will arise in the future over its potential misuse.

Enron files for bankruptcy
Enron, a leading energy company, had been falsifying their books and manipulating the market. Enron employees lose billions in their company retirement plan.

2002

Bush names the Axis of Evil
President Bush uses his State of the Union Address to label Iran, Iraq, and North Korea the new "Axis of Evil."

Steve Fossett circles the globe in a balloon
He completes the first solo balloon trip around the world.

Department of Homeland Security created
This new department is designed to help the U.S. fight terrorism and respond to natural disasters. It combines 22 existing agencies, including Immigration and Naturalization, the Coast Guard, and the Border Patrol.

2003

Space shuttle *Columbia* explodes

The shuttle explodes upon reentry due to missing heat tiles, killing all seven astronauts. The diverse crew included an Israeli astronaut and a woman from India.

2003 ┼ **U.S. attacks Iraq in Second Gulf War**

After a decade of continued violations of the peace agree- #116
ment ending the first Gulf War, and after evidence of WMD
(weapons of mass destruction), the U.S. begins a bombing
campaign against Iraq. Baghdad is captured after a ground
war lasting only a few weeks with less than 200 Allies killed.
The war will drag on until the end of the decade with roadside
bombs and terrorist attacks killing thousands of U.S. soldiers.

President Bush signs $350 billion tax cut bill

Sadaam Hussein captured

On December 14, Sadaam is found hiding in an underground hole. He will be executed 3 years later by the Iraqis
for his crimes against humanity.

2004 ┼ **NATO gets new members**

NATO admits former Communist bloc countries to their organization, including Bulgaria, Estonia, Latvia, Lithuania,
Romania, Slovakia, and Slovenia.

★2004★ GEORGE W. BUSH RE-ELECTED

Candidate	Party	Electoral Vote	Popular Vote
George W. Bush Dick Cheney	Republican	286	62,040,610
John Kerry John Edwards	Democratic	251	59,028,444

Bush and Cheney run again for the Republicans. Bush focuses
on fighting terrorism and privatizing part of social security.
Bush was transformed into a war president by the September 11, 2001 attacks, and his approval rating remained high
through the invasion of Afghanistan and start of the invasion
of Iraq. However, as the war drags on in Iraq and more soldiers are killed, his approval rating drops. Democrats have to
pick a candidate from a large field. It narrows down to Howard
Dean, John Kerry, John Edwards, and Richard Gephardt. Dean
is hurt by a screaming cheer he makes at the Iowa caucus that
is recorded. Kerry finally gets the nod and picks Edwards as
his running mate. He emphasizes his Vietnam War experience,
though later ads by the *Swift Vets* and *POWs for Truth* claim
Kerry is exaggerating his war experience and combat wounds.
Bush's National Guard service is brought into question with
documents aired on CBS's *60 Minutes* which are later found
to be fraudulent, resulting in the producer's dismissal. The
election is not as contentious as 2000, but the victor is not
determined until the Ohio results are finalized the next day.
Kerry decides not to dispute Ohio, though he feels there are irregularities, even though the margin is 120,000 votes. Twelve
million more votes are cast in 2004 than four years earlier,
and this time, Bush wins both the electoral and popular vote.

2004

Indonesian tsunami kills 230,000

An underwater earthquake on December 26 creates massive waves that destroy coastal towns in one of the deadliest natural disasters in history. The 9.1 magnitude earthquake lasts longer than any on record, more than 8 minutes.

2005

Elections in Iraq

Iraq holds their first free elections in 50 years.

Hurricane Katrina devastates New Orleans

New Orleans sits well below the surrounding level of the Mississippi River and Lake Pontchartrain. When the surrounding levees failed, the city was flooded.

The huge hurricane hits New Orleans on August 29 and becomes the costliest in our nation's history. It floods most of New Orleans and kills 1,800. There is much finger pointing in the aftermath, as all levels of government failed, particularly the city and state.

2006

Democrats retake Congress

Nancy Pelosi becomes the first female Speaker of the House as Democrats retake the House and Senate.

2007

Virginia Tech shooting kills 32

A crazed shooter at Virginia Tech in Blacksburg kills 32 students. Ironically, the school is in a "gun free" zone.

Troop surge in Iraq is a success

Facing a deteriorating situation in Iraq, Bush orders an additional 20,000 troops into Iraq ("the surge") to provide stability and security. The surge is successful and violence decreases, allowing a transition of control back to the Iraqis.

2008

Michael Phelps sweeps the Beijing Olympics

He becomes the first athlete to win eight gold medals in one Olympics by winning all his swimming events. His eight gold medals tops Mark Spitz's 1972 record of seven. His Olympic medal count now totals sixteen.

Emergency Economic Stabilization Act passes

Faced with an economic crisis and possible collapse of major financial companies, Congress passes a massive $700 billion Troubled Asset Relief Program (TARP) to purchase failing bank assets. Following the vote, the Dow Jones Average falls 777 points in one day, its largest drop ever.

★2008★ BARACK H. OBAMA 44

Candidate	Party	Electoral Vote	Popular Vote
Barack H. Obama Joe Biden	*Democratic*	365	69,456,897
John McCain Sarah Palin	*Republican*	173	59,934,814

This historic election returns a Democrat to the White House. It is the first time since 1952 that neither the incumbent president or vice president run again. This leaves the Republicans looking for a candidate. They finally pick Senator McCain, a respected former Vietnam POW. He selects the Governor of Alaska, Sarah Palin, as his running mate, the first time the Republicans have nominated a woman. She brings new energy to the campaign but many feel she is not qualified for the position. The Democrat nomination is a neck-and-neck race between Senator Hillary Clinton, former President Bill Clinton's wife, and Barack Obama, a black Senator from Illinois. Either will make history if elected. They fight each other until Obama finally clinches the nomination on June 3. He runs on a platform of change, though Clinton emphasizes Obama's inexperience during the primaries. The Republicans suffer from continued opposition to the conflict in Iraq, and low approval numbers for Bush. It is the first time two sitting senators run against each other, and the first time both candidates are born outside of the contiguous 48 states. The voter turnout is the highest in history and Obama easily wins the election.

2009 $787 stimulus bill

Obama signs the most expensive bill in the history of the country to try to pump money into the economy. However, the cost of the bill rises (to $862 billion), and unemployment keeps rising.

The government takes over private companies

Obama uses executive powers to place several auto and financial companies under government control.

Fort Hood shooting

A disgruntled Muslim U.S. Army officer kills 13 soldiers at Fort Hood in Texas. Political correctness has kept his superiors from removing him from the service.

2010 Approval of Congress hits new low of 13%

Nancy Pelosi's House and Harry Reid's Senate receive the lowest approval rating ever as just 13% of the American public approve of their work.

2010

Congress passes Health Care bill
After nationwide debates, Congress passes the Affordable Care Act, having to use controversial legislative procedures.

Offshore BP oil well disaster
An offshore oil well run by British Petroleum catches on fire, killing eleven workers and spilling thousands of barrels of oil into the Gulf until it is plugged months later.

Republicans win back the House
In an historic mid-term election, Democrats lose 63 seats in the House, the most lost since 1948, to give up control to the Republicans. They lose 6 Senate seats but retain control. Nancy Pelosi loses her position as Speaker of the House.

2011

Representative Gabrielle Giffords shot by gunman
Giffords and 17 others shot by gunman in Arizona.

Defense of Marriage Act declared unconstitutional
Obama administration nullifies act which had defined marriage as between one man and one woman.

Tornado devastates Joplin, Missouri
An EF5 tornado strikes Joplin killing 158 people and causing 2.8 billion in damages.

Osama Bin Laden killed by U.S. Seals

In a daring night raid of four helicopters carrying 40 Navy Seals into a fortified compound in Pakistan, Bin Laden is killed. He has been hunted by our military ever since he orchestrated the September 11, 2001 terror bombings in New York and Washington. His body is taken for DNA verification, and then buried at sea.

Final shuttle mission after 30 years of space flight
Shuttle *Atlantis* makes the 135th and final shuttle flight. It lands at the Kennedy Space Center on July 21.

U.S. credit rating lowered for first time in history
Rating is lowered from AAA to AA+ due to the ongoing debate over debt ceiling.

Last U.S. troops leave Iraq
In agreement with the 2008 U.S.-Iraq Status of Forces Agreement, the last troops leave Iraq on December 18.

2012

Self-driving cars move closer to reality
Google receives license in Nevada for driver-less cars.

2012 — **Terrorists attack U.S. consulate in Benghazi, Libya**
They kill four Americans including Ambassador Stevens. The White House initially blames the unrest on an Internet video. The mishandling of the situation by President Obama and Secretary of State Hillary Clinton will remain in the news for years and impact Hillary's 2016 presidential bid.

Hurricane *Sandy* wallops the Northeast
The third costliest storm in U.S. history (after hurricanes Irma and Katrina) causes more than 130 deaths and over $80 billion in damage. It affects 24 states with flooding and wind damage.

★2012★BARACK H. OBAMA RE-ELECTED

CANDIDATE	PARTY	ELECTORAL VOTE	POPULAR VOTE
Barack H. Obama Joe Biden	Democratic	332	65,915,796
Mitt Romney Paul Ryan	Republican	206	60,933,500

Obama runs for President again with Joe Biden as his running mate. He essentially has no opposition in the Democratic primary. The Republicans pick Mitt Romney after opposition from conservative opponents including Newt Gingrich, Ron Paul, and Rick Santorum. By early June, Romney clinches the nomination and chooses Paul Ryan as his running mate.

The campaign focuses on budget issues, foreign policy and the Affordable Care Act. Terrorism is on the agenda as is dealing with Iran over nuclear weapons. Obama wins with a narrower margin than his 2008 election becoming the first incumbent president since FDR to win a reelection with fewer electoral votes and a lower popular vote percentage than in the previous election. The total turnout percentage decreases from the previous election as well, due in part to Hurricane Sandy.

Sandy Hook Elementary School shooting in Newton, CT
20-year-old Adam Lanza enters the school and shoots and kills 29 children and 6 adults after earlier killing his mother. He ends the siege by killing himself.

2013 — **Boston Marathon bombing kills 3 and injures 170**
Two Chechen brothers set off home-made bombs near the finish line of the Boston Marathon. One brother dies in a subsequent shoot out, and the other will receive the death penalty in a 2015 trial.

2013 IRS targeting scandal
IRS admits to targeting conservative groups by applying extra scrutiny to tax-exempt applications.

2014 Parts of Affordable Care Act goes into effect
Enacted in 2010, a number of important provisions go into effect for all Americans

Troops ordered back to Iraq
The rise of the Islamic State of Iraq and Syria (ISIS) makes it a major threat in the Mideast. Obama orders troops back to Iraq to counter the threat.

Ebola outbreak spreads around the world
A new outbreak of the deadly disease spreads to the U.S. after claiming more than 9,000 lives in Africa. Two die in this country after contracting the disease during travel abroad. The outbreak is the largest outbreak of Ebola in history.

New World Trade Center tower opens in NYC
The 104-floor, 1,776 foot tall "Freedom Tower" opens after eight years of construction. It occupies the location of the Twin Towers destroyed by terrorists on 9/11/2001. It becomes the tallest building in America.

Fall elections give Republicans control of Congress
Republicans take control of Senate while maintaining their control of the House

2015 Custody death leads to *Black Lives Matter* movement
A black man, Freddie Gray, dies in police custody in Baltimore leading to protests that spread around the country. This event, along with a number of police shootings of black men around the U.S., leads to the creation of the *Black Lives Matter* movement.

Terrorists attack Texas art display
Two Islamist terrorists attack the Curtis Culwell Center during a showing of drawings of the prophet Muhammad. Both terrorists are killed by a SWAT team.

American Pharoah wins the Triple Crown

American Pharoah becomes the first horse since 1978 to win the Triple Crown, winning at Belmont after previous wins in the Preakness and the Kentucky Derby.

Weapons sent to eastern Europe
The U.S. responds to aggressive Russian actions in the Ukraine by placing additional weapons in eastern Europe.

2015

Diplomatic ties with Cuba restored

Ties had been severed since 1961 after Castro rose to power and moved his nation towards the Soviet Union after the U.S. had imposed trade sanctions.

BP settlement largest in U.S. history

British Petroleum pays a $18 billion settlement over damages caused by their 2010 oil well spill in the Gulf of Mexico. This is the largest ever paid by one company in the U.S.

San Bernardino massacre

A Muslim couple kills 14 people at a San Bernardino center for the disabled. Fleeing the scene, they are both killed by police. The attack follows similar attacks in Paris and elsewhere in the world. Their mobile phone becomes a subject of controversy as the FBI attempts to break its security.

2016

Flint, Michigan water supply emergency declared

A state-appointed manager switched the city's water supply to the local Flint River in 2014. Residents develop rashes and a host of health problems due to high levels of lead in the water. Officials continue to maintain that the water is safe but an emergency is finally declared. Residents are instructed to use bottled water and it will take more than a year for lead levels to return to a safe level.

President Obama visits Cuba

He becomes the first sitting President since 1928 to visit the island nation.

America sends warplanes to Iceland and Europe

The U.S. builds up military assets abroad to answer Russian threats in Europe.

Treasury announces changes to $20 bill

Bowing to public pressure, the Treasury announces it will replace Andrew Jackson's portrait with that of the Civil War abolitionist Harriet Tubman. She becomes the first black, and the first woman in 100 years, to appear on American currency. The Treasury decides against replacing Hamilton's picture on the $10.

First U.S. death from Zika virus

An elderly Utah resident dies from the Zika virus. The virus had been picked up during travel abroad.

President Obama visits Hiroshima, Japan

He becomes the first U.S. President to visit the site of the first atomic bomb explosion in World War II.

2016 ⊤ **Boxing legend Muhammad Ali dies**

Born Cassius Clay, he was an Olympic champion and one of the best (and most famous) professional boxers ever. He was named as the greatest athlete of the 20th century. He had been fighting Parkinson's disease for a number of years. He carried the Olympic flag at the 2012 games in London.

Deadliest mass shooting in U.S. history

An Islamic terrorist shoots and kills 49 people at the Pulse nightclub in Orlando, Florida. He pledges allegiance to ISIS before being killed by police.

Police shootings continue across the country

More shootings of suspects by police continue across the country. During a Black Lives Matter rally in Dallas, a sniper shoots and kills five Dallas police officers. Three officers are later killed in a shooting in Baton Rouge, Louisiana.

2016 Rio de Janeiro Summer Olympics

Amid troubles from the Zika virus, unfinished structures, and polluted water, the first South American Summer Olympics succeeds. The U.S. wins 46 gold medals and Brazil wins seven golds, their most ever. Swimmer Michael Phelps finishes his Olympic career winning another five gold medals. His total medal count in five Olympics reaches 28 with 23 golds, making him the most decorated Olympian in history.

Dakota Access Pipeline construction halted

The controversial project, started in 2014, is designed to transport oil from the Bakken shale oil fields in North Dakota to storage tanks in Illinois. Protested from the start by environmental protection and native American groups, construction is halted by federal order in September. Opponents are concerned of possible environmental  damage, though transporting the oil via trucks or trains could be equally dangerous. Native American tribes are concerned about its impact on the Standing Rock Sioux reservation, even though the pipeline does not cross their land. This controversy is in addition to that over the Keystone Pipeline designed to bring oil from Canada to the U.S.

Chicago Cubs win World Series to end 108-year drought

They defeat the Cleveland Indians who had the second-longest World Series drought, overcoming a 3-1 deficit.

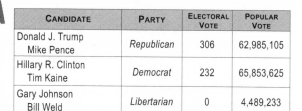

★2016★   Donald J. Trump   45

Candidate	Party	Electoral Vote	Popular Vote
Donald J. Trump Mike Pence	Republican	306	62,985,105
Hillary R. Clinton Tim Kaine	Democrat	232	65,853,625
Gary Johnson Bill Weld	Libertarian	0	4,489,233

The electoral votes actually cast in December for the candidates differed. Trump received only 304 votes and Clinton 227. Seven votes were spread around others including the first Native American to get an electoral vote, Faith Spotted Eagle.

The most contentious election in history starts with the most Republican candidates in history(17). Donald Trump starts as the prohibitive longshot, but outlasts them all, including the last two, Ted Cruz and John Kasich. At the convention, Trump picks Indiana Governor Mike Pence for his VP.

The Democratic field includes former Secretary of State and First Lady Hillary Clinton, frontrunner and presumptive winner. VP Joe Biden decides not to run, but she faces a serious challenge from Independent Senator Bernie Sanders. Sanders wins a large number of state primaries, some by wide margins. Clinton finally clinches the nomination and selects Virginia Senator Tim Kaine as her VP. She becomes the first female major presidential candidate.

Clinton focuses on the Affordable Care Act, women's rights, and economy. Trump appeals to his base with his slogan, *Make America Great Again*, with a populist appeal similar to Andrew Jackson's and promises to 'drain the D.C. swamp'. His talks about revising the tax code, building the wall on the southern border, and stopping illegal immigration.

Both candidates have historically low approval rates. Clinton is troubled by leaks connected to her private email server. Trump's often scandalous behavior and comments continue to hurt him. Clinton alienates voters by calling Trump supporters 'deplorables', while Trump is hurt by the release of a 10-year old audio containing obscene and sexist remarks. Trump shocks the pollsters, the country, and the world by pulling off the biggest upset in election history.

Trump becomes the fifth President in history to win without winning the popular vote, receiving almost 3 million votes less than Clinton. He wins by taking the formerly Democratic states of Michigan, Pennsylvania and Wisconsin. It was the first electoral vote split in Maine since Andrew Jackson's 1828 victory. Trump becomes the first President without prior public or military experience.

2016 — **Fire at party in Oakland warehouse kills 36**
An overcrowded event with more than 100 people at a non-permitted warehouse known as *Ghost Ship* turns deadly. The deadliest building fire since the 1906 earthquake claims 36 lives. The party-goers were unable to escape the building and many died by smoke inhalation.

Carrie Fisher and Debbie Reynolds die one day apart
The *Star Wars* actress Carrie Fisher dies on December 27 after experiencing a heart attack on a flight to LA. and her famous actress mother Debbie Reynolds dies the next day. Reynolds was perhaps best known for her role in the movie *Singin' in the Rain*.

2017 — **FBI report details Russian hacking efforts in U.S. election**
The report outlines their hacking into Democratic National Committee and other email accounts. However, there is no evidence of any attempt to tamper with actual voting machines or ballots.

Trump signs a number of executive orders
Many of these overturn some of Obama's executive orders and aim to fulfill some of Trump's campaign promises. These include orders to start building the wall along the Mexican border and a controversial order that temporarily bans immigration from seven specific countries linked to terrorism. This order is blocked by a federal appellate court.

Dow hits 20,000
The Dow Jones Industrial Average tops 20,000 for the first time in history.

U.S. targets Syria
The United States launches airstrikes against Syria in response to Syrian use of chemical weapons.

Trump fires the FBI Director
In response to his mishandling of the investigation into Hillary Clinton's email servers, President Trump fires FBI Director James Comey.

Robert Mueller appointed Special Investigator
Robert Mueller is selected by Justice Department to conduct an investigation into alleged Russian interference in the last election. The investigation will continue into 2019 and will end up clearing President Trump of any collusion.

Neil Gorsuch appointed to Supreme Court
Senate confirms Neil Gorsuch to the Supreme Court. A conservative judge, he is confirmed mostly along party lines.

2017

U.S. withdraws from the Paris Climate Agreement

Signed by the U.S. in 2016, President Trump indicates that the U.S. will withdraw from the agreement as soon as possible.

Protests lead to an accidental death in Virginia

Violent protests in Charlottesville, Virginia over civil rights and removal of Confederate-era statues lead to one death from a speeding car. The removal of a statue of Robert E. Lee sparked the confrontations.

Total solar eclipse

A total solar eclipse crosses the entire United States for the first time in 99 years.

North Korea releases captive American

Otto Warmbier, an American student detained in North Korean custody for a year, is finally released but dies of complications from his custody.

Bad hurricane season hit the U.S. and Puerto Rico

A record-breaking hurricane season smashes the east coast with Hurricanes Harvey dumping 51 inches of rain (a record) and Hurricane Irma adding to the damage. Hurricane Maria strikes Puerto Rico causing more death and destruction. The dark areas on the map mark all of the landslides created on Puerto Rico.

Deadly shooting on Las Vegas strip

A shooter in Las Vegas fires on a music concert crowd of 22,000 people from the 32nd floor of a downtown hotel killing 58 people and injuring over 500 before killing himself.

Sexual predators exposed

Sexual harassment charges are brought against movie producer Harvey Weinstein resulting in his arrest. This is the start of the #MeToo social media movement that draws attention to sexual assault and harassment. His arrest is followed later in the year by the downfalls of a number of well-known people, including TV hosts Charlie Rose and Matt Lauer over sexual assault allegations.

Another gunman opens fire in Texas

A gunman in Sutherland Springs, Texas opens fire on a church congregation, killing 26 people.

2017 **U.S. recognizes Jerusalem as capital of Israel**
President Trump defies critics by recognizing Jerusalem as the capital of Israel and moves the U.S. embassy to that city.

Life expectancy falls again
Life expectancy in the U.S. falls for the second year in a row due mainly to deaths from the worsening opioid crisis.

2018 **Record cold hits the U.S.**
A record cold wave strikes the American Mid-West and East Coast.

Deadly school shooting in Florida
A deadly shooting at Parkland High School in Florida leaves 17 dead. It is the deadliest high school shooting in U.S. history.

Large tariffs placed on China
President Trump announces a set of large tariffs on Chinese goods and plans to limit their investment in the U.S. China replies with tariffs on U.S. products.

Diplomats expelled
U.S. expels 60 Russian diplomats following the poisoning of an ex-spy. Russia retaliates by expelling a similar number of U.S. diplomats.

Unemployment rate drops again
The U.S. unemployment rate drops to 3.9%, the lowest since 2000. It will fall to 3.6%, the lowest in 49 years.

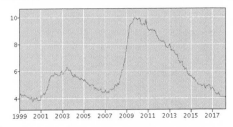

Trump announces withdrawal from Iran Treaty
The President announces a plan to withdraw from the Iranian nuclear agreement, set up by the Obama administration.

Coldest month in ten years
April 2018 was the coldest month in U.S. since 1997.

President Trump meets North Korean Leader

President Trump meets with North Korea's Leader, Kim Jong-un, This is the first time that a current United States President has met with that country's leader.

2018

California burns
Wildfires in California are declared the largest in the state's history.

Supreme Court hearings captivate the nation
The hearings for Supreme Court Justice nominee Brett Kavanaugh are held with sexual misconduct allegations brought by Christine Ford and others. The hearings drag on until Kavanaugh is finally confirmed along party lines.

Soldiers reinforce the border
Soldiers are sent to the Mexican border as part of Operation Faithful Patriot in anticipation of large incoming migrant caravans.

Democrats retake the House
Democrats regain control of the House of Representatives in mid-term elections but lose two seats in the Senate.

2019

Government shuts down over political impasse
Government shutdown continues for 35 days making it longest in U.S. history.

National emergency declared to get wall built
Trump declares a national emergency to free up funds to build the southern wall with the military.

Democrats line up to run for President
Democrat field for President in 2020 gets crowded with more than 20 candidates declaring, including Joe Biden, Elizabeth Warren, and Bernie Sanders.

Robert Mueller submits his report
Robert Mueller submits his report of his two-year investigation into Russian interference in the 2016 election. He reports that there was no finding of collusion by President Trump.

ISIS no longer controls territory in Syria
Department of Defense reports that the terrorist group ISIS no longer controls any territory in Syria.

More deployments to the Middle East

U.S. deploys additional ships and planes to the Middle East amidst increased tension with Iran over ship seizures and drone downings. U.S. sanctions on Iran are increasingly taking a heavy toll on the Iranian economy.

2019 **Trump approval rating hits new high**
President Trump's approval rating reaches 46%, its highest to date.

Measles outbreak underscores importance of immunizations
A measles outbreak hits the U.S. resulting in highest number of cases in 25 years. This accompanies warnings about the lack of immunizations for infectious diseases.

President Trump visits North Korea DMZ
Trump becomes first sitting U.S. President to visit North Korea as he meets the North Korean leader in the DMZ.

Social media companies undergo more scrutiny
Investigation and fines against social media and search engine companies continue with a $5 billion fine against Facebook. Google also comes under scrutiny.

The Future
It is up to every citizen to help write the future. Whether this country will endure, or whether it will join the other failed civilizations of history, depends on how well this and future generations heed the lessons of history, stay faithful to the concepts of the Constitution, and stay involved in their government.

History is a ribbon, always unfurling. History is a journey. And as we continue our journey, we think of those who traveled before us... and we see and hear again the echoes of our past: a general falls to his knees in the hard snow of Valley Forge; a lonely president paces the darkened halls and ponders his struggle to preserve the Union; the men of the Alamo call out encouragement to each other; a settler pushes west and sings a song, and the song echoes out forever and fills the unknowing air. It is the American sound. It is hopeful, big-hearted, idealistic, daring, decent, and fair. That's our heritage, that's our song. We sing it still. For all our problems, our differences, we are together as of old.
—Ronald Reagan, 2nd Inaugural Address

George Washington
The Father of our Country

2008 #69

❧

When King George asked an American in London what Washington would do after the war, the man answered that he would probably go back home to his Virginia farm. "If he does that," said the astonished king, "he will be the greatest man in the world."

—King George

First in war, first in peace and first in the hearts of his countrymen, he was second to none in the humble and endearing scenes of private life. Pious, just, humane, temperate and sincere—uniform, dignified and commanding—his example was as edifying to all around him as were the effects of that example lasting. . . Correct throughout, vice shuddered in his presence and virtue always felt his fostering hand. The purity of his private character gave effulgence to his public virtues. . . Such was the man for whom our nation mourns.

—Henry Lee at Washington's funeral, 1799

Chapter 2

U.S. Presidents

❧

PRESIDENTIAL ELECTIONS are held every four years in November with the victor being inaugurated early the next year. The following information lists the years the president served in office, starting with the year they were elected (not inaugurated), except for cases when a president died, was killed in office, or resigned. The state of birth is shown along with their dates of birth and death. The history timeline in the preceding chapter lists more details about each Presidential election.

GEORGE WASHINGTON	1
Virginia	**1789-1796**
Feb 22, 1732 - Dec 14, 1799	

Washington was tall, strong, and one of the richest colonists. He had fought alongside the British during the Indian wars and served in the House of Burgesses. He was President of the Constitutional Convention and was picked by the Continental Congress to lead the American troops against the British, and it was only his fierce determination and belief in his new country that kept the rag-tag Continental Army together. After the war, he left public life but was unanimously selected to be the new country's first President. He wisely turned down requests to act as its King. As the first President, he had an enormous responsibility to set the precedents that would guide America in the future. He had no government buildings—he had only the Constitution. He declined a third term, feeling that a President should only serve two terms. Sadly, he died a few years after leaving office.

#70 2008
#86 2020

JOHN ADAMS

Massachusetts
Oct 30, 1735 - Jul 4, 1826

2

1796-1800

Adams was Washington's vice president. He had been instrumental in the founding of the new country and had long supported the concept of an independent nation and the signing of the Declaration of Independence, but he was not as popular as Washington or Jefferson. He was a strong Federalist and was constantly fighting anti-Federalists like Jefferson. His passage of the Alien and Sedition Laws of 1789 met with great disapproval and increased the fear of a strong central government. He died on the 50th anniversary of the signing of the Declaration, on July 4, 1826—the same day that Jefferson died.

THOMAS JEFFERSON

Virginia
Apr 13, 1743 - Jul 4, 1826

3

1800-1808

The builder of Monticello in Virginia and the founder of the University of Virginia, Jefferson was crucial in the creation of the Declaration of Independence. He was a member of the Virginia House of Burgesses and the Continental Congress, Governor of Virginia, 1st Secretary of State, and vice president under Adams. He was one of the most accomplished and talented Presidents in our history. He was a strong believer in state and individual rights. His term in office was highlighted by three key events—the purchase of the Louisiana territory from the French; the backing of the Lewis and Clark expedition that explored the new territory; and the rise of the American Navy that successfully fought the Barbary pirates in Africa. He died on the same day as John Adams, July 4, 1826, 50 years after the signing of the Declaration.

U.S. **Presidential Trivia**

TRIVIA Which presidents were born or died on the Fourth of July?

Born: Calvin Coolidge on July 4, 1872.

Died: Three of the first five presidents died on July 4: Thomas Jefferson and John Adams on July 4, 1826, the fiftieth anniversary of the signing of the Declaration; and James Monroe on July 4, 1831.

JAMES MADISON | 4

Virginia | **1808-1816**

Mar 16, 1751 - Jun 28, 1836

#88 2020 Madison believed in many of the same principles as Jefferson. He was instrumental in the creation of the Constitution and, along with John Jay and Alexander Hamilton, wrote the Federalist Papers to help convince the nation to adopt the Constitution. Madison had introduced the Bill of Rights which was crucial in getting final ratification from all thirteen states. Maritime conflict with Britain led to the War of 1812 and he, along with his wife Dolly, were forced to flee the new capital of Washington when the British invaded. He was unpopular, but the successful conclusion of the war with Britain helped restore his legacy. Washington was the Father of his Country, but Madison was the Father of the Constitution.

JAMES MONROE | 5

Virginia | **1816-1824**

Apr 28, 1758 - Jul 4, 1831

Monroe presided over 8 years of peace. He purchased Florida from Spain, made the Canadian border peaceful, and issued the Monroe Doctrine declaring the Western Hemisphere off-limits to European powers. He also helped pass the Missouri Compromise which outlawed slavery north of the Mason-Dixon line. He was the last of three consecutive Virginian Presidents. He helped further Jefferson's beliefs in state and individual rights.

JOHN QUINCY ADAMS | 6

Massachusetts | **1824-1828**

Jul 11, 1767 - Feb 23, 1848

Son of the 2nd President, John Adams, John Quincy was a lawyer who held a number of positions prior to the Presidency. He helped write the Monroe Doctrine under the previous President. The election in 1824 produced no clear winner, and the House of Representatives had to decide between Adams and Andrew Jackson. Henry Clay supported Adams and the dispute resulted in the creation of two political parties. After leaving the White House, Adams served in Congress for seventeen years until he died on the floor of the House. He spent his last years opposing slavery.

Andrew Jackson
South Carolina
Mar 15, 1767 - Jun 8, 1845

7

1828-1836

Jackson fought the British during the Revolution as a 13-year-old boy and was taken prisoner and permanently scarred by a British officer's sword. As a General during the War of 1812, he soundly defeated the British at the Battle of New Orleans. He had a large following and became the first real President of the "people." He exercised federal authority and prevented the recharter of the Bank of the United States. He also vetoed more bills than all the previous presidents put together.

Martin van Buren
New York
Dec 5, 1782 - Jul 24, 1862

8

1836-1840

Van Buren helped organize the Democrat Party that Andrew Jackson brought to power in 1828. He ran a political machine in New York before becoming President. After becoming President, he was faced with the financial Panic of 1837, and formed the basis of the Treasury Department.

William H. Harrison
Virginia
Feb 9, 1773 - Apr 4, 1841

9

1840-1841

The Whig party nominated the 68-year-old Harrison but didn't count on him giving a 3-hour inauguration speech in the rain. Harrison died one month later—the shortest term of any President. His father, Benjamin Harrison, had been a signer of the Declaration of Independence. He was succeeded by his vice president, John Tyler. Harrison's election heralded in a new era of national politics as the Whigs ran an organized campaign which pictured Harrison as a war hero at the Battle of Tippecanoe. The Whigs pushed the slogan "Tippecanoe and Tyler, too" at their rallies.

JOHN TYLER

Virginia

Mar 29, 1790 - Jan 18, 1862

10

1841-1844

Assuming office after the untimely death of President Harrison, Tyler became the first vice president to take over for an elected President. The Whigs most likely would not have nominated him for vice president if they had known this would happen as Tyler's policies were not consistent with the Whig party platform. He vetoed a bill for the Bank of the U.S. causing almost the entire original cabinet to resign. His main accomplishment was the annexation of Texas which became a state in 1845. After leaving the White House, he supported state's rights and joined the Confederate Congress.

JAMES POLK

North Carolina

Nov 2, 1795 - Jun 15, 1849

11

1844-1848

Perhaps one of the most under-rated Presidents, Polk came from obscurity to beat the well-known Henry Clay and head a fairly successful presidency. He presided over one of the most expansionist eras in the country. He led the country in the Mexican-American War which resulted in the addition of territory from Texas to California. He also resolved the Oregon Territory dispute with Great Britain, and acquired full rights to what became Oregon, Washington and Idaho. He served only one term and died 3 months after leaving office.

ZACHARY TAYLOR

Virginia

Nov 24, 1784 - Jul 9, 1850

12

1848-1850

Taylor was the first career Army officer to become President. He had been fighting since 1812 and became a national hero fighting the Mexicans in 1846 and 1847, crushing a larger army under Santa Anna at Buena Vista. He was unskilled at politics and soon ran into trouble over the issue of slavery and the admission of California as a free state. He was the last President to actually own slaves while in office. He died of unknown causes halfway through his term.

MILLARD FILLMORE

New York
Jan 7, 1800 - Mar 8, 1874

13
1850-1852

Fillmore was born in a log cabin and, upon President Taylor's death, became the last Whig to be President. He signed the Compromise of 1850 and the Fugitive Slave Act which favored the South but angered the North and helped keep the country divided. He kept the French from annexing the Hawaiian Islands. After leaving the White House, he later opposed President Lincoln.

FRANKLIN PIERCE

New Hampshire
Nov 23, 1804 - Oct 8, 1869

14
1852-1856

Pierce was a reluctant dark-horse candidate who received the Democratic nomination after 35 stalemated ballots. He had served in the House and Senate, but had retired to private life before being thrust back into politics. His support of the 1850 Compromise and the Fugitive Slave Act alienated the North, and the passage of the Kansas-Nebraska Act created new problems. A plan to buy Cuba from Spain was successfully opposed by anti-slavery interests. His presidency is usually viewed as one of the most ineffective in history, and his reputation was further tarnished by his support for the Confederacy.

JAMES BUCHANAN

Pennsylvania
Apr 23, 1791 - Jun 1, 1868

15
1856-1860

Born in a log cabin and the only bachelor President, Buchanan was also one of the oldest. He was unable to handle the slavery issue and his attempts at compromise only alienated both sides and earned him a position as one of our worst Presidents.

U.S.	Presidential Trivia
TRIVIA	Which presidents have been elected with fewer popular votes than their opponents?

Donald J. Trump (2016), George W. Bush (2000), Benjamin Harrison (1888), Rutherford Hayes (1876), John Q. Adams (1824)

ABRAHAM LINCOLN
Kentucky
Feb 12, 1809 - Apr 15, 1865

16

1860-1865

#75 **2008**

#94 **2020**

Born in a log cabin in Kentucky, Lincoln overcame adversity to become one of the greatest U.S. Presidents. He was a lawyer, state legislator, and national representative, but lost his two attempts to became a Senator. He campaigned against slavery and won the presidential election without a majority, or a single southern state—they started seceding as soon as he was elected. His entire presidency was consumed by the Civil War. His overriding goal was to preserve the Union at any cost. His Gettysburg Address encapsulated his vision for America. His perseverance won the war, preserved the Union, and ended slavery. Unfortunately, he was assassinated just 6 days after General Lee surrendered his Army.

ANDREW JOHNSON
North Carolina
Dec 29, 1808 - Jul 31, 1875

17

1865-1868

Johnson became vice president in 1864 and was thrust into the Presidency when Lincoln was shot. Lacking formal education, he was previously a Tennessee Senator, and the only southern Senator to keep his seat when the south seceded. He opposed Republicans who wanted to crush the southern states, and was impeached but acquitted by only one vote. After leaving office, he returned to the Senate and continued to fight Reconstruction policies.

ULYSSES S. GRANT
Ohio
Apr 27, 1822 - Jul 23, 1885

18

1868-1876

Raised on a farm and educated at West Point, Grant was picked by Lincoln to head the Northern armies after his victories at Vicksburg and Chattanooga. He used brute force to finally defeat the South, suffering enormous casualties in the process. He was picked by the Republicans for president even though he had no political experience. He made a number of mistakes early in office and assisted in events that led up to the Panic of 1873. His two terms were marred by corruption and incompetence, though he continued to fight for the civil rights of freed slaves.

RUTHERFORD B. HAYES

Ohio

Oct 4, 1822 - Jan 17, 1893

19

1876-1880

Picked in part for his honesty after the corrupt Grant administration, Hayes had served in the military and was Governor of Ohio when picked for President. His election was hotly disputed as he lost the popular vote. A compromise with the Democrats gave him the 20 disputed votes needed to become President. The price of this compromise was the end of the military occupation of the South, the end of Reconstruction, and the subsequent loss of voting rights for former southern slaves.

JAMES A. GARFIELD

Ohio

Nov 19, 1831 - Sep 19, 1881

20

1880-1881

As the last "log cabin" president, Garfield started out as a teacher and college president. He was a Union officer and a member of Congress for 18 years. The Republican convention deadlocked for 35 ballots before the dark-horse Garfield got the nomination. Unfortunately, an assassin killed him after only four months in office.

CHESTER A. ARTHUR

Vermont

Oct 5, 1829 - Nov 18, 1886

21

1881-1884

Garfield's vice president was associated with the New York political machine and many feared he would bring that to the White House. But he changed course and worked for the good of the country. His support of the Civil Service Reform Act led to federal employment based on examinations and merit, not political connections.

GROVER CLEVELAND

New Jersey

Mar 18, 1837 - Jun 24, 1908

22

1884-1888

A self-taught lawyer and governor of New York, Cleveland had fought corruption in his own Democrat party before becoming president. He helped protect civil service and fought against a high import tariff. He also created the Interstate Commerce Commission and started to modernize the navy.

BENJAMIN HARRISON

Ohio

Aug 20, 1833 - Mar 13, 1901

23

1888-1892

Grandson of the 9th President, Harrison had been a lawyer and Union army officer. His was the first administration to spend one billion dollars, and his McKinley Tariff was one of the most protective ever. The Sherman Antitrust Act was passed but his office did little to enforce its terms. Six states were admitted during his tenure.

GROVER CLEVELAND

New Jersey

Mar 18, 1837 - Jun 24, 1908

24

1892-1896

Cleveland was the only man to be elected President for two non-consecutive terms. His first successor, Benjamin Harrison, could not overcome the economic conditions to win a second term. Cleveland quickly inherited the Panic of 1893, a depression across the entire country that ruined the Democrat party. Cleveland supported the gold standard and used government forces to crush the Pullman Strike of 1894.

WILLIAM MCKINLEY

Ohio

Jan 29, 1843 - Sep 14, 1901

25

1896-1901

A supporter of high tariffs, McKinley pushed the gold standard and represented big business. Pressure grew to interfere in Cuba, fed by yellow journalism from some major newspapers. The USS *Maine* was sunk in Havana and war broke out. The Spanish-American War ended quickly and the U.S. acquired Puerto Rico, Guam, and the Philippines from Spain, and also annexed Hawaii in 1898. He named the hero Teddy Roosevelt as his vice president in the 1900 election, a move that would soon have consequences since Roosevelt was not as pro-business as McKinley. McKinley was shot and killed by an anarchist in 1901.

TEDDY ROOSEVELT

New York
Oct 27, 1858 - Jan 6, 1919

26
1901-1908

Teddy Roosevelt had served in many positions prior to becoming President, including governor of New York. He was multifaceted, similar to Thomas Jefferson, being a scientist, hunter, and family man. He was a strong reformer but popular enough to earn a spot on Mount Rushmore. He personally led the Rough Riders to victory in the Spanish-American War. When he took over for president, he became the youngest President ever at 42. He attacked business trusts, started major conservation projects, and established the United States Forest Service. He acquired the Panama Canal Zone and sent the Great White Fleet of battleships around the world to project American power. Roosevelt helped negotiate the end to the Russo-Japanese War, becoming the first American Nobel Peace Prize winner.

WILLIAM HOWARD TAFT

Ohio
Sep 15, 1857 - Mar 8, 1930

27
1908-1912

Roosevelt had promised not to run for a third term, and he was succeeded by his Secretary of War, William Taft. Taft continued Roosevelt's policies of fighting trusts and reforming the civil service, but alienated his friends. Roosevelt finally took to publicly attacking him. Taft lost his bid for a second term. He later became the tenth Chief Justice of the United States, the only President to hold both positions.

U.S. TRIVIA	Presidential Trivia
	Which presidents did not finish their elected term of office and why?

Assassinated: Abraham Lincoln (1865), James Garfield (1881), William McKinley (1901), John Kennedy (1963)

Resigned: Richard Nixon (1974)

Died from illness: William Harrison (1841), Zachary Taylor (1850), Warren Harding (1923), Franklin Roosevelt (1945)

Assassination attempts: Andrew Jackson (1835), Theodore Roosevelt (1912), FDR (1933), Harry Truman (1950), Gerald Ford (1975-twice), Ronald Reagan (1981)

WOODROW WILSON

Virginia

Dec 28, 1856 - Feb 3, 1924

28

1912-1920

Teddy Roosevelt, upset by Taft's performance, tried to win the Republican nomination, and won the majority of the primaries before being outmaneuvered at the convention with the nomination going to Taft. Roosevelt formed a new Progressive party resulting in splitting the national vote, giving the election to the Democrat Wilson with only 42% of the popular vote. Wilson had been a history professor, president of Princeton, and governor of New Jersey. After his election, he launched a number of progressive programs, including the Federal Reserve Act, Federal Trade Commission Act, the Clayton Antitrust Act, the Federal Farm Loan Act, and a progress federal income tax. He also helped segregate federal agencies.

Wilson barely won re-election in 1916, campaigning on keeping the U.S. out of war. But German submarine warfare and a secret German alliance with Mexico finally forced a declaration of war against Germany. Wilson re-instituted the draft, took over the railroads, promoted labor unions, and suppressed anti-war movements. He pushed his Fourteen-Points vision of a peaceful post-war world, helped shape the Treaty of Versailles, and pushed for the creation of a League of Nations. However, he alienated his opposition, refused to compromise, and finally was stopped by a stroke. The U.S. never joined the League of Nations.

WARREN G. HARDING

Ohio

Nov 2, 1865 - Jul 2, 1923

29

1920-1923

Running on a platform similar to Teddy Roosevelt's, Harding came into office promising a return to normalcy. He favored big business, but his term became embroiled in corruption. Upon his return from a trip to Alaska, he died under suspicious circumstances in San Francisco.

U.S.	Presidential Trivia
TRIVIA	Which president was never elected to the office?

Gerald Ford: When Spiro Agnew resigned in 1973, President Nixon picked Gerald Ford for his Vice President. When Nixon resigned in 1974, Ford became President.

CALVIN COOLIDGE

Vermont
Jul 4, 1872 - Jan 5, 1933

30
1923-1928

As governor of Massachusetts, Coolidge reduced the number of departments from 118 to 18. He took over the high office favoring big business, stating "The business of America is business." He ran an efficient administration, and business prospered as he continued his laissez-faire policies. He ran a budget surplus each year and reduced top tax rates from 73% to 25%, enabling his reelection the following year. Even though he was popular, he decided not to run for re-election in 1928, and left office while times were good.

HERBERT HOOVER

Iowa
Aug 10, 1874 - Oct 20, 1964

31
1928-1932

Hoover had no previous elected office experience. He used his engineering background to eliminate waste in the government. However, the 1929 Stock Market Crash heralded in a decade-long depression, and Hoover's efforts were for naught. His inability to turn the country around was seen very unfavorably by voters. Homeless camps around the country came to be called "Hoovervilles."

FRANKLIN D. ROOSEVELT

New York
Jan 30, 1882 - Apr 12, 1945

32
1932-1945

Educated at Harvard, Roosevelt was crippled with polio before serving two terms as New York governor. He launched a 4-term project of transforming America during the height of the Depression. A liberal social reformer, he used the hard times to justify his actions. His government programs were designed to provide jobs and secu- `2008` #80 rity, but also created a government dependence that still exists. He formed numerous agencies and spent billions, but ten years of effort did not end the Depression. However, he recognized the danger of German and Japanese aggression, and did what he could to help the Allies, particularly by implementing the Lend-Lease Act. After the Pearl Harbor attack, he worked with Churchill and Stalin to plot the war's course and plan the post-war world. He died suddenly in 1945 before the war ended. He was the only president to serve 4 terms, leading to an Amendment limiting the president to two terms.

HARRY S. TRUMAN

Missouri

May 8, 1884 - Dec 26, 1972

33

1945-1952

Roosevelt's death thrust his vice president into a mass of problems—ending the war, dealing with post-war Russia, and the atomic bomb. Truman dealt with these problems in a straight-forward manner, approving the use of the atomic bomb to end the war. He successfully dealt with the Russians in a divided Germany, established NATO, and upset Thomas Dewey in the 1948 election. He ratified the U.N. charter and used the Marshall Plan to help Europe recover. He oversaw the Korean War and relieved General MacArthur for insubordination.

DWIGHT D. EISENHOWER

Texas

Oct 14,1890 - Mar 28, 1969

34

1952-1960

The leader of Allied forces in World War II had never held public office, but his popularity thrust him into public office. Communism was on the march, with North Vietnam falling to Communists,

#82 **2008**
#107 **2020**

and the Russians crushing the Hungary uprising, but Americans were content to regain prosperity after the lean years of the Depression and the war. Civil rights became a major issue and Eisenhower ordered troops to Little Rock, Arkansas to protect school children. He also created the Interstate System.

JOHN F. KENNEDY

Massachusetts

May 29, 1917 - Nov 22, 1963

35

1960-1963

The first president born in the 20th century, he was a war hero and part of the Kennedy dynasty. He outshone his opponent, Richard Nixon, in the first televised presidential debate, and narrowly won victory. He was the first Catholic president which had worried many Americans. His book, *Profiles in Courage*, won a Pulitzer Prize. He backed the disastrous Bay of Pigs invasion of Cuba, and faced the placing of Russian missiles in Cuba. The world was brought to the brink of nuclear war, but the blockade of Cuba turned back the Russians, and the missiles were removed from Cuba. His challenge to put a man on the moon by the end of the decade inspired the effort that placed Neil Armstrong on the moon in 1969. While in Dallas on November 22, 1963, he was killed by Lee Harvey Oswald—an event that shocked the world.

LYNDON B. JOHNSON

Texas

Aug 27, 1908 - Jan 22, 1973

36

1963-1968

The eighth vice president to take over for a dead president, Johnson was sworn into office on a plane ready to return to Washington after the assassination in Texas. He was a seasoned politician who had vehemently opposed Kennedy in the 1960 Democratic primaries, but was placed on the ticket to help secure Southern votes and leverage Johnson's considerable influence. After winning re-election in 1964, he pushed his plan for a "Great Society" resulting in a number of social programs like Medicare and Medicaid. He signed the historic Civil Rights Act of 1964, overcoming stubborn opposition, mainly from southern Democrats. However, his escalation of the war in Vietnam let to riots at home and a decline in popularity which led him to withdraw from the 1968 election.

RICHARD NIXON

California

Jan 9, 1913 - Apr 22, 1994

37

1968-1974

Nixon was Eisenhower's vice president, but lost to Kennedy in one of the closest races in history. He lost a race for California governor two years later and retired from politics until his 1968 bid for the presidency. Opposition to the Vietnam War continued, but he had success in other foreign policy efforts, being the first president to visit Communist China leading to an agreement with that country. He also signed an anti-ballistic missile treaty with the USSR in 1972. However, a bungled 1972 break-in at Democratic Headquarters at the Watergate building eventually led to his downfall. Ironically, he easily won that election and needed no help from any underhanded methods. Troops started withdrawing from Vietnam the next year but the nation became engrossed with the Watergate hearings and revelations of secret White House tapes including a crucial tape that was missing 18½ minutes of audio. The Supreme Court ordered his tapes released and he resigned in 1974 to avoid impeachment.

GERALD FORD
Nebraska
Jul 14, 1913 - Dec 26, 2006

38
1974-1976

Gerald Ford was the only President who was never elected. Nixon had appointed him vice president when Spiro Agnew left office due to corruption charges. When Nixon resigned, Ford took over the top job. A college football player, he had been a Representative in Congress for twenty years. He started office by pardoning Richard Nixon for all his crimes, a move that most likely helped heal the country, but brought sharp criticism. He signed the Helsinki Accords with the Soviets, and presided over the final U.S. withdrawal from Vietnam.

JIMMY CARTER
Georgia
Oct 1, 1924 -

39
1976-1980

The first president from the deep South since the Civil War, Carter used televised debates to overcome his relative obscurity. An intelligent former Navy officer, Carter owned a large peanut farm in Georgia and was governor of Georgia in 1970. He created the Department of Energy but signed over control of the Panama Canal to Panama, a move that angered many. His 1978 Camp David Accords worked towards Middle East peace between Egypt and Israel. However, soaring inflation and rising oil prices greatly harmed the economy. In 1979, the Iranians seized the American Embassy in Tehran, starting a hostage crisis that would not end until the inauguration of Ronald Reagan. The Soviets invaded Afghanistan, prompting a grain embargo and a boycott of the 1980 Moscow Olympics. Barely beating Ted Kennedy for the Democratic nomination in 1980, he was soundly defeated by Ronald Reagan.

U.S. Presidential Trivia

TRIVIA Which presidents have been related to each other?

Fifth Cousin (1): Theodore Roosevelt/Franklin D. Roosevelt.

Second Cousin (1): James Madison/Zachary Taylor.

Grandfather/Grandson (1): William H. Harrison/Benjamin Harrison.

Father/Son (2): John Adams/John Quincy Adams, George H. W. Bush/George W. Bush.

RONALD REAGAN

Illinois
Feb 6, 1911 - Jun 5, 2004

40

1980-1988

Reagan started as a Hollywood actor making more than 40 movies before serving as governor of California. He brought an upbeat belief in the greatness of America to the office, based on conservative and traditional values. He became known as "The Great Communicator." His term started with the release of the Iranian hostages on the day of his inauguration. A failed assassination attempt several months into office left him with the belief that God had spared him for some great task. He nominated the first female Supreme Court judge, Sandra O'Connor. His trickle-down economic policies and huge tax cuts (top rates fell from 70% to 28%) spurred a decade-long expansion of the economy. His conservative policies and aggressive expansion of the military led to a landslide victory in 1984, winning every state except one. He used the military to bomb Libya, invade Grenada, and confront the Soviets whenever possible. He demanded that Gorbachev tear down the Berlin Wall, and kept funding the space defense program, ultimately leading to the collapse of the Soviet Union without a shot being fired. The later years of his term were marred by the Iran Contra crisis but he left office on a high note.

GEORGE H. W. BUSH

Massachusetts
June 12, 1924 -

41

1988-1992

Bush had been the youngest Navy pilot in World War II. He was shot down in the Pacific and rescued by a submarine. He became the first sitting vice president to be elected president since Martin van Buren. He had experience in government and had been director of the CIA. He started his term carrying on many of the policies of Reagan but had to fight a Democrat Congress. He won election on a promise of no new taxes, but his major tax increases soon cost him support. The Soviet Union collapsed during his tenure and he put together a successful international coalition in the Gulf War to remove Sadaam Hussein from Kuwait after Sadaam had invaded that country. But Bush's failure to restore the economy and his lack of support for true conservative ideals cost him the next election.

BILL CLINTON

Arkansas
Aug 19, 1946 -

[42]
[1992-2000]

Clinton won only 43% of the popular vote due to the candidacy of Ross Perot. Clinton had been governor of Arkansas and a Rhodes Scholar. Coming into office, he passed the "Don't ask, don't tell" policy to allow gays in the military, but suffered a setback when his wife, Hillary, was unable to push new health care measures. He lost control of both houses of Congress in 1994, causing him to moderate his policies, but, banking on his personal popularity, won re-election in 1996. Clinton was caught in a sex scandal involving an intern at the White House, and his subsequent lies to a Grand Jury resulted in impeachment hearings. He was acquitted on charges, but the affair tainted his presidency. Clinton had served two terms, so his vice president, Al Gore, was the 2000 Democratic nominee.

GEORGE W. BUSH

Connecticut
Jul 6, 1946 -

[43]
[2000-2008]

The son of the 41st president, George W. Bush was a Harvard MBA, National Guard pilot, and Texas governor. The 2000 election was so close it would not be decided for weeks. Gore won the popular vote, but vote counting problems in Florida left the electoral vote undecided. Incorrect and miscounted ballots, and prematurely announced results clouded the election. The Supreme Court finally decided the outcome. Before Bush's first year was over, Islamic terrorists attacked New York and Washington on September 11, 2001, and Bush's presidency was redefined. When Afghanistan refused to turn over the attack's planner Osama Bin Laden, Bush attacked the country. Two years later, the U.S. invaded Iraq to finish the job started ten years earlier. The U.S. was still involved in both countries at the end of his 2nd term in 2008. He passed extensive tax cuts and withdrew from the Kyoto protocol on Global Warming. He was continually attacked about his policies on enhanced interrogation and the Patriot Act. He narrowly beat Senator Kerry in 2004. His administration was denounced for its handling of Hurricane Katrina, though state and local governments were also to blame. The Democrats gained control of both houses of Congress in 2006, and the end of his presidency was marked by a worsening economy.

BARACK H. OBAMA

Hawaii
Aug 4, 1961 -

44
2008-2016

Barack Obama made history by becoming America's first black president after serving as an Illinois and U.S. Senator. A financial crisis, triggered in part by problems with home mortgages and foreclosures, forced the passage of costly economic stimulus and job creation acts. Obama had complete Democrat control of both houses of Congress, so acts could pass Congress without fear of a presidential veto. He came to the office on a wave of enthusiasm about his ability to change Washington, but his initial popularity was put to the test by the debate over the new healthcare bill that was finally passed by a divided Congress. He also ran into difficulty fulfilling other campaign promises, such as the closing of the Guantanamo Bay detention facility, and removing troops from Iraq and Afghanistan. The Congress under Harry Reid and Nancy Pelosi sank to new lows of popularity and the elections of 2010 resulted in the Democrats losing control of the House and almost losing the Senate. Obama received a surge of support by the country in 2011 when the terrorist Osama bin Laden was killed by U.S. troops in Pakistan after a 9-year search.

Obama runs for President again in 2012 keeping Joe Biden as his running mate and wins with a narrower margin than his 2008 election. He focuses his second term on managing his healthcare implementation, working on climate change initiatives, and handling the continuing war on terror with American troops still in Iraq and Afghanistan. This term also witnesses the rise of ISIS as the major terror threat to the world. The Republicans win control of the Senate in 2014 so Obama must deal with an opposition Senate for his last two years. He signs the Paris Agreement on Climate Change in 2016. Obama leaves office at the end of his term with the Republicans maintaining control of Congress and the controversial Donald Trump as the new President-elect.

Donald J. Trump

New York
June 14, 1946 -

45

2016-2020

Donald Trump clinched the presidency after the most controversial and contentious election in memory. He rose from being a businessman to the most powerful office in the world. In 1971 he took over the his family's real estate empire and was involved in a number of office buildings, hotels, casinos, and golf courses in his career. He was also involved in the Miss USA and Miss Universe pageants as well as a TV show, *The Apprentice*. His personal wealth of over $4 billion makes him the wealthiest U.S. President.

Trump ran on a populist platform whose slogan was *Make America Great Again*. He was very outspoken and was often accused of making offensive remarks. Against the NAFTA and the TPP trade agreements, he supported stricter immigration laws and building the wall along the U.S.-Mexican border. He vowed to repeal Obamacare and simplify the tax code if elected. He beat out 16 other Republican contenders to face Hillary Clinton in November. Every mainstream media outlet and poll had Clinton up by 5 points or more on election day but Trump shocked the country and the world by winning the electoral college, but became the fifth President in history to lose the popular vote, this time to Hillary Clinton by almost three million votes. He becomes the oldest first term President. The election was followed by anti-Trump protests across the country and third party candidate Jill Stein filed requests to recount several states that had very close votes but the recounts showed little differences.

Trump started his term with a majority in the Senate and House and quickly signed a number of executive orders to start building the wall on the Mexican border, start the repeal of Obamacare,and temporarily stopped immigration from a number of countries linked to terrorism. His cabinet picks included outsiders and more retired military generals than any other President.

JOSEPH BIDEN

Pennsylvania
November 20, 1942

46

2020-

In April 2019, Biden announced his candidacy in the 2020 presidential election. He became the presumptive Democratic nominee in April 2020 and reached the delegate threshold needed to secure the nomination in June 2020. Biden and his running mate Kamala Harris defeated incumbent president Donald Trump and vice president Mike Pence in the general election. Biden is the oldest elected president, the first from Delaware, and the second Catholic. His early activity as president centered around a series of executive orders. In addition to emergency actions pertaining to the ongoing COVID-19 pandemic, Biden's orders reversed several Trump administration policies. His reversals included rejoining the Paris Agreement on climate change, reaffirming protections for Deferred Action for Childhood Arrivals recipients, halting construction of the Trump border wall, ending the national emergency at the southern border declared by the Trump administration, ending the Trump travel ban imposed on predominantly Muslim countries, and revoking permits for the construction of the Keystone XL pipeline.

Chapter 3

U.S. MAPS

❧

THE ORIGINAL 13 STATES made up less than 10% of the total land area of the future country. Some of the original states had claims to additional territory, but most of the continent was still claimed by various European nations, including England, France, Spain, and Russia. The United States had received a huge parcel of land, the Northwest Territory, in the treaty that ended the Revolutionary War, and the founders knew they had to set up procedures to handle the admission of new states as the nation grew. The procedures in the Northwest Ordinance and the Constitution would govern how those new states were to be admitted.

The path to our manifest destiny of 50 states would be long and tortuous. It involved wars, treaties, purchases, conflicts with the Native Americans, the discovery of gold, and, most importantly, the resolution of the slavery issue. The growth of the new Union was reflected in how the country was referenced, changing from "the United States *are*" to "the United States *is*."

Northwest Ordinance of 1787

The Northwest Ordinance of 1787, passed under the Articles of Confederation, established the policy used, with minor exceptions, for admitting future states. Its guidelines included:

- Congress appoints a territorial governor, territorial secretary, and three judges.

- When there are 5,000 free adult males in each territory, they can elect a general assembly legislature. (Remember women don't have the vote yet and slavery still existed.)

- When the population reaches 60,000, they can write their constitution and apply for statehood.

- New states are admitted on equal footing with old states.

- Slavery was prohibited in the Northwest territory.

THE GROWTH OF AMERICA

Native American Tribes

2008 #59,87
2020 #74,117

The map shows some of the major tribes prior to European settlement. These are also hundreds of smaller ones. You'll recognize future state and city names among the tribe names. Columbus had mistakenly called the natives "Indians" thinking he had reached the East Indies.

1 Delaware (1787)	8 South Carolina (1788)
2 Pennsylvania (1787)	9 New Hampshire (1788)
3 New Jersey (1787)	10 Virginia (1788)
4 Georgia (1788)	11 New York (1788)
5 Connecticut (1788)	
6 Massachusetts (1788)	12 North Carolina (1789)
7 Maryland (1788)	13 Rhode Island (1790)

2008 #64
2020 #81

The 13 colonies become states when their state legislatures ratify the new Constitution. Several states do not ratify until they have been assured that a Bill of Rights will be included. Delaware takes the title as "The First State." Massachusetts also claims what is present-day Maine, and Kentucky and West Virginia are part of Virginia. The treaty ending the Revolution gives the U.S. the Northwest Territory.

14 Vermont (1791)   **16** Tennessee (1796)
15 Kentucky (1792)   **17** Ohio (1803)

Jefferson doubles the size of the country by purchasing the Louisiana Territory from France. Kentucky separates from Virginia and becomes the 15th state, and Ohio becomes the first state from the Northwest Territory.

18 Louisiana (1812)   **22** Alabama (1819)
19 Indiana (1816)
20 Mississippi (1817)   **23** Maine (1820)
21 Illinois (1818)   **24** Missouri (1821)

The Louisiana Territory is renamed the Missouri Territory when Louisiana becomes a state. It then becomes an unorganized territory when Missouri becomes a state. Arkansas is originally spelled "Arkansaw" before the spelling is later changed. Maine is admitted as a free state to balance the new slave state Missouri. The 1819 Adams-Onis Treaty grants Florida and surrounding area to the U.S. The Anglo-American Convention of 1818 gives the Red River Basin to the U.S. since it is south of the new border with Canada at latitude 49°.

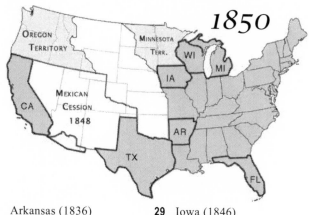

25	Arkansas (1836)	29	Iowa (1846)
26	Michigan (1837)	30	Wisconsin (1848)
27	Florida (1845)		
28	Texas (1845)	31	California (1850)

The treaty ending the Mexican war in 1848, along with a payment of $18 million, gives the U.S. control of the Mexican Cession area. Texas (a slave state) has to wait to become a state until a Northern non-slave state can also be added. The 1846 Oregon Treaty sets the 49th parallel as our border with Canada.

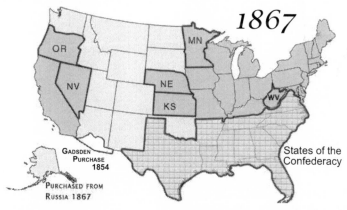

32	Minnesota (1858)	35	West Virginia (1863)
33	Oregon (1859)	36	Nevada (1864)
34	Kansas (1861)	37	Nebraska (1867)

As a result of the Kansas-Nebraska Act, Kansas draws up an anti-slavery constitution and is allowed into the Union as a free state. Nebraska has to wait until after the Civil War to be admitted as a free state. West Virginia votes itself independent of Virginia (which it had been a part of) and applies for statehood with the Union. The U.S. gets the Gadsden area from Mexico for $10 million in 1854, and purchases Alaska from Russia for $7.2 million in 1867.

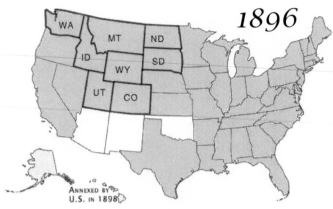

38 Colorado (1876)
39 North Dakota (1889)
40 South Dakota (1889)
41 Montana (1889)

42 Washington (1889)
43 Idaho (1890)
44 Wyoming (1890)
45 Utah (1896)

Utah enters the Union with a large population that is 90% Mormon. Wyoming women had been given the right to vote which almost kept Wyoming from acquiring statehood. North and South Dakota achieve statehood on the same day, but are recorded in alphabetical order.

46 Oklahoma (1907)
47 New Mexico (1912)

48 Arizona (1912)

Attempts to split the Oklahoma Territory into two states, a regular U.S. state and the Native American state of Sequoyah, fall short. A combined Oklahoma is admitted to the Union. New Mexico and Arizona fulfill the promise of Manifest Destiny as the United States now spreads continuously from sea to sea.

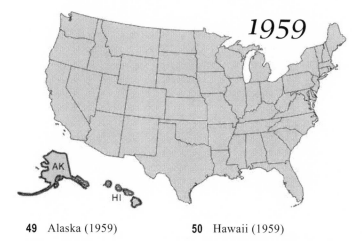

49 Alaska (1959)   **50** Hawaii (1959)

The Alaska territory, bought from the Russians in 1867 for $7.2 million, finally becomes the largest state in the Union. Hawaii had been annexed to the United States in 1898 and becomes the last state in 1959—the United States now has a fifty-star flag.

Regions and rivers of America

The map above shows the major rivers of the country, and the names of the general regions used to describe parts of the country. The names overlap and represent general areas and not exact collections of states. The Mississippi and Missouri rivers are the longest, each being over 2,000 miles long.

2008 #90

2008 #88

Continental Divide

The vertical line running through the Rocky Mountains divides the two major watersheds of the continental United States. All rivers to the west of the divide drain into the Pacific Ocean, while all rivers to the east drain into the Atlantic Ocean or Gulf of Mexico.

[#]44 **2008** ## States, capitals(★), major cities, and time zones

[#]62 **2020** How many city nicknames can you recognize in this list?

Beantown	Big Apple	Big Easy
Motor City	Music City	City of Angels
Windy City	City by the Bay	Gateway to the West
Steel City	Mile High City	City of Brotherly Love

Pittsburgh	*Denver*	*Philadelphia*
Chicago	*San Francisco*	*St. Louis*
Detroit	*Nashville*	*Los Angeles*
Boston	*New York*	*New Orleans*

CENTRAL TIME ZONE 5PM

EASTERN TIME ZONE 6PM

U.S. Territories and Possessions

These islands are overseen directly by the United States government and are not part of any U.S. state.

Puerto Rico	Wake Island
U.S. Virgin Islands	Kingman Reef
Northern Mariana Islands	Navassa Island
American Samoa	Palmyra Atoll
Johnston Atoll	Midway Islands
Baker, Howland, Jarvis Islands	Guam

2008 #91

National Parks, Monuments, and attractions

Washington, D.C.
FDR Memorial, Korean War Veterans Memorial, Lincoln Memorial, National Mall, Thomas Jefferson Memorial, Vietnam Veterans Memorial, Washington Monument, White House, U.S. Capitol, World War II Memorial, Smithsonian Museum

Philadelphia, Pennsylvania
Liberty Bell, Independence Hall

New York City
Statue of Liberty, Ellis Island, Empire State Building

CENTRAL
TIME ZONE
5PM

EASTERN
TIME ZONE
6PM

United States facts (Source: CIA Factbook 2016)

Highest point (50 states): Mt. McKinley, AK (20,320 ft.)

Highest point (48 states): Mt. Whitney, CA (14,494 ft.)

Lowest point: Death Valley, CA (-282 ft.) 100 miles from Whitney

Square Area (50 states): 3,794,101 sq. mi. (3rd largest in world)

Population (2011): 323,995,528 (3rd largest in world) White: 79%; Black: 13%; Asian: 4.4%; Hispanic: 15% (overlaps w/others)

Largest Metropolitan Areas: New York (19,300,000) Los Angeles (12,675,000) Chicago (9,134,000)

Religion: Protestant: 46%, Catholic: 21%, Mormon: 1.6%, Jewish: 1.9%, Buddhist: 0.7%, Muslim: 0.9%, other/none: 24%

Signing of the Mayflower Compact
Plymouth Harbor—November 11, 1620
by Jean Leon Gerome Ferris

We on this continent should never forget that men first crossed the Atlantic not to find soil for their ploughs but to secure liberty for their souls.

—Robert J. McCracken

America is much more than a geographical fact. It is a political and moral fact—the first community in which men set out in principle to institutionalize freedom, responsible government, and human equality.

—Adlai Stevenson

Signing of the Constitution of the United States
Independence Hall, Philadelphia—September 17, 1787
by Howard Chandler Christy

Chapter 4

OUR FOUNDING DOCUMENTS

❧

O UR FORM OF GOVERNMENT can trace its roots back through English law, the Magna Carta of 1215, and the civilizations of Rome and Greece. The early settlers of the new land knew the importance of the rule of law, and soon produced documents protecting individual rights and ensuring that the will of the people would always be heard. Some of America's most important documents are the Mayflower Compact, Articles of Confederation, the Declaration of Independence, the Northwest Ordinance of 1787, Federalist Papers, Virginia Declaration of Rights, and the U.S. Constitution. The full text of all these is included, except the Northwest Ordinance which is an important but often overlooked document establishing the procedures for territories to achieve statehood.

2020 #14

Declaration of Independence BY JOHN TRUMBULL

This famous painting depicts the Declaration being presented to the Continental Congress by the drafting committee on June 28, 1776. Trumbull included 42 of the 56 signers of the Declaration in the picture. The 18x12-foot painting hangs in the U.S. Capitol and is reproduced on the back of the $2 bill. It does *not* depict the actual signing of the document.

Documents Grow Longer as Government Grows

Mayflower Compact
1 PAGE

Declaration of Independence
1 BIG PAGE

U.S. Constitution
4 PAGES

2010 Health Bill
2,100 PAGES

U.S. Tax Code
16,845 PAGES

MAYFLOWER COMPACT

PILGRIMS   NOVEMBER 11, 1620

Before the colonists landed at Plymouth, Massachusetts in 1620, they all signed a document since known as the Mayflower Compact. This social contract established the right of the people to form a new government in the new land based on the consent of those same people. This eventually led to the Declaration of Independence and the American Constitution more than 150 years later. The *Mayflower* was supposed to land in Northern Virginia which explains their reference to Virginia in this document.

In the name of God, Amen. We whose names are underwritten, the loyal subjects of our dread Sovereign Lord King James, by the Grace of God of Great Britain, France and Ireland, King, Defender of the Faith, etc.

Having undertaken, for the Glory of God and advancement of the Christian Faith and Honour of our King and Country, a Voyage to plant the First Colony in the Northern Parts of Virginia, do by these presents solemnly and mutually in the presence of God and one of another, Covenant and Combine ourselves together into a Civil Body Politic, for our better ordering and preservation and furtherance of the ends aforesaid; and by virtue hereof to enact, constitute and frame such just and equal Laws, Ordinances, Acts, Constitutions and Offices, from time to time, as shall be thought most meet and convenient for the general good of the Colony, unto which we promise all due submission and obedience.

In witness whereof we have hereunder subscribed our names at Cape Cod, the 11th of November, in the year of the reign of our Sovereign Lord King James, of England, France and Ireland the eighteenth, and of Scotland the fifty-fourth. Anno Domini 1620.

I sought for the greatness and genius of America in her commodious harbors and her ample rivers, and it was not there. In the fertile fields and boundless prairies, and it was not there. In her rich mines and her vast world commerce, and it was not there. Not until I went into the churches of America and heard her pulpits, aflame with righteousness, did I understand the secret of her genius and power. America is great because she is good, and if America ever ceases to be good, America will cease to be great.

—attributed to Alexis de Tocqueville

#63 `2008`
#79 `2020`

Declaration of Independence

Second Continental Congress   **July 4, 1776**

#8, 62 `2008`
#8, 9, 78 `2020`

The colonies had been fighting with British forces for a year when the Continental Congress met in Philadelphia to formally declare their separation from England. A draft, composed primarily by Thomas Jefferson, was presented on June 28 and approved on July 4. British forces were landing in New York and threatening Philadelphia, so there was no time to lose. Copies were rushed by land and sea to all the colonies. The original, signed copy is in the Washington National Archives. It states that all people are created equal.

In CONGRESS, July 4, 1776
The Unanimous Declaration of the
Thirteen United States of America

WHEN IN THE COURSE OF HUMAN EVENTS it becomes necessary for one people to dissolve the political bands which have connected them with another and to assume among the powers of the earth, the separate and equal station to which the Laws of Nature and of Nature's God entitle them, a decent respect to the opinions of mankind requires that they should declare the causes which impel them to the separation.

#9 `2008`
#11 `2020`

We hold these truths to be self-evident, that all men are created equal, that they are endowed by their Creator with certain unalienable Rights, that among these are Life, Liberty and the pursuit of Happiness. — That to secure these rights, Governments are instituted among Men, deriving their just powers from the consent of the governed, — That whenever any Form of Government becomes destructive of these ends, it is the Right of the People to alter or to abolish it, and to institute new Government, laying its foundation on such principles and organizing its powers in such form, as to them shall seem most likely to effect their Safety and Happiness. Prudence, indeed, will dictate that Governments long established should not be changed for light and transient causes; and accordingly all experience hath shewn that mankind are more disposed to suffer, while evils are sufferable than to right themselves by abolishing the forms to which they are accustomed. But when a long train of abuses and usurpations, pursuing invariably the same Object evinces a design to reduce them under absolute Despotism, it is their right, it is their duty, to throw off such Government, and to provide new Guards for their future security. — Such has been the patient sufferance of these Colonies; and such is now the necessity which constrains them to alter their former

Systems of Government. The history of the present King of Great Britain is a history of repeated injuries and usurpations, all having in direct object the establishment of an absolute Tyranny over these States. To prove this, let Facts be submitted to a candid world.

He has refused his Assent to Laws, the most wholesome and necessary for the public good. He has forbidden his Governors to pass Laws of immediate and pressing importance, unless suspended in their operation till his Assent should be obtained; and when so suspended, he has utterly neglected to attend to them.

He has refused to pass other Laws for the accommodation of large districts of people, unless those people would relinquish the right of Representation in the Legislature, a right inestimable to them and formidable to tyrants only.

He has called together legislative bodies at places unusual, uncomfortable, and distant from the depository of their Public Records, for the sole purpose of fatiguing them into compliance with his measures. He has dissolved Representative Houses repeatedly, for opposing with manly firmness his invasions on the rights of the people.

He has refused for a long time, after such dissolutions, to cause others to be elected, whereby the Legislative Powers, incapable of Annihilation, have returned to the People at large for their exercise; the State remaining in the mean time exposed to all the dangers of invasion from without, and convulsions within.

He has endeavoured to prevent the population of these States; for that purpose obstructing the Laws for Naturalization of Foreigners; refusing to pass others to encourage their migrations hither, and raising the conditions of new Appropriations of Lands.

He has obstructed the Administration of Justice by refusing his Assent to Laws for establishing Judiciary Powers. He has made Judges dependent on his Will alone for the tenure of their offices, and the amount and payment of their salaries.

He has erected a multitude of New Offices, and sent hither swarms of Officers to harass our people and eat out their substance. He has kept among us, in times of peace, Standing Armies without the Consent of our legislatures. He has affected to render the Military independent of and superior to the Civil Power.

He has combined with others to subject us to a jurisdiction foreign to our constitution, and unacknowledged by our laws; giving his Assent to their Acts of pretended Legislation:

For Quartering large bodies of armed troops among us: For protecting them, by a mock Trial, from punishment for any Murders which they should commit on the Inhabitants of these States:

For cutting off our Trade with all parts of the world: For imposing Taxes on us without our Consent: For depriving us in many cases, of the benefit of Trial by Jury: For transporting us beyond Seas to be tried for pretended offences:

For abolishing the free System of English Laws in a neighbouring Province, establishing therein an Arbitrary government, and enlarging its Boundaries so as to render it at once an example and fit instrument for introducing the same absolute rule into these Colonies

For taking away our Charters, abolishing our most valuable Laws and altering fundamentally the Forms of our Governments: For suspending our own Legislatures, and declaring themselves invested with power to legislate for us in all cases whatsoever.

He has abdicated Government here, by declaring us out of his Protection and waging War against us. He has plundered our seas, ravaged our coasts, burnt our towns, and destroyed the lives of our people. He is at this time transporting large Armies of foreign Mercenaries to compleat the works of death, desolation, and tyranny, already begun with circumstances of Cruelty & Perfidy scarcely paralleled in the most barbarous ages, and totally unworthy the Head of a civilized nation.

He has constrained our fellow Citizens taken Captive on the high Seas to bear Arms against their Country, to become the executioners of their friends and Brethren, or to fall themselves by their Hands.

He has excited domestic insurrections amongst us, and has endeavoured to bring on the inhabitants of our frontiers, the merciless Indian Savages whose known rule of warfare, is an undistinguished destruction of all ages, sexes and conditions.

In every stage of these Oppressions We have Petitioned for Redress in the most humble terms: Our repeated Petitions have been answered only by repeated injury. A Prince, whose character is thus marked by every act which may define a Tyrant, is unfit to be the ruler of a free people.

Nor have We been wanting in attentions to our British brethren. We have warned them from time to time of attempts by their legislature to extend an unwarrantable jurisdiction over us. We have reminded them of the circumstances of our emigration and settlement here. We have appealed to their native justice and magnanimity, and we have conjured them by the ties of our common kindred to disavow these usurpations, which would inevitably interrupt our connections and correspondence. They too have been deaf to the voice of justice and of consanguinity. We must, therefore, acquiesce in the necessity, which denounces our Separation, and hold them, as we hold the rest of mankind, Enemies in War, in Peace Friends.

We, therefore, the Representatives of the united States of America, in General Congress, Assembled, appealing to the Supreme Judge of the world for the rectitude of our intentions, do, in the Name, and by Authority of the good People of these Colonies, solemnly publish and declare, **That these united Colonies are, and of Right ought to be Free and Independent States,** that they are Absolved from all Allegiance to the British Crown, and that all political connection between them and the State of Great Britain, is and ought to be totally dissolved; and that as Free and Independent States, they have full Power to levy War, conclude Peace, contract Alliances, establish Commerce, and to do all other Acts and Things which Independent States may of right do. **— And for the support of this Declaration, with a firm reliance on the protection of Divine Providence, we mutually pledge to each other our Lives, our Fortunes, and our sacred Honor.**

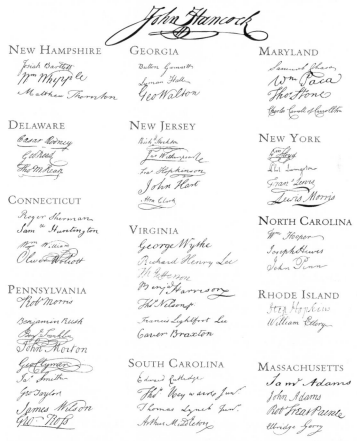

NEW HAMPSHIRE
Josiah Bartlett
Wm Whipple
Matthew Thornton

DELAWARE
Cæsar Rodney
Geo Read
Tho M:Kean

CONNECTICUT
Roger Sherman
Sam.el Huntington
Wm Williams
Oliver Wolcott

PENNSYLVANIA
Robt Morris
Benjamin Rush
Benj.a Franklin
John Morton
Geo Clymer
Ja.s Smith
Geo Taylor
James Wilson
Geo. Ross

GEORGIA
Button Gwinnett
Lyman Hall
Geo Walton

NEW JERSEY
Richd Stockton
Jno Witherspoon
Fras Hopkinson
John Hart
Abra Clark

VIRGINIA
George Wythe
Richard Henry Lee
Th Jefferson
Benja Harrison
Thos Nelson jr.
Francis Lightfoot Lee
Carter Braxton

SOUTH CAROLINA
Edward Rutledge
Tho.s Heyward Junr.
Thomas Lynch Junr.
Arthur Middleton

MARYLAND
Samuel Chase
Wm Paca
Thos Stone
Charles Carroll of Carrollton

NEW YORK
Wm Floyd
Phil. Livingston
Frans Lewis
Lewis Morris

NORTH CAROLINA
Wm Hooper
Joseph Hewes
John Penn

RHODE ISLAND
Step Hopkins
William Ellery

MASSACHUSETTS
Sam.l Adams
John Adams
Robt Treat Paine
Elbridge Gerry

Northwest Ordinance of 1787

CONGRESS OF THE CONFEDERATION   JULY 13, 1787

In one of its last official acts, the Confederation passed the Northwest Ordinance earlier in the same year that they passed the Constitution. This document was of upmost importance to the subsequent expansion of the country as it set the general procedures for statehood. The 1783 Peace Treaty had granted a large territory to the new country, consisting of present-day Ohio, Indiana, Illinois, Michigan, Wisconsin, and Minnesota. However, there were no procedures in place to handle new states. On July 13, the Congress passed this new ordinance which set the rules for establishing new states in this territory, as well as prohibiting slavery in those states. It also encouraged schools, protected property rights, guaranteed religious freedom, and protected the rights of Native Americans. All new states would be admitted as equals with existing states. Excerpts from the Ordinance follow:

That there shall be appointed from time to time by Congress, a governor, whose commission shall continue in force for the term of three years, unless sooner revoked by Congress; he shall reside in the district, and have a freehold estate therein in 1,000 acres of land, while in the exercise of his office...There shall also be appointed a court to consist of three judges, any two of whom to form a court, who shall have a common law jurisdiction, and reside in the district, and have each therein a freehold estate in 500 acres of land while in the exercise of their offices; and their commissions shall continue in force during good behavior...

The governor, for the time being, shall be commander in chief of the militia, appoint and commission all officers in the same below the rank of general officers; all general officers shall be appointed and commissioned by Congress...

So soon as there shall be five thousand free male inhabitants of full age in the district, upon giving proof thereof to the governor, they shall receive authority, with time and place, to elect a representative from their counties or townships to represent them in the general assembly...

As soon as a legislature shall be formed in the district, the council and house assembled in one room, shall have authority, by joint ballot, to elect a delegate to Congress, who shall have a seat in Congress, with a right of debating but not voting during this temporary government.

And, for extending the fundamental principles of civil and religious liberty...and for their admission to a share in the federal councils on an equal footing with the original States, at as early periods as may be consistent with the general interest...

Art. 1. No person, demeaning himself in a peaceable and orderly manner, shall ever be molested on account of his mode of worship or religious sentiments, in the said territory.

Art. 2. The inhabitants of the said territory shall always be entitled to the benefits of the writ of habeas corpus, and of the trial by jury; of a proportionate representation of the people in the legislature; and of judicial proceedings according to the course of the common law...No man shall be deprived of his liberty or property, but by the judgment of his peers or the law of the land; ...

Art. 3. Religion, morality, and knowledge, being necessary to good government and the happiness of mankind, schools and the means of education shall forever be encouraged. The utmost good faith shall always be observed towards the Indians; their lands and property shall never be taken from them without their consent; and, in their property, rights, and liberty, they shall never be invaded or disturbed, unless in just and lawful wars authorized by Congress; but laws founded in justice and humanity, shall from time to time be made for preventing wrongs being done to them, and for preserving peace and friendship with them...

Art. 5. There shall be formed in the said territory, not less than three nor more than five States; and the boundaries of the States, as soon as Virginia shall alter her act of cession, and consent to the same, shall become fixed....

And, whenever any of the said States shall have sixty thousand free inhabitants therein, such State shall be admitted, by its delegates, into the Congress of the United States, on an equal footing with the original States in all respects whatever, and shall be at liberty to form a permanent constitution and State government: Provided, the constitution and government so to be formed, shall be republican, and in conformity to the principles contained in these articles; and, so far as it can be consistent with the general interest of the confederacy, such admission shall be allowed at an earlier period, and when there may be a less number of free inhabitants in the State than sixty thousand.

Art. 6. There shall be neither slavery nor involuntary servitude in the said territory, otherwise than in the punishment of crimes whereof the party shall have been duly convicted: Provided, always, That any person escaping into the same, from whom labor or service is lawfully claimed in any one of the original States, such fugitive may be lawfully reclaimed and conveyed to the person claiming his or her labor or service as aforesaid...

United States Constitution

<table>
<tr><td>Constitutional Convention</td><td>March 4, 1789</td></tr>
</table>

After the Revolutionary War, it became obvious that the Articles of Confederation were not capable of running the new country. Its national government was too weak to hold the country together. There was no provision for taxation or handling the national debt. Its form of weak central government was only natural due to the country's recent problems with, and separation from, the British monarchy.

#65 **2008**
#82 **2020**

A Constitutional Convention met in Philadelphia in May of 1787 to amend the Articles of Confederation, but decided instead that an entirely new document was needed. A new plan from Virginia called for a 3-branch government, but there were concerns about a legislative body based solely on population. A compromise led to the creation of a bicameral body with a House based on population, and a Senate with equal representation from each state. The Three-Fifths Compromise counted slaves as only 3/5 of a person for determining representation, but this was mainly to reduce the influence of southern states.

#1, 66 **2008**

By September of 1787, they had produced a draft of a new Constitution. It received the required ratification by nine states on June 21, 1788, and became effective on March 4, 1789. It was the first time that a nation's people had peacefully decided on their new form of government, and the document they produced is the oldest written constitution still in effect. Only 12 states initially signed the Constitution. Rhode Island did not even attend the convention as she was the smallest state and felt that the new government would take away too much of her power as a state. The Constitution is now the supreme law of the land. Note: The original text is shown below with sections that have been changed or superseded by amendments shown in **_bold italic_**. There is one grammar mistake that has been copied from the original document. See if you can find it (it is not an old or British spelling like chuse).

#3 **2008**
#4 **2020**

We the People of the UNITED STATES, in Order to form a more perfect Union, establish Justice, insure domestic Tranquility, provide for the common defence, promote the general Welfare, and secure the Blessings of Liberty to ourselves and our Posterity, do ordain and establish this Constitution for the United States of America.

Article I

Section 1. All legislative Powers herein granted shall be vested in a Congress of the United States, which shall consist of a Senate and House of Representatives.

Section 2. The House of Representatives shall be composed of Members chosen every second Year by the People of the several States, and the Electors in each State shall have the Qualifications requisite for Electors of the most numerous Branch of the State Legislature.

No Person shall be a Representative who shall not have attained to the Age of twenty five Years, and been seven Years a Citizen of the United States, and who shall not, when elected, be an Inhabitant of that State in which he shall be chosen.

Representatives and direct Taxes shall be apportioned among the several States which may be included within this Union, according to their respective Numbers, which shall be determined by adding to the whole Number of free Persons, including those bound to Service for a Term of Years, and excluding Indians not taxed, three fifths of all other Persons. *(Modified by 14 amendment.)* The actual Enumeration shall be made within three Years after the first Meeting of the Congress of the United States, and within every subsequent Term of ten Years, in such Manner as they shall by Law direct. The Number of Representatives shall not exceed one for every thirty Thousand, but each State shall have at Least one Representative; and until such enumeration shall be made, the State of New Hampshire shall be entitled to chuse three, Massachusetts eight, Rhode Island and Providence Plantations one, Connecticut five, New York six, New Jersey four, Pennsylvania eight, Delaware one, Maryland six, Virginia ten, North Carolina five, South Carolina five and Georgia three.

When vacancies happen in the Representation from any State, the Executive Authority thereof shall issue Writs of Election to fill such Vacancies.

The House of Representatives shall chuse their Speaker and other Officers; and shall have the sole Power of Impeachment.

SECTION 3. The Senate of the United States shall be composed of two Senators from each State, *chosen by the Legislature thereof,* *(modified by the 17th Amendment)* for six Years; and each Senator shall have one Vote.

Immediately after they shall be assembled in Consequence of the first Election, they shall be divided as equally as may be into three Classes. The Seats of the Senators of the first Class shall be vacated at the Expiration of the second Year, of the second Class at the Expiration of the fourth Year, and of the third Class at the Expiration of the sixth Year, so that one third may be chosen every second Year; *and if Vacancies happen by Resignation, or otherwise, during the Recess of the Legislature of any State, the Executive thereof may make temporary Appointments until the next Meeting of the Legislature, which shall then fill such Vacancies.* *(modified by the 17th amendment)*

No person shall be a Senator who shall not have attained to the Age of thirty Years, and been nine Years a Citizen of the United States, and who shall not, when elected, be an Inhabitant of that State for which he shall be chosen.

The Vice President of the United States shall be President of the Senate, but shall have no Vote, unless they be equally divided.

The Senate shall chuse their other Officers, and also a President pro tempore, in the absence of the Vice President, or when he shall exercise the Office of President of the United States.

The Senate shall have the sole Power to try all Impeachments. When sitting for that Purpose, they shall be on Oath or Affirmation. When the President of the United States is tried, the Chief Justice shall preside: And no Person shall be convicted without the Concurrence of two thirds of the Members present.

Judgment in Cases of Impeachment shall not extend further than to removal from Office, and disqualification to hold and enjoy any Office of honor, Trust or Profit under the United States: but the Party convicted shall nevertheless be liable and subject to Indictment, Trial, Judgment and Punishment, according to Law.

SECTION 4. The Times, Places and Manner of holding Elections for Senators and Representatives, shall be prescribed in each State by the Legislature thereof; but the Congress may at any time by Law make or alter such Regulations, except as to the Place of Chusing Senators.

The Congress shall assemble at least once in every Year, and such Meeting shall be *on the first Monday in December,* (superseded by the 20th amendment) unless they shall by Law appoint a different Day.

SECTION 5. Each House shall be the Judge of the Elections, Returns and Qualifications of its own Members, and a Majority of each shall constitute a Quorum to do Business; but a smaller number may adjourn from day to day, and may be authorized to compel the Attendance of absent Members, in such Manner, and under such Penalties as each House may provide.

Each House may determine the Rules of its Proceedings, punish its Members for disorderly Behavior, and, with the Concurrence of two-thirds, expel a Member.

Each House shall keep a Journal of its Proceedings, and from time to time publish the same, excepting such Parts as may in their Judgment require Secrecy; and the Yeas and Nays of the Members of either House on any question shall, at the Desire of one fifth of those Present, be entered on the Journal.

Neither House, during the Session of Congress, shall, without the Consent of the other, adjourn for more than three days, nor to any other Place than that in which the two Houses shall be sitting.

SECTION 6. *The Senators and Representatives shall receive a Compensation for their Services, to be ascertained by Law, and paid out of the Treasury of the United States.* (modified by the 27th Amendment.) They shall in all Cases, except Treason, Felony and Breach of the Peace, be privileged from Arrest during their Attendance at the Session of their respective Houses, and in going to and returning from the same; and for any Speech or Debate in either House, they shall not be questioned in any other Place.

No Senator or Representative shall, during the Time for which he was elected, be appointed to any civil Office under the Authority of the United States which shall have been created, or the Emoluments whereof shall have been increased during such time; and no Person holding any Office under the United States, shall be a Member of either House during his Continuance in Office.

Section 7. All bills for raising Revenue shall originate in the House of Representatives; but the Senate may propose or concur with Amendments as on other Bills.

Every Bill which shall have passed the House of Representatives and the Senate, shall, before it become a Law, be presented to the President of the United States; If he approve he shall sign it, but if not he shall return it, with his Objections to that House in which it shall have originated, who shall enter the Objections at large on their Journal, and proceed to reconsider it. If after such Reconsideration two thirds of that House shall agree to pass the Bill, it shall be sent, together with the Objections, to the other House, by which it shall likewise be reconsidered, and if approved by two thirds of that House, it shall become a Law. But in all such Cases the Votes of both Houses shall be determined by Yeas and Nays, and the Names of the Persons voting for and against the Bill shall be entered on the Journal of each House respectively. If any Bill shall not be returned by the President within ten Days (Sundays excepted) after it shall have been presented to him, the Same shall be a Law, in like Manner as if he had signed it, unless the Congress by their Adjournment prevent its Return, in which Case it shall not be a Law.

Every Order, Resolution, or Vote to which the Concurrence of the Senate and House of Representatives may be necessary (except on a question of Adjournment) shall be presented to the President of the United States; and before the Same shall take Effect, shall be approved by him, or being disapproved by him, shall be repassed by two thirds of the Senate and House of Representatives, according to the Rules and Limitations prescribed in the Case of a Bill.

Section 8. The Congress shall have Power To lay and collect Taxes, Duties, Imposts and Excises, to pay the Debts and provide for the common Defence and general Welfare of the United States; but all Duties, Imposts and Excises shall be uniform throughout the United States;

To borrow money on the credit of the United States;

To regulate Commerce with foreign Nations, and among the several States, and with the Indian Tribes;

To establish an uniform Rule of Naturalization, and uniform Laws on the subject of Bankruptcies throughout the United States;

To coin Money, regulate the Value thereof, and of foreign Coin, and fix the Standard of Weights and Measures;

To provide for the Punishment of counterfeiting the Securities and current Coin of the United States;

To establish Post Offices and Post Roads;

To promote the Progress of Science and useful Arts, by securing for limited Times to Authors and Inventors the exclusive Right to their respective Writings and Discoveries;

To constitute Tribunals inferior to the supreme Court;

To define and punish Piracies and Felonies committed on the high Seas, and Offenses against the Law of Nations;

To declare War, grant Letters of Marque and Reprisal, and make Rules concerning Captures on Land and Water;

To raise and support Armies, but no Appropriation of Money to that Use shall be for a longer Term than two Years;

To provide and maintain a Navy; To make Rules for the Government and Regulation of the land and naval Forces;

To provide for calling forth the Militia to execute the Laws of the Union, suppress Insurrections and repel Invasions;

To provide for organizing, arming, and disciplining, the Militia, and for governing such Part of them as may be employed in the Service of the United States, reserving to the States respectively, the Appointment of the Officers, and the Authority of training the Militia according to the discipline prescribed by Congress;

To exercise exclusive Legislation in all Cases whatsoever, over such District (not exceeding ten Miles square) as may, by Cession of particular States, and the acceptance of Congress, become the Seat of the Government of the United States, and to exercise like Authority over all Places purchased by the Consent of the Legislature of the State in which the Same shall be, for the Erection of Forts, Magazines, Arsenals, dock-Yards, and other needful Buildings; And

To make all Laws which shall be necessary and proper for carrying into Execution the foregoing Powers, and all other Powers vested by this Constitution in the Government of the United States, or in any Department or Officer thereof.

SECTION 9. The Migration or Importation of such Persons as any of the States now existing shall think proper to admit, shall not be prohibited by the Congress prior to the Year one thousand eight hundred and eight, but a tax or duty may be imposed on such Importation, not exceeding ten dollars for each Person.

The privilege of the Writ of Habeas Corpus shall not be suspended, unless when in Cases of Rebellion or Invasion the public Safety may require it.

No Bill of Attainder or ex post facto Law shall be passed.

No capitation, or other direct, Tax shall be laid, unless in Proportion to the Census or Enumeration herein before directed to be taken. (Clarified by the 16th Amendment.)

No Tax or Duty shall be laid on Articles exported from any State.

No Preference shall be given by any Regulation of Commerce or Revenue to the Ports of one State over those of another: nor shall Vessels bound to, or from, one State, be obliged to enter, clear, or pay Duties in another.

No Money shall be drawn from the Treasury, but in Consequence of Appropriations made by Law; and a regular Statement and Account of the Receipts and Expenditures of all public Money shall be published from time to time.

No Title of Nobility shall be granted by the United States: And no Person holding any Office of Profit or Trust under them, shall, without the Consent of the Congress, accept of any present, Emolument, Office, or Title, of any kind whatever, from any King, Prince or foreign State.

SECTION 10. No State shall enter into any Treaty, Alliance, or Confederation; grant Letters of Marque and Reprisal; coin Money; emit Bills of Credit; make any Thing but gold and silver Coin a Tender in Payment of Debts; pass any Bill of Attainder, ex post facto Law, or Law impairing the Obligation of Contracts, or grant any Title of Nobility.

No State shall, without the Consent of the Congress, lay any Imposts or Duties on Imports or Exports, except what may be absolutely necessary for executing it's inspection Laws: and the net Produce of all Duties and Imposts, laid by any State on Imports or Exports, shall be for the Use of the Treasury of the United States; and all such Laws shall be subject to the Revision and Controul of the Congress.

No State shall, without the Consent of Congress, lay any duty of Tonnage, keep Troops, or Ships of War in time of Peace, enter into any Agreement or Compact with another State, or with a foreign Power, or engage in War, unless actually invaded, or in such imminent Danger as will not admit of delay.

ARTICLE II

SECTION 1. The executive Power shall be vested in a President of the United States of America. He shall hold his Office during the Term of four Years, and, together with the Vice President chosen for the same Term, be elected, as follows:

Each State shall appoint, in such Manner as the Legislature thereof may direct, a Number of Electors, equal to the whole Number of Senators and Representatives to which the State may be entitled in the Congress: but no Senator or Representative, or Person holding an Office of Trust or Profit under the United States, shall be appointed an Elector.

The Electors shall meet in their respective States, and vote by Ballot for two persons, of whom one at least shall not be an Inhabitant of the same State with themselves. And they shall make a List of all the Persons voted for, and of the Number of Votes for each; which List they shall sign and certify, and transmit sealed to the Seat of the Government of the United States, directed to the President of the Senate. The President of the Senate shall, in the Presence of the Senate and House of Representatives, open all the Certificates, and the Votes shall then be counted. The Person having the greatest Number of Votes shall be the President, if such Number be a Majority of the whole Number of Electors appointed; and if there be more than one who have such Majority, and have an equal Number of Votes, then the House of Representatives shall immediately chuse by Ballot one of them for President; and if no Person have a Majority, then from the five highest on the List the said House shall in like Manner chuse the President. But in chusing the President, the Votes shall be taken by States, the Representation from each State having one Vote; a quorum for this Purpose shall consist of a Member or Members from two-thirds of the States, and a Majority of all the States shall be necessary to a Choice. In every Case, after the Choice of the President, the Person having the greatest Number of Votes of the Electors shall be the Vice President. But if there should remain two or more who have equal Votes, the Senate shall chuse from them by Ballot the Vice-President. (superseded by the 12th Amendment.)

The Congress may determine the Time of chusing the Electors, and the Day on which they shall give their Votes; which Day shall be the same throughout the United States.

No person except a natural born Citizen, or a Citizen of the United States, at the time of the Adoption of this Constitution, shall be eligible to the Office of President; neither shall any Person be eligible to that Office who shall not have attained to the Age of thirty-five Years, and been fourteen Years a Resident within the United States.

In Case of the Removal of the President from Office, or of his Death, Resignation, or Inability to discharge the Powers and Duties of the said Office, the same shall devolve on the Vice President, and the Congress may by Law provide for the Case of Removal, Death, Resignation or Inability, both of the President and Vice President, declaring what Officer shall then act as President, and such Officer shall act accordingly, until the Disability be removed, or a President shall be elected. (modified by the 20th and 25th Amendments.)

The President shall, at stated Times, receive for his Services, a Compensation, which shall neither be increased nor diminished during the Period for which he shall have been elected, and he shall not receive within that Period any other Emolument from the United States, or any of them.

Before he enter on the Execution of his Office, he shall take the following Oath or Affirmation:

"I do solemnly swear (or affirm) that I will faithfully execute the Office of President of the United States, and will to the best of my Ability, preserve, protect and defend the Constitution of the United States."

SECTION 2. The President shall be Commander in Chief of the Army and Navy of the United States, and of the Militia of the several States, when called into the actual Service of the United States; he may require the Opinion, in writing, of the principal Officer in each of the executive Departments, upon any subject relating to the Duties of their respective Offices, and he shall have Power to Grant Reprieves and Pardons for Offenses against the United States, except in Cases of Impeachment.

He shall have Power, by and with the Advice and Consent of the Senate, to make Treaties, provided two thirds of the Senators present concur; and he shall nominate, and by and with the Advice and Consent of the Senate, shall appoint Ambassadors, other public Ministers and Consuls, Judges of the supreme Court, and all other Officers of the United States, whose Appointments are not herein otherwise provided for, and which shall be established by Law: but the Congress may by Law vest the Appointment of such inferior Officers, as they think proper, in the President alone, in the Courts of Law, or in the Heads of Departments.

The President shall have Power to fill up all Vacancies that may happen during the Recess of the Senate, by granting Commissions which shall expire at the End of their next Session.

SECTION 3. He shall from time to time give to the Congress Information of the State of the Union, and recommend to their Consideration such Measures as he shall judge necessary and expedient; he may, on extraordinary Occasions, convene both Houses, or either of them, and in Case of Disagreement between them, with Respect to the Time of Adjournment, he may adjourn them to such Time as he shall think proper; he shall receive Ambassadors and other public Ministers; he shall take Care that the Laws be faithfully executed, and shall Commission all the Officers of the United States.

SECTION 4. The President, Vice President and all civil Officers of the United States, shall be removed from Office on Impeachment for, and Conviction of, Treason, Bribery, or other high Crimes and Misdemeanors.

Article III

Section 1. The judicial Power of the United States, shall be vested in one supreme Court, and in such inferior Courts as the Congress may from time to time ordain and establish. The Judges, both of the supreme and inferior Courts, shall hold their Offices during good Behavior, and shall, at stated Times, receive for their Services a Compensation which shall not be diminished during their Continuance in Office.

Section 2. *The judicial Power shall extend to all Cases, in Law and Equity, arising under this Constitution, the Laws of the United States, and Treaties made, or which shall be made, under their Authority; to all Cases affecting Ambassadors, other public Ministers and Consuls; to all Cases of admiralty and maritime Jurisdiction; to Controversies to which the United States shall be a Party; to Controversies between two or more States; between a State and Citizens of another State; between Citizens of different States; between Citizens of the same State claiming Lands under Grants of different States, and between a State, or the Citizens thereof, and foreign States, Citizens or Subjects.* (modified by the 11th Amendment.)

In all Cases affecting Ambassadors, other public Ministers and Consuls, and those in which a State shall be Party, the supreme Court shall have original Jurisdiction. In all the other Cases before mentioned, the supreme Court shall have appellate Jurisdiction, both as to Law and Fact, with such Exceptions, and under such Regulations as the Congress shall make.

The Trial of all Crimes, except in Cases of Impeachment, shall be by Jury; and such Trial shall be held in the State where the said Crimes shall have been committed; but when not committed within any State, the Trial shall be at such Place or Places as the Congress may by Law have directed.

Section 3. Treason against the United States, shall consist only in levying War against them, or in adhering to their Enemies, giving them Aid and Comfort. No Person shall be convicted of Treason unless on the Testimony of two Witnesses to the same overt Act, or on Confession in open Court.

The Congress shall have power to declare the Punishment of Treason, but no Attainder of Treason shall work Corruption of Blood, or Forfeiture except during the Life of the Person attainted.

Article IV

Section 1. Full Faith and Credit shall be given in each State to the public Acts, Records, and judicial Proceedings of every other State. And the Congress may by general Laws prescribe the Manner in which such Acts, Records and Proceedings shall be proved, and the Effect thereof.

SECTION 2. The Citizens of each State shall be entitled to all Privileges and Immunities of Citizens in the several States.

A Person charged in any State with Treason, Felony, or other Crime, who shall flee from Justice, and be found in another State, shall on demand of the executive Authority of the State from which he fled, be delivered up, to be removed to the State having Jurisdiction of the Crime.

No Person held to Service or Labour in one State, under the Laws thereof, escaping into another, shall, in Consequence of any Law or Regulation therein, be discharged from such Service or Labour, But shall be delivered up on Claim of the Party to whom such Service or Labour may be due. (superseded by the 13th Amendment.)

SECTION 3. New States may be admitted by the Congress into this Union; but no new States shall be formed or erected within the Jurisdiction of any other State; nor any State be formed by the Junction of two or more States, or parts of States, without the Consent of the Legislatures of the States concerned as well as of the Congress.

The Congress shall have Power to dispose of and make all needful Rules and Regulations respecting the Territory or other Property belonging to the United States; and nothing in this Constitution shall be so construed as to Prejudice any Claims of the United States, or of any particular State.

SECTION 4. The United States shall guarantee to every State in this Union a Republican Form of Government, and shall protect each of them against Invasion; and on Application of the Legislature, or of the Executive (when the Legislature cannot be convened) against domestic Violence.

ARTICLE V

The Congress, whenever two thirds of both Houses shall deem it necessary, shall propose Amendments to this Constitution, or, on the Application of the Legislatures of two thirds of the several States, shall call a Convention for proposing Amendments, which, in either Case, shall be valid to all Intents and Purposes, as part of this Constitution, when ratified by the Legislatures of three fourths of the several States, or by Conventions in three fourths thereof, as the one or the other Mode of Ratification may be proposed by the Congress; Provided that no Amendment which may be made prior to the Year One thousand eight hundred and eight shall in any Manner affect the first and fourth Clauses in the Ninth Section of the first Article; and that no State, without its Consent, shall be deprived of its equal Suffrage in the Senate.

Article VI

All Debts contracted and Engagements entered into, before the Adoption of this Constitution, shall be as valid against the United States under this Constitution, as under the Confederation.

This Constitution, and the Laws of the United States which shall be made in Pursuance thereof; and all Treaties made, or which shall be made, under the Authority of the United States, shall be the supreme Law of the Land; and the Judges in every State shall be bound thereby, any Thing in the Constitution or Laws of any State to the Contrary notwithstanding.

The Senators and Representatives before mentioned, and the Members of the several State Legislatures, and all executive and judicial Officers, both of the United States and of the several States, shall be bound by Oath or Affirmation, to support this Constitution; but no religious Test shall ever be required as a Qualification to any Office or public Trust under the United States.

Article VII

The Ratification of the Conventions of nine States, shall be sufficient for the Establishment of this Constitution between the States so ratifying the Same.

Done in Convention by the Unanimous Consent of the States present the Seventeenth Day of September in the Year of our Lord one thousand seven hundred and Eighty seven and of the Independence of the United States of America the Twelfth.

In Witness whereof We have hereunto subscribed our Names.

Go Washington
President and deputy from Virginia

DELAWARE	NEW HAMPSHIRE	PENSYLVANIA
Geo. Read	*John Langdon*	*B Franklin*
Gunning Bedford, Jr.	*Nicholas Gilman*	*Thomas Mifflin*
John Dickinson	MARYLAND	*Robt Morris*
Richard Bassett	*James McHenry*	*Geo. Clymer*
Jaco. Broom	*Dan of St Tho Jenifer*	*Thos FitzSimons*
VIRGINIA	*Danl Carroll*	*Jared Ingersoll*
John Blair	CONNECTICUT	*James Wilson*
James Madison Jr.	*Wm Saml Johnson*	*Gouv Morris*
NEW JERSEY	*Roger Sherman*	MASSACHUSETTS
Wil Livingston	NORTH CAROLINA	*Nathaniel Gorham*
David Brearley	*Wm Blount*	*Rufus King*
Wm Paterson	*Richd Dobbs Spaight*	SOUTH CAROLINA
Jona. Dayton	*Hu Williamson*	*J. Rutledge*
GEORGIA	NEW YORK	*Charles Cotesworth Pinckney*
William Few	*Alexander Hamilton*	*Charles Pinckney*
Abr Baldwin		*Pierce Butler*

Attest: *William Jackson*, Secretary

Amendments to the Constitution

CONGRESS   1791 - TODAY

The Constitution allowed for changes or additions to be made using state-approved amendments. Several states were concerned about the potential power of the new federal government, and agreed to ratify the new Constitution only if some changes were made to protect state and individual rights. These became the first ten amendments to the Constitution, commonly referred to as the Bill of Rights, protect the basic rights of Americans. The dates shown below are the dates the amendments were ratified by the states. Amendments must be approved by 2/3 of Congress and 3/4 of the states.

2008	#4
2020	#5
2008	#5
2020	#6

BILL OF RIGHTS - AMENDMENTS 1 TO 10

AMENDMENT I   1791

FREEDOM OF RELIGION, SPEECH, PRESS, PEACEFUL ASSEMBLY

Congress shall make no law respecting an establishment of religion, or prohibiting the free exercise thereof; or abridging the freedom of speech, or of the press; or the right of the people peaceably to assemble, and to petition the Government for a redress of grievances.

2008	#6, 10
2008	#51
2020	#65

AMENDMENT II   1791

RIGHT TO BEAR ARMS

A well regulated Militia, being necessary to the security of a free State, the right of the people to keep and bear Arms, shall not be infringed.

AMENDMENT III   1791

NO QUARTERING OF SOLDIERS

No Soldier shall, in time of peace be quartered in any house, without the consent of the Owner, nor in time of war, but in a manner to be prescribed by law.

AMENDMENT IV   1791

PROTECTION AGAINST UNREASONABLE SEARCHES AND SEIZURES

The right of the people to be secure in their persons, houses, papers, and effects, against unreasonable searches and seizures, shall not be violated, and no Warrants shall issue, but upon probable cause, supported by Oath or affirmation, and particularly describing the place to be searched, and the persons or things to be seized.

AMENDMENT V   1791

NO SELF-INCRIMINATION OR DOUBLE JEOPARDY, RIGHT TO GRAND JURY

No person shall be held to answer for a capital, or otherwise infamous crime, unless on a presentment or indictment of a Grand Jury, except in cases arising in the land or naval forces, or in the Militia, when in actual service in time of War or public danger; nor shall any person be subject for the same offense to be twice put in jeopardy of life or limb; nor shall be compelled in any criminal case to be a witness against himself, nor be deprived of life, liberty, or property, without due process of law; nor shall private property be taken for public use, without just compensation.

Amendment VI   1791

Right to speedy trial, confrontation of witnesses

In all criminal prosecutions, the accused shall enjoy the right to a speedy and public trial, by an impartial jury of the State and district wherein the crime shall have been committed, which district shall have been previously ascertained by law, and to be informed of the nature and cause of the accusation; to be confronted with the witnesses against him; to have compulsory process for obtaining witnesses in his favor, and to have the Assistance of Counsel for his defence.

Amendment VII   1791

Right to a trial by jury for civil cases

In Suits at common law, where the value in controversy shall exceed twenty dollars, the right of trial by jury shall be preserved, and no fact tried by a jury, shall be otherwise re-examined in any Court of the United States, than according to the rules of the common law.

Amendment VIII   1791

Protection from cruel and unusual punishment

Excessive bail shall not be required, nor excessive fines imposed, nor cruel and unusual punishments inflicted.

Amendment IX   1791

Extent of enumerated rights in Constitution

The enumeration in the Constitution, of certain rights, shall not be construed to deny or disparage others retained by the people.

Amendment X   1791

#60 2020

Undelegated powers reside in the states and the people

The powers not delegated to the United States by the Constitution, nor prohibited by it to the States, are reserved to the States respectively, or to the people.

End of Bill of Rights

Amendment XI — 1795

Judicial limits

The Judicial power of the United States shall not be construed to extend to any suit in law or equity, commenced or prosecuted against one of the United States by Citizens of another State, or by Citizens or Subjects of any Foreign State.

Amendment XII — 1804

Choosing the President and Vice President

The Electors shall meet in their respective states, and vote by ballot for President and Vice President, one of whom, at least, shall not be an inhabitant of the same state with themselves; they shall name in their ballots the person voted for as President, and in distinct ballots the person voted for as Vice President, and they shall make distinct lists of all persons voted for as President, and of all persons voted for as Vice President and of the number of votes for each, which lists they shall sign and certify, and transmit sealed to the seat of the government of the United States, directed to the President of the Senate;

The President of the Senate shall, in the presence of the Senate and House of Representatives, open all the certificates and the votes shall then be counted;

The person having the greatest Number of votes for President, shall be the President, if such number be a majority of the whole number of Electors appointed; and if no person have such majority, then from the persons having the highest numbers not exceeding three on the list of those voted for as President, the House of Representatives shall choose immediately, by ballot, the President. But in choosing the President, the votes shall be taken by states, the representation from each state having one vote; a quorum for this purpose shall consist of a member or members from two-thirds of the states, and a majority of all the states shall be necessary to a choice. And if the House of Representatives shall not choose a President whenever the right of choice shall devolve upon them, before the fourth day of March next following, then the Vice President shall act as President, as in the case of the death or other constitutional disability of the President.

The person having the greatest number of votes as Vice President, shall be the Vice President, if such number be a majority of the whole number of Electors appointed, and if no person have a majority, then from the two highest numbers on the list, the Senate shall choose the Vice President; a quorum for the purpose shall consist of two-thirds of the whole number of Senators, and a majority of the whole number shall be necessary to a choice. But no person constitutionally ineligible to the office of President shall be eligible to that of Vice President of the United States.

Amendment XIII   1865

Abolishment of slavery

1. Neither slavery nor involuntary servitude, except as a punishment for crime whereof the party shall have been duly convicted, shall exist within the United States, or any place subject to their jurisdiction.

2. Congress shall have power to enforce this article by appropriate legislation.

Amendment XIV   1868

Citizenship rights
Apportionment of representatives; oaths

1. All persons born or naturalized in the United States, and subject to the jurisdiction thereof, are citizens of the United States and of the State wherein they reside. No State shall make or enforce any law which shall abridge the privileges or immunities of citizens of the United States; nor shall any State deprive any person of life, liberty, or property, without due process of law; nor deny to any person within its jurisdiction the equal protection of the laws.

2. Representatives shall be apportioned among the several States according to their respective numbers, counting the whole number of persons in each State, excluding Indians not taxed. But when the right to vote at any election for the choice of electors for President and Vice President of the United States, Representatives in Congress, the Executive and Judicial officers of a State, or the members of the Legislature thereof, is denied to any of the male inhabitants of such State, being twenty-one years of age, and citizens of the United States, or in any way abridged, except for participation in rebellion, or other crime, the basis of representation therein shall be reduced in the proportion which the number of such male citizens shall bear to the whole number of male citizens twenty-one years of age in such State.

3. No person shall be a Senator or Representative in Congress, or elector of President and Vice President, or hold any office, civil or military, under the United States, or under any State, who, having previously taken an oath, as a member of Congress, or as an officer of the United States, or as a member of any State legislature, or as an executive or judicial officer of any State, to support the Constitution of the United States, shall have engaged in insurrection or rebellion against the same, or given aid or comfort to the enemies thereof. But Congress may by a vote of two-thirds of each House, remove such disability.

4. The validity of the public debt of the United States, authorized by law, including debts incurred for payment of pensions and bounties for services in suppressing insurrection or rebellion, shall not be

questioned. But neither the United States nor any State shall assume or pay any debt or obligation incurred in aid of insurrection or rebellion against the United States, or any claim for the loss or emancipation of any slave; but all such debts, obligations and claims shall be held illegal and void.

5. The Congress shall have power to enforce, by appropriate legislation, the provisions of this article.

AMENDMENT XV   1870

VOTING RIGHTS EXTENDED
TO EX-SLAVES AND ALL RACES AND COLORS

1. The right of citizens of the United States to vote shall not be 2020 #98 denied or abridged by the United States or by any State on account of race, color, or previous condition of servitude.

2. The Congress shall have power to enforce this article by appropriate legislation.

AMENDMENT XVI   1913

CONGRESS GIVEN RIGHT TO COLLECT INCOME TAX

The Congress shall have power to lay and collect taxes on incomes, from whatever source derived, without apportionment among the several States, and without regard to any census or enumeration.

AMENDMENT XVII   1913

SENATORS ELECTED BY POPULAR VOTE

The Senate of the United States shall be composed of two Senators from each State, elected by the people thereof, for six years; and each Senator shall have one vote. The electors in each State shall have the qualifications requisite for electors of the most numerous branch of the State legislatures.

When vacancies happen in the representation of any State in the Senate, the executive authority of such State shall issue writs of election to fill such vacancies: Provided, That the legislature of any State may empower the executive thereof to make temporary appointments until the people fill the vacancies by election as the legislature may direct.

This amendment shall not be so construed as to affect the election or term of any Senator chosen before it becomes valid as part of the Constitution.

Amendment XVIII   1919

PROHIBITS MANUFACTURE, SALE AND TRANSPORTATION OF ALCOHOL

1. After one year from the ratification of this article the manufacture, sale, or transportation of intoxicating liquors within, the importation thereof into, or the exportation thereof from the United States and all territory subject to the jurisdiction thereof for beverage purposes is hereby prohibited.

2. The Congress and the several States shall have concurrent power to enforce this article by appropriate legislation.

3. This article shall be inoperative unless it shall have been ratified as an amendment to the Constitution by the legislatures of the several States, as provided in the Constitution, within seven years from the date of the submission hereof to the States by the Congress.

Amendment XIX   1920

#102 `2020`

WOMEN GIVEN THE RIGHT TO VOTE

The right of citizens of the United States to vote shall not be denied or abridged by the United States or by any State on account of sex.

Congress shall have power to enforce this article by appropriate legislation.

Amendment XX   1933

DEFINES TERMS OF PRESIDENT AND CONGRESS

1. The terms of the President and Vice President shall end at noon on the 20th day of January, and the terms of Senators and Representatives at noon on the 3d day of January, of the years in which such terms would have ended if this article had not been ratified; and the terms of their successors shall then begin.

2. The Congress shall assemble at least once in every year, and such meeting shall begin at noon on the 3d day of January, unless they shall by law appoint a different day.

3. If, at the time fixed for the beginning of the term of the President, the President elect shall have died, the Vice President elect shall become President. If a President shall not have been chosen before the time fixed for the beginning of his term, or if the President elect shall have failed to qualify, then the Vice President elect shall act as President until a President shall have qualified; and the Congress may by law provide for the case wherein neither a President elect nor a Vice President elect shall have qualified, declaring who shall then act as President, or the manner in which one who is to act shall be selected, and such person shall act accordingly until a President or Vice President shall have qualified.

4. The Congress may by law provide for the case of the death of any of the persons from whom the House of Representatives may choose a President whenever the right of choice shall have devolved upon them, and for the case of the death of any of the persons from whom the Senate may choose a Vice President whenever the right of choice shall have devolved upon them.

5. Sections 1 and 2 shall take effect on the 15th day of October following the ratification of this article.

6. This article shall be inoperative unless it shall have been ratified as an amendment to the Constitution by the legislatures of three-fourths of the several States within seven years from the date of its submission.

AMENDMENT XXI   1933

REPEALS 18TH AMENDMENT; LEGALIZES ALCOHOL AGAIN

1. The eighteenth article of amendment to the Constitution of the United States is hereby repealed.

2. The transportation or importation into any State, Territory, or possession of the United States for delivery or use therein of intoxicating liquors, in violation of the laws thereof, is hereby prohibited.

3. The article shall be inoperative unless it shall have been ratified as an amendment to the Constitution by conventions in the several States, as provided in the Constitution, within seven years from the date of the submission hereof to the States by the Congress.

AMENDMENT XXII   1951

LIMITS PRESIDENT TO TWO TERMS IN OFFICE

1. No person shall be elected to the office of the President more than twice, and no person who has held the office of President, or acted as President, for more than two years of a term to which some other person was elected President shall be elected to the office of the President more than once. But this Article shall not apply to any person holding the office of President, when this Article was proposed by the Congress, and shall not prevent any person who may be holding the office of President, or acting as President, during the term within which this Article becomes operative from holding the office of President or acting as President during the remainder of such term.

2. This article shall be inoperative unless it shall have been ratified as an amendment to the Constitution by the legislatures of three-fourths of the several States within seven years from the date of its submission to the States by the Congress.

AMENDMENT XXIII   1961

GIVES PRESIDENTIAL VOTE TO DISTRICT OF COLUMBIA

1. The District constituting the seat of Government of the United States shall appoint in such manner as the Congress may direct: A number of electors of President and Vice President equal to the whole number of Senators and Representatives in Congress to which the District would be entitled if it were a State, but in no event more than the least populous State; they shall be in addition to those appointed by the States, but they shall be considered, for the purposes of the election of President and Vice President, to be electors appointed by a State; and they shall meet in the District and perform such duties as provided by the twelfth article of amendment.

2. The Congress shall have power to enforce this article by appropriate legislation.

AMENDMENT XXIV   1964

OUTLAWS POLL TAX

1. The right of citizens of the United States to vote in any primary or other election for President or Vice President, for electors for President or Vice President, or for Senator or Representative in Congress, shall not be denied or abridged by the United States or any State by reason of failure to pay any poll tax or other tax.

2. The Congress shall have power to enforce this article by appropriate legislation.

AMENDMENT XXV   1967

SETS PRESIDENTIAL DISABILITY AND SUCCESSION RULES

1. In case of the removal of the President from office or of his death or resignation, the Vice President shall become President.

2. Whenever there is a vacancy in the office of the Vice President, the President shall nominate a Vice President who shall take office upon confirmation by a majority vote of both Houses of Congress.

3. Whenever the President transmits to the President pro tempore of the Senate and the Speaker of the House of Representatives his written declaration that he is unable to discharge the powers and duties of his office, and until he transmits to them a written declaration to the contrary, such powers and duties shall be discharged by the Vice President as Acting President.

4. Whenever the Vice President and a majority of either the principal officers of the executive departments or of such other body as Congress may by law provide, transmit to the President pro tempore of the Senate and the Speaker of the House of Representatives their written declaration that the President is unable to discharge the powers

and duties of his office, the Vice President shall immediately assume the powers and duties of the office as Acting President.

Thereafter, when the President transmits to the President pro tempore of the Senate and the Speaker of the House of Representatives his written declaration that no inability exists, he shall resume the powers and duties of his office unless the Vice President and a majority of either the principal officers of the executive department or of such other body as Congress may by law provide, transmit within four days to the President pro tempore of the Senate and the Speaker of the House of Representatives their written declaration that the President is unable to discharge the powers and duties of his office. Thereupon Congress shall decide the issue, assembling within forty eight hours for that purpose if not in session. If the Congress, within twenty one days after receipt of the latter written declaration, or, if Congress is not in session, within twenty one days after Congress is required to assemble, determines by two thirds vote of both Houses that the President is unable to discharge the powers and duties of his office, the Vice President shall continue to discharge the same as Acting President; otherwise, the President shall resume the powers and duties of his office.

Amendment XXVI   1971

Sets voting age to 18 years

2008 #54

1. The right of citizens of the United States, who are eighteen years of age or older, to vote shall not be denied or abridged by the United States or by any State on account of age.

2. The Congress shall have power to enforce this article by appropriate legislation.

Amendment XXVII   1992

2008 #7

Limits Congressional pay increases

2020 #7

No law, varying the compensation for the services of the Senators and Representatives, shall take effect, until an election of Representatives shall have intervened.

The 27th amendment was first proposed in 1789 and took 203 years to be ratified. Michigan was the 38th state to ratify the amendment in 1992. There have been over 10,000 amendments introduced in Congress, and there are still four amendments that have passed Congress and are awaiting ratification by the states. The Equal Rights Amendment (ERA) was never ratified and has expired.

───────────────── ❀ ─────────────────

The Constitution is not an instrument for government to restrain the people, it is an instrument for the people to restrain the government—lest it come to dominate our lives and interests.

—Patrick Henry

Inauguration of
George Washington
April 30, 1789
New York City
by Ramon de Elorriaga

Humanity has won its battle. Liberty now has a country.
—*Marquis de Lafayette*

Inauguration of
Abraham Lincoln
March 4, 1861
Washington, D.C.

The ballot is stronger than the bullet.
—*Abraham Lincoln*

To live under the American Constitution is the greatest political privilege that was ever accorded to the human race.
—*Calvin Coolidge*

Inauguration of
Barack Obama
January 20, 2009
Washington, D.C.

The orderly transfer of authority as called for in the Constitution routinely takes place, as it has for almost two centuries, and few of us stop to think how unique we really are. In the eyes of many in the world, this every-four-year ceremony we accept as normal is nothing less than a miracle.
—*Ronald Reagan*

Chapter 5

HOW OUR GOVERNMENT WORKS

❧

T HE Declaration of Independence and the Constitution were based on the belief in the equality of everyone and the natural `2020` #10 right to liberty and self-government.

What the Founders Were Thinking

The founders of this country were very aware of how other forms of government had fared throughout the world, going back to ancient Greece and Rome. They knew the tyranny of monarchs and tyrants, just as they realized the tyranny of pure democracies. The founders were products of the Age of Enlightenment, the Renaissance, and an increased reliance on science and reason. They were also descendants of settlers fleeing religious persecution, so they knew the danger of state religion and intolerance. They shared an almost universal belief in a God, whether they were Deists or devout Christians. These views manifested themselves in the Declaration of Independence and the Constitution, and their entire approach to the new country.

What does the Preamble to the Constitution mean?

Gouverneur Morris attended the Convention as a delegate from Pennsylvania. He had strong beliefs opposing slavery in the states, and helped write parts of the Constitution. He is best remembered, however, for writing the Preamble to the Constitution. The Preamble assigns no powers, nor does it directly stipulate any function of government. It does, however, describe the principles behind the document, and has even been used by the courts to help establish the meaning of the Constitution and the intent of the Founding Fathers.

The phrases in the short preamble were carefully chosen to convey the intent of the men crafting this historic document. Just the inclusion of the words "We the People" was historic. The phrases of the preamble are:

We the People of the United States
This was the first country in the world to form a government based on the consent of the people.

in Order to form a more perfect Union
The Articles of Confederation were ineffective, primarily due to lack of power in the central government, and the founders knew they could never produce a perfect nation, just a "more" perfect one.

establish Justice
The new nation had to be based on equal justice for all citizens. The people can enjoy their freedom and rights, but they are not free to violate the rights of others.

insure domestic Tranquility
The Confederation had been unable to control domestic unrest and the founders knew the new government had to be able to control the country.

provide for the common defence
The new country would be threatened on all sides, and the states all needed to band together to stand any chance of success.

promote the general Welfare
The founders knew that government's role was not to guarantee success or happiness, but to provide the framework required to make it happen.

and secure the Blessings of Liberty to ourselves and our Posterity
The founders had fought for their liberty, and knew they were creating a government that should last for centuries.

do ordain and establish this Constitution
"Ordaining" this document implies a higher power similar to the reference in the Declaration to unalienable rights flowing from a Creator.

for the United States of America.
This closing clause formalizes the name for the new nation: The United States of America.

What Kind of Government Do We Have

The United States was formed as a **Federal Constitutional Republic**. It is democratic, but it is not a democracy. This distinction is very important. These three words mean: `2020` [1]

Federal: comprised of states united by a central government.

Constitutional: bound by a formal constitution adopted by the citizens and only changed with their consent.

Republic: run by representatives elected by the citizens rather than by direct vote, and not run by a monarch or dictator.

America is not a true democracy

It is democratic in the sense that the citizens can all vote for their officials. It is a representative democracy in the sense that the citizens elect officials who actually create and pass the laws. However, it is not a pure democracy, nor is it a pure representative democracy. In a pure democracy, a majority may impose their will over the minority with nothing to protect those minorities. What makes America work is the protection of the Constitution. A constitutional republic protects the unalienable rights and liberties of all its citizens, including any minority. A majority cannot simply `2020` [2] exercise their will over the minority by simply voting their desires—that is mob rule. Laws passed in this country must be both approved by the voters, and be constitutional. The Constitution is `2008` [1] the supreme law of the land.

It is critical for every citizen to understand the importance of the Constitution, and not assume that a majority may pass any law they desire. It is interesting that the word "democracy" does not appear anywhere in either the Declaration or the Constitution.

The founding fathers knew the dangers of a pure democracy and also knew the importance of a strong Constitution. Alexander Hamilton, arguing in 1788 for the approval of the Constitution, said:

> It has been observed that a pure democracy, if it were practicable, would be the most perfect government. Experience has proved that no position is more false than this. The ancient democracies in which the people themselves deliberated never possessed one good feature of government. Their very character was tyranny; their figure deformity.

As so clearly stated in the Declaration of Independence, our rights are unalienable and come from our Creator, not from any government. Any government that thinks they must pass laws to "give" rights to individuals will be the same government that "takes" those rights away. The government's only purpose is to protect the rights each person already possesses. Allowing a majority vote to violate anyone's unalienable rights is no different than allowing a tyrant or dictator to do the same.

A quotation often attributed to Alexander Tytler states, "A democracy cannot exist as a permanent form of government. It can only exist until a majority of voters discover that they can vote themselves largesse out of the public treasury." Our government today is perilously close to this tipping point.

The government often mischaracterizes itself as a democracy. President Wilson called World War I the war "to make the world safe for democracy," and President Roosevelt called America "the great arsenal of democracy." An accurate description of the perils of a pure democracy was outlined in the *1928 U.S. Training Manual*:

> **Democracy:** A government of the masses. Authority derived through mass meeting or any other form of "direct" expression. Results in mobocracy. Attitude toward property is communistic—negating property rights. Attitude toward law is that the will of the majority shall regulate, whether it be based upon deliberation or governed by passion, prejudice, and impulse, without restraint or regard to consequences. Results in demagogism, license, agitation, discontent, anarchy.

The Creation of the Constitution

The *Articles of Confederation*, created at the start of the Revolution, proved to be completely unusable in running the new country. A convention was convened to fix the Articles, but the founders ended up creating a novel new form of government. It was not a straight forward or easy process. There were strong arguments on all sides. There was a basic split between those favoring a strong central government, and those favoring state and individual rights. Some of the more important compromises during the debating included:

1. **Great Compromise of 1787:** The rights of small and large states were balanced by creating a Senate with equal state representation, and a House with representation proportional to population.

2. **Bill of Rights:** The concerns of several states about an overly strong central government led to the promise of the creation of the Bill of Rights (the first ten amendments) to protect the rights of states and individuals. The Constitution was finally ratified because of this promise.

3. **Slavery:** Slaves could be imported only until 1808, but the Fugitive Slave Clause allowed southern owners to reclaim runaway slaves. To keep southern states from acquiring too much power in the new House, slaves were counted as 3/5 of a person in determining state representation.

4. **Electoral College:** The president would be elected by electors in the Electoral College, and not by a direct vote.

The ultimate innovation was the process of how the Constitution was to be changed. The Constitution stipulated that it can only be changed by a formal process of "amendments," and provided the mechanism to make those changes in a manner that is difficult enough to ensure it will be used only when absolutely necessary. And the tenth amendment itself states that any powers not specifically granted to the federal government by the Constitution revert to the states or to the people. There have been twenty-seven amendments to date, although there have been over 10,000 amendments proposed.

Once the Constitution was finished and approved by the members, it had to be sent to the thirteen states for ratification. It was decided that only nine states had to ratify the new document for it to take effect. New Hampshire became the ninth state to ratify the Constitution on June 21, 1788, and the new nation finally had a government. The Constitution defined the structure of the new government, and protected the rights of its citizens, but it was up to the early leaders to actually put that government into action.

`2008` #2
`2020` #3

On April 30, 1789, George Washington was inaugurated as the first president in New York City. He has been the only unanimous selection for president. He was essential in setting the tone for our government since the Constitution did not detail every specific process, position, or department. Washington named cabinet positions, created a national bank, established a precedent for dealing with Congress, and stuck with his belief that a president should not serve more than 2 terms.

Lord Acton of England wrote of the Constitution,

> They had solved with astonishing ease and unduplicated success two problems which had heretofore baffled the capacity of the most enlightened nations. They had contrived a system of federal government which prodigiously increased national power and yet respected local liberties and authorities, and they had founded it on a principle of equality without surrendering the securities of property or freedom.

Three Equal Branches

#13 `2008`
#15, 16 `2020`
Our particular republic government was created with another crucial safeguard—its three separate, but equal, Executive, Legislative, and Judicial branches. The Constitution was very clear on this separation of powers. Each branch has very specific duties, responsibilities, and limits.

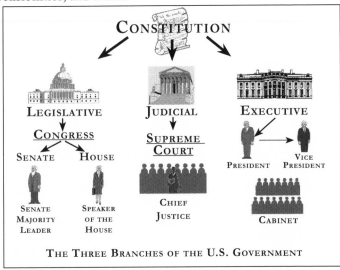

CONSTITUTION

LEGISLATIVE · JUDICIAL · EXECUTIVE

CONGRESS · SUPREME COURT

SENATE · HOUSE · PRESIDENT · VICE PRESIDENT

SENATE MAJORITY LEADER · SPEAKER OF THE HOUSE · CHIEF JUSTICE · CABINET

THE THREE BRANCHES OF THE U.S. GOVERNMENT

Executive branch

#15, 26 `2008`
#17,36 `2020`
#45,46 `2020`
#32,33 `2008`
#41,43 `2020`
#34 `2008`
#42,44 `2020`
#37 `2020`

This branch consists of the President, Vice President and 15 cabinet level departments. The president and vice president are elected every four years. The president appoints Supreme Court justices and Cabinet members who all have to be approved by the Senate. The executive branch is in charge of ensuring laws are carried out, collecting taxes, and keeping the country safe. The president submits the federal budget to Congress every year. Most of the work is accomplished by the various departments, such as the Attorney General, State Department, Defense Department, etc. The president can sign bills given to him for signature and make them law, or veto the bill, which then requires a 2/3 vote in Congress to overcome the veto. The president also serves as Commander-in-Chief of the military. To be eligible for president, a candidate must be 35 years or older, a natural-born citizen, and have lived in the U.S. for at least 14 consecutive years. Since the passage of the 22nd amendment, the president can serve only two terms in office.

Legislative Branch

The Senate and the House of Representatives are collectively known as Congress. This branch is responsible for creating, passing, and funding the laws of the country, and approving presidential nominations and Cabinet selections. After passing laws, they send them to the President for approval or veto. The president has limited powers to use the military, but wars can only be declared by Congress. There are no term limits now for any member of Congress, and some have served for decades—Senator Byrd served for 51 years. Sixteen Senators have gone on to become president. Washington, D.C. has no representation in the Senate and can't vote on the House floor.

2020 [19]

2008 [16]

2020 [18,20]

Senate

The Senate consists of 100 Senators, two from each state. Senators serve six-year terms, with 1/3 of them being elected every two years. They are elected to represent the entire state. The Senate gives equal representation to each state regardless of their population. The Vice President acts as *President of the Senate,* casting the deciding vote in case of ties. The *president pro tempore* presides in his absence. The Senate Majority Leader normally controls the Senate. The Senate can approve treaties, confirm judges and Cabinet picks, and confirm impeachments. Senators must be 30 years of age, a citizen of the U.S. for the previous nine years, and a resident of the state they represent.

2008 [17,18]

2020 [21,27]

2008 [19,24]

2020 [22,31]

2020 [28,32]

House of Representatives

The number of representatives varies with the population of each state and are elected by voters of each district. The members elect their leader, the Speaker of the House. The party not in control elects a Minority Leader. The House represents the interests of smaller groups of citizens, and small congressional districts around the country. Serving 2-year terms, they have to stay in touch with their constituents back home and continue to earn their support. A Representative must be 25 years or older, a citizen for seven years before the election, and a resident of the state of their election, but not necessarily the district to which they are elected. The Apportionment Act of 1911 fixed the total number of representatives at 435. The number allocated each state is calculated using the National Census every ten years. Some states may lose representatives and some may gain, but the total number remains fixed at 435. The House originates all revenue bills, starts impeachments and elects the president in case of an electoral tie.

2008 [25]

2020 [34,35]

2008 [22]

2020 [25,33]

2020 [26]

2008 [21]

2020 [24]

Judicial Branch

#37,38 `2008`
#50,52 `2020`
#39 `2008`
#53,54 `2020`
#12 `2008`
#51,55 `2020`
#13 `2020`

The judiciary consists of the U.S. Supreme Court (the highest court in the land) and all the lower federal courts. It hears cases to interpret the constitutionality of legislation. There are nine justices on the Supreme Court, appointed by the president for their lifetime, but confirmed by the Senate. It takes at least 5 justices to decide a case. The Chief Justice of the United States, one of the nine judges, heads the Supreme Court. The Executive Branch enforces the laws, but the Judicial Branch ensures that the laws are constitutional. Our Constitution and our laws are the backbone of our system of government. We are a nation that honors the "rule of law." Every citizen, no matter what position they hold, how rich they are, or what their social status is, must obey the law—it is equal justice for all.

Checks and balances keep the government honest

#14 `2008`
#56 `2020`

The founders crafted the government to include a separation of powers to prevent any one branch or any one person from seizing control of the government or causing harm to its citizens. The president's power is kept in check by Congress which can turn down his appointments, override his veto, or impeach him. Congress passes laws that the president can veto, though they can override the veto with enough votes. Or their laws may be declared unconstitutional by the Supreme Court. Congress has to approve Supreme Court judges and can attempt to amend the Constitution, but this requires approval of two-thirds of Congress and three-fourths of all the states. Supreme Court justices are appointed for life to help ensure they are independent of politics.

Sometimes the checks do not work as they should, particularly when one party controls the White House and both houses of Congress. One attempt to upset the balance occurred in 1937 when Franklin Roosevelt proposed enlarging the Supreme Court by adding more hand-picked justices who would rule in favor of some of his more radical programs. But a different "check" saved the day when Congress refused to approve FDR's request.

The Executive Cabinet

The "Cabinet" refers to the heads of the various departments that exist in the Executive Branch of the government. George Washington appointed four cabinet members—Secretary of State, Secretary of the Treasury, Secretary of War, and Attorney General. Today, there are 15 members who head their corresponding departments. These positions are filled by the President with Senate approval. Besides running their respective departments, the Cabinet members advise and assist the President. The Departments, with the year they were formed, are:

2008 #35

2020 #47

Agriculture (1862): helps promote our agriculture at home and abroad, researches new crops, manages food programs like Food Stamps, and ensures the safety of our food.

2008 #36

2020 #48

Commerce (1903): promotes international trade, works to prevent unfair trade and business practices, forecasts the weather, regulates patents, and conducts the census every ten years.

Defense (1789): originally named the War Department, manages all military forces, including Navy, Army, and Air Force.

Education (1979): administers federal education programs, handles student loans, and works to eliminate discrimination in education.

Energy (1977): researches and encourages the development of energy and energy conservation, oversees nuclear energy and nuclear weapons, and regulates energy allocation.

Health and Human Services (1953): administers Social Security, Medicare, and Medicaid, manages social programs for the needy, conducts medical research, and ensures safety of drugs and non-meat food products.

Homeland Security (2002): formed from 22 separate agencies after the 9/11 attacks, it protects the country from terrorist attacks and natural disasters. It includes the Coast Guard, Immigration, Customs and Border protection, and the Secret Service.

Housing and Urban Development (1965): encourages affordable housing and community development, administers fair housing laws, oversees and insures mortgages.

Interior (1849): manages federal land, forests, monuments, and parks, runs federal dams, encourages resource conservation, and manages U.S. territories.

Justice (1789): enforces federal laws, supervises federal marshals, administers immigration laws, and runs federal prisons.

Labor (1913): protects workers' rights, gathers employment statistics, and improves working conditions.

State (1789): handles U.S. foreign policy; negotiates treaties; represents U.S. internationally; supervises foreign embassies and consulates.

Transportation (1966): sets transportation policy for the nation including land, sea, and air.

Treasury (1789): regulates banks, prints money, collects Federal income taxes (IRS), and prints stamps for Post Office.

Veterans Affairs (1989): handles government programs and hospitals that assist veterans and their families, and operates national cemeteries.

Other cabinet-level positions

There are other cabinet level positions that are not officially cabinet departments. Presidents can decide which positions are accorded cabinet-level status. Currently, they include:

Chief of Staff: responsible for the White House staff and managing the president's schedule.

Environmental Protection Agency (EPA): protects the health and environment of the country.

Office of Management and Budget (OMB): helps the president prepare the federal budget.

U.S. Trade Representative: helps promote economic growth and open-market policies.

Ambassador to the U.N.: leader of the U.S. delegation to the United Nations.

Director of National Intelligence: added in February, 2017

Directory of the CIA: added in February, 2017

Small Business Administration: added in January, 2012.

Vice President of the United States: A cabinet-level position.

Other well-known agencies

United States Postal Service (USPS): an independent government agency that provides postal service to the entire country. Authorized by the Constitution, it is not paid for by taxes.

Federal Bureau of Investigation (FBI): an agency of the Department of Justice whose job it is to defend against terrorism and uphold the country's criminal laws.

Central Intelligence Agency (CIA): a civilian agency reporting to the Director of National Intelligence. It collects information about foreign governments and individuals.

National Security Agency: Department of Defense intelligence agency that collects and analyzes foreign communications.

Presidential Succession

A clear path of succession is outlined in the Constitution, the 25th Amendment, and the Presidential Succession Act of 1947. If the president dies, resigns, is impeached, or is incapacitated for any reason, the duties of the office pass to the next person in the line of succession. The list includes the Vice President, leaders of both houses of Congress, and all 15 cabinet members. These rules were used when Nixon resigned from office, when Reagan was shot, and when presidents have died in office. This peaceful and clearly-defined process displays the strength of our system. Where many countries experience turmoil, uncertainty, and even violence whenever a leader dies, America peacefully moves on. After the first three positions, the order is determined by the year the department was formed, the older departments being higher in the list. During State of the Union addresses, at least one member in the list is not present--the designated survivor. Today, the line of succession is:

1. **Vice President**   2008 #30,31
2. **Speaker of the House**   2020 #40
3. **President pro tempore of the Senate**
4. **Secretary of State**
5. **Secretary of the Treasury**
6. **Secretary of Defense**
7. **Attorney General**
8. **Secretary of the Interior**
9. **Secretary of Agriculture**
10. **Secretary of Commerce**
11. **Secretary of Labor**
12. **Secretary of Health and Human Services**
13. **Secretary of Housing and Urban Development**
14. **Secretary of Transportation**
15. **Secretary of Energy**
16. **Secretary of Education**
17. **Secretary of Veterans Affairs**
18. **Secretary of Homeland Security**

Joint Chiefs of Staff

A group of senior military officers appointed by the President who advise the President, Secretary of Defense, National Security Council, and the Homeland Security Council on matters of national defense. Besides a chairman and vice chairman, the group consists of the leaders of the Army, Navy, Air Force, and Marine Corps. The Pentagon in Arlington, Virginia, houses the Department of Defense. It is the world's largest office building with 6.5 million square feet of floor area.

THE FEDERAL BUDGET

The spending budget for the country is prepared by the president and submitted to Congress every year. The federal fiscal year goes from October 1 to September 30 of the following year. The 2015 budget was $3.8 trillion, more than double what it was in 1999. Shown another way, that's: **$3,800,000,000,000**. Remember this every April 15th when you have to send in your annual income tax payment. It is important to pay taxes because it is required by law and it is your civic duty. Social security, Medicare, and Medicaid spending consumed more than twice what was spent by the Defense Department. The 2015 budget included the following items:

#56 2008

#71 2020

NOTE: Numbers are in Billions of dollars

$ 1,280	**Social Security, Unemployment, Labor**
1,050	**Medicare and Health**
609	**Military**
229	**Interest on National Debt**
160	**Veteran's Benefits**
136	**Food and Agriculture**
102	**Education**
85	**Transportation**
61	**Housing and Community**
50	**International Affairs**
45	**Energy and Environment**
30	**Science**

(Source: OMB, National Priorities Project)

STATES' RIGHTS AND POWERS

The Supremacy Clause of Article VI of the Constitution essentially declares federal law supreme over any laws of the states. However, this applies only if the federal acts are constitutional. **2008** #41 The federal government can print money, declare war, create an **2020** #58 army, and make treaties. But the 10th Amendment reserves to the states all powers that are not delegated to the federal government by the Constitution. Powers that are exercised by the states today include: issuing licenses, conducting state elections, ratifying Constitutional amendments, providing education and local services such as fire and police, and approving land use. But they are **2008** #42 prohibited from other actions, such as printing their own money. **2020** #59

THE ELECTORAL COLLEGE

When Americans vote every four years for president, they are not actually directly electing that person. Instead, the voters of each state vote for "electors" who then cast the actual vote for the president and vice president later. The only vote **2020** #49

Electoral votes based on 2010 census

that counts is the electoral vote. Presidents can win the electoral vote but lose the popular vote. This has happened five times in our history, most recently in 2016 when Donald Trump beat Hillary Clinton in the electoral count, but lost the popular vote.

Each state is represented by the same number of electors as that state has Representatives and Senators in the U.S. Congress. Some less populated states have only three electors, while California has the most with fifty-five. Today, the total number is fixed at 538, which includes one vote for each of the 435 Representatives, one vote for each of the 100 Senators, and 3 votes for the District of Columbia. The number of Representatives has been fixed at 435 since the Apportionment Act of 1911.

States have different rules on how the electors for that state must vote. Most states require that all electoral votes for that state be cast for the presidential candidate that wins the popular vote in that state. A candidate must receive at least 270 electoral votes to win. If no one receives that many votes, the House of Representatives selects the winner.

Though many have talked about removing the Electoral College from the election process and relying on just the popular vote, there are important reasons to keep this method.

- It is a cornerstone of federalism in this country. It helps protect the rights of small states and prevents a few large urban population centers from deciding the fate of the country.

#49 `2020`
- It is one more barrier between our present, successful form of government, and mob rule.

- It reduces or eliminates the need for recounts in more than one or two states in close elections, as was seen in Florida in 2000. Examine the timeline in this book to see how close the popular vote has been in the past. If that was the sole method used to select the president, the vote counts from every state could easily be challenged, and recounts ordered in every state.

- It has worked for over 200 years.

The founders provided further protection for states by requiring that Constitutional amendments to change the electoral process require three-fourths of the states to approve. The smaller states would almost certainly never agree to that.

When are elections?

Local and state elections generally have their elections at the same time that the national government has
#27 `2008` theirs, which is the Tuesday following the first Monday in November. It was originally set to this date to be after the crops had all been harvested, thus allowing farmers to have the time to travel and vote in the election. It was set on Tuesday, not Monday, so no voters would have to start travel on Sunday. There are other local and special elections held throughout the year in the states. National elections are held every two years in even-numbered years. Those years divisible by four (such as 2012 and 2016) are also presidential elections. The new president is sworn into office the following January, as stipulated in the 20th amendment.

Who can vote?

Generally, you must be a U.S. citizen who is 18 years or older, and a legal resident of the state you are voting in. There are restrictions on current or former felons. And, most importantly, you must register to vote—you can't just show up on Election Day, although this is, unfortunately, changing in some states.

Registering for the Selective Service

All males must register with the Selective Service System within 30 days of their 18th birthday. This information will be used if the country ever re-institutes the military draft in order to make a fair draft.

2008 #57
2020 #72

THE HISTORY OF VOTING IN AMERICA

The new federal government in the 1700s was elected by only 15-20% of the total population, due mainly to voting restrictions against women, slaves, and those not owning land. But as the country grew and conditions changed, the Constitution allowed the system to adapt. Over the following two centuries, voting rights expanded as restrictions were gradually removed. States are still responsible for determining who votes, but amendments to the Constitution and legal decisions bar states from denying the right to vote to certain groups of citizens. Unfortunately, in the aftermath of the Civil War, many states adopted various methods to restrict the rights of ex-slaves to vote, including literacy tests and poll taxes. But all the restrictions have been slowly peeled away. Amendments affecting voting include 15, 18, 23, 24 and 26.

2008 #48
2020 #63

- **Property-owning requirements**: These were dropped by most states shortly after the birth of the country.

- **Race and color:** Slaves had been freed after the Civil War, and the 15th amendment in 1870 gave the vote to men of all races and colors.

- **Sex**: The 19th amendment in 1920 gave all women the vote. Women had been voting in certain states, primarily in the West, for years before this amendment. Women in Wyoming had been voting since 1869. In an interesting twist, women actually ran for president in 1872 and 1884. Even though they were not allowed to vote, there were no laws preventing them from running for president.

- **District of Columbia**: The 23rd amendment in 1961 restored presidential voting rights to Washington, D.C. residents.

- **Poll tax:** The 24th amendment in 1964 prohibited states from denying the right to vote in federal elections due to failure to pay a poll tax. Several southern states had adopted poll taxes starting in 1889.

- **Age:** The 26th amendment in 1971 barred states from deny-ing voting rights to anyone 18 years of age or older. States can still individually grant voting rights to younger voters.

- **Election of Senators:** The 17th amendment in 1913 changed the election of Senators from being made by the State Legis-latures to being made directly by the people.

- **Literacy tests:** These were adopted by several southern states in the late 1800s to deny the vote to freed slaves. When the tests were found to exclude too many white voters, the southern states changed the law, adding a loophole allow-ing whites failing the test to still vote. The change allowed citizens whose father or grandfather could vote in 1867 to be allowed to vote (this is the origin of the phrase: *grand-father clause*). Since slaves had not been given the right to vote until 1870, this prohibited their descendants use of this allowance. The Supreme Court declared literacy tests uncon-stitutional in 1915, but they were still in use until outlawed by the Voting Rights Act of 1965.

- **Native Americans:** As a group, they finally received full citi-zenship rights in 1924 when the Indian Citizenship Act gave them the right to vote in federal elections. A number of west-ern states would still obstruct their ability to vote for decades.

Our country has a checkered history of fulfilling the dream of its Declaration of Independence that "all men are created equal." The important point is that these rights were eventually granted using procedures set up by the Constitution. And our country's record should be viewed in the context of other countries in the world—many of which still prohibit its citizens from voting at all, or treat women or other groups as second-class citizens.

POLITICAL PARTIES

George Washington was first elected before he formally be-longed to a political party, but the presidential elections after that pitted members of one party against another (and sometimes against each other). A number of political parties have come and gone, including the Whigs and the Federalists, but today we basi-cally have a two-party system consisting of the Republican Party and the Democratic Party. Many other parties run candidates, with the strongest showings usually belonging to the Libertarian, Green, and Constitution parties. Ross Perot ran as an Independent in 1992 and 1996, winning millions of popular votes and possibly changing the outcome of those elections.

There is nothing in the Constitution about political parties. The original method of electing the vice president was to name the candidate receiving the highest number of votes president, and name as vice president the candidate getting the second highest number of votes. However, this could lead to a president having a vice president from a different party, as in 1796, or, in the case of the 1800 election, the candidate running for vice president could actually get as many votes as his presidential running mate. The confusion of the 1800 election led to the adoption of the 12th amendment modifying how vice-presidents were elected. From that point forward, the presidential elections have consisted of president/vice-president pairs of candidates running against each other.

Major political parties in America today

There are two dominant political parties in the country today that have been shaping American politics for more than 150 years—the Democratic Party and the Republican Party.

2008 #45

Democratic Party: The 1790s saw the Democratic-Republican Party form to face the Federalist Party. This eventually becomes the Democratic Party, while the Federalist Party disbanded and was replaced by the Whig Party. The Democratic platform is considered liberal and progressive and on the left of the political spectrum. Besides the current president, Barack Obama, other well-known Democrat presidents include Franklin Roosevelt, John F. Kennedy, and Bill Clinton. They are often associated with a donkey, and are represented by the color "blue" on political maps.

Republican Party: This party was started in 1854 as an anti-slavery party before the Civil War. Their platform is conservative and on the right side of the political spectrum. Well-known Republican presidents include Abraham Lincoln, Dwight Eisenhower, George Bush, and Ronald Reagan. They are associated with an elephant, called the *GOP* (Grand Old Party), and are represented by the color "red" on political maps.

Primaries and the national conventions

Since 1832, the major parties had used national conventions as the method of selecting their best candidates for president and vice president. These would usually consist of party officials meeting to determine who they thought the best candidate was. This made it difficult to gauge the actual popular support for any candidate. Starting in 1910, the parties started holding primary elections in a number of states. These elections selected the delegates that would go to the national convention to vote for their candidate. The parties follow this procedure today, though each party and state handle the process differently. Normally each state has a primary election for each party early in the same year as the presidential election. These primary elections are usually open only to registered voters of that party. Some states hold more informal *caucuses* to select candidates.

The elected delegates meet at their national convention later that year to cast their votes for their party's candidate. Normally, if no candidate gets the required number of votes on the first ballot, the delegates are free to vote for anyone. Conventions in the past have held up to 100 ballots before finally selecting a candidate. These stalemates often result in a relatively unknown *"dark horse"* candidate finally winning the vote. The conventions also formalize their party's platform, which is their formal stand on the important issues of the day.

STATE AND LOCAL GOVERNMENTS

The state and local governments generally duplicate the federal structure, though there are local variations. This creates a very orderly structure as laws and rulings can move from the top of the structure down to the local level, and other issues, such as legal disputes over certain laws, can travel back up the structure, all the way to the Supreme Court if needed. The general structure throughout the country is:

Type	Location	Executive	Legislative	Judicial
National	Washington, D.C.	President	U.S. Senate U.S. House	Supreme Court Federal Courts
State	State Capitol	Governor	State Senate State House	State courts
City	City Hall	Mayor	City Council	Municipal courts

RESPONSIBILITIES OF A U.S. CITIZEN

Being a United States citizen gives you some of the most valued rights in the world. You can become a citizen by being born in America, being naturalized, or deriving your citizenship. You [2008] #50 can vote, bring family to this country, travel with a U.S. passport, [2020] #64,68 run for federal office, get a federal job, enjoy the rights guaranteed to you under the Constitution, receive help from the federal government, and be protected by that government and its military anywhere in the world. And what are your responsibilities? Not many, but they are important:

- Serve on a jury when called
- Vote
- Serve your country when required   [2008] #49
- Obey the laws   [2020] #70
- Pay taxes
- Respect the rights, beliefs, and opinions of others
- Defend the Constitution

UNITED STATES OATH OF ALLEGIANCE

Citizens born in this country often take it for granted how special their country is. Immigrants fleeing repressive governments and oppressive conditions don't have that problem, and most likely appreciate their responsibilities as well. Oaths of Allegiance have been used since the Revolutionary War. Naturalized citizens must take the following oath before they can become a citizen. Every native-born citizen should be prepared to take the same oath.

I hereby declare, on oath,

that I absolutely and entirely renounce and abjure all allegiance and fidelity to any foreign prince, potentate, state, [2008] #53 or sovereignty of whom or which I have heretofore been [2020] #67 a subject or citizen;

that I will support and defend the Constitution and laws of the United States of America against all enemies, foreign and domestic; that I will bear true faith and allegiance to the same;

that I will bear arms on behalf of the United States when required by the law;

that I will perform noncombatant service in the Armed Forces of the United States when required by the law;

that I will perform work of national importance under civilian direction when required by the law; and that I take this obligation freely without any mental reservation or purpose of evasion; so help me God.

AMERICAN HOLIDAYS

The celebration of common holidays is important to this country. These celebrations help unite an increasingly diverse population in shared activities that serve as links to the past. This ensures that we never forget the people and events that made this country, and the sacrifices that have been made by our ancestors. Holidays mark the passage of time, and frame each year with indelible markers. Unfortunately, they often have become just excuses for 3-day vacation weekends, or time off from work, which is why we need to be reminded of their meanings. Halloween is not devil worship but a rite of passage for children, and a time that adults can dress up and laugh at themselves. Thanksgiving, in particular, is woven into American life as a time for all families to gather and give thanks for the bounty this country has given them. It has no religious connotations and can be celebrated by everyone. The following list includes Federal holidays, some state holidays, and unofficial holidays and observances. The official national holidays are marked with an asterisk (*).

#100 2008
#126 2020

April Fools Day (April 1): Known as *All Fools Day*, this is a time to play pranks and practical jokes on friends and relatives.

* Christmas (December 25): An important Christian holiday celebrating the birth of Jesus Christ. Almost all schools have a 2-week recess around Christmas. It has also become an important secular holiday with Christmas trees and gift giving.

* Columbus Day (2nd Monday in October): Celebrates Columbus' arrival in the new world on October 12, 1492.

Earth Day (April 22): Celebrated since 1970 to promote interest in cleaning up the earth's soil, air, and water.

Easter (1st Sunday after 1st full moon after spring equinox): A Christian holiday celebrating the resurrection of Jesus Christ. Along with Christmas, it is the most important Christian holiday. Many attend sunrise services and hide colored Easter eggs.

Father's Day (3rd Sunday in June): Celebrated since 1909 and made an official holiday in 1966, it is a day to honor fathers.

Flag Day (June 14): Celebrates the adoption of the American Flag in 1777 by the Continental Congress. Citizens are encouraged to fly the national flag on this day.

Groundhog Day (February 2): Celebrated since 1887. If the groundhog Punxsutawney Phil emerges from his burrow in Pennsylvania and sees his shadow, there will be six more weeks of winter weather.

Halloween (October 31): The night before All Hallows Day, it is celebrated by children dressing in costumes and "trick or treating" around their neighborhood to receive candy. It also involves carved pumpkins, haunted houses, and scary tales.

* *Independence Day (July 4):* Our most important holiday celebrates the signing of the Declaration of Independence in 1776. It is celebrated by parades and massive firework demonstrations. **2008** #99 **2020** #125

* *Labor Day (1st Monday in September):* Celebrates the labor movement in America and marks the end of summer vacations.

Lincoln's Birthday (February 12): A legal holiday in some states honoring the 16th President's birthday in 1809. Never a federal holiday, it is often combined with the Washington's Birthday celebration and called President's Day.

* *Martin Luther King, Jr. Day (3rd Monday in January):* Celebrates the birth of the slain civil rights leader, January 15, 1929.

* *Memorial Day (last Monday of May):* Honors Americans who have given their lives fighting for their country. Originally known as *Decoration Day* in 1868, it was observed on May 30 until moved to this day in 1968. Americans usually use it to celebrate the first day of summer vacation. **2020** #127

Mother's Day (2nd Sunday in May): President Wilson started this day of thanks in 1914. Besides giving cards and flowers, wise husbands also take their wives out to dinner.

National Arbor Day (last Friday in April): Started in 1970 to encourage tree planting across the country.

* *New Year's Day (January 1):* New Year's Eve his is normally marked by parties and celebrations at midnight to mark the end of the Gregorian calendar year. The most famous celebration is at Times Square in New York City. New Years Day is a holiday normally filled with parades and football games.

Pearl Harbor Remembrance Day (December 7): Honors the military personnel who died in the surprise attack on December 7, 1941, resulting in the U.S. entering World War II.

* *Presidents' Day:* see *Washington's Birthday*. Presidents' day is not an official holiday.

* *Thanksgiving Day (4th Thursday in November):* Started by colonial settlers in New England in 1621 to give thanks for their harvest, it is a traditional day of family gatherings and turkey dinners. It also has the heaviest air travel of the year. President Lincoln declared Thanksgiving to be the last Thursday in November. This was observed until President Roosevelt moved it to the second to last Thursday of November to allow for more shopping days before Christmas. The ensuing national furor resulted in some states ignoring the new date until Congress finally passed a 1941 law setting the official date as the fourth Thursday.

Valentine's Day (February 14): Named after St. Valentine, a day for loved ones to give each other cards, candy, and flowers.

[#]128 **2020** * ***Veterans Day (November 11):*** Honors all veterans of the armed forces. Originally called Armistice Day, it calls for a moment of silence at 11:00 am commemorating the start of the World War I armistice on 11/11/1918 at 11:00 am.

* ***Washington's Birthday (3rd Monday in February):*** The birthday of the first president is February 22. The holiday was moved to its present day in 1968, and sometimes called Presidents' Day.

Heritage Days

A number of celebrations are not official holidays, but honor the heritage or country of origin of various groups. These include:

Native American Heritage Day (Friday after Thanksgiving): Celebrates the culture and traditions of Native Americans.

Chinese New Year (varies): The start of a new year in the Chinese calendar is usually marked by large parades and celebrations.

Cinco de Mayo (May 5): The victory of the Mexican Army over the French in 1862 is marked by parades and parties, often larger in the United States than in Mexico. It does not celebrate Mexican Independence, which was on September 16, 1810.

Kwanzaa (December 26): Established in 1966 for African-Americans to celebrate their heritage, it lasts for seven days.

Mardi Gras (varies, the day before Ash Wednesday): *Mardi Gras* is French for "Fat Tuesday" describing the last day of overeating before beginning the fasting period of Lent the next day. First celebrated in this country in Mobile, Alabama in 1703, it is marked by a week of wild celebrations and parades, epitomized by the New Orleans celebration.

Rosh Hashanah (varies): A Jewish holiday marking the start of a new year in the Jewish calendar, usually in September or October.

St. Lucia's Day (December 13): A Scandinavian holiday that honors Saint Lucia. It is usually celebrated by processions of girls in white robes carrying candles or with crowns of candles.

St. Patrick's Day (March 17): An Irish holiday celebrating St. Patrick who brought Christianity to Ireland and drove the snakes from that island. It is marked in this country by parties, wearing of something green, and the greening of everything including the Chicago River. Nineteen presidents, including Barack Obama, and 36 million Americans claim Irish ancestry.

History of the American Flag

George Washington and the Continental Army were laying siege to Boston at the start of 1776. On January 1st, he flew the Grand Union flag at his headquarters.

Grand Union Flag

Later that year, Betsy Ross is purported to have created the first flag containing 13 5-pointed stars, and 13 stripes. That flag was not made official until June 14, 1777 (later celebrated as Flag Day) when the Continental Congress passed the Flag Act.

Betsy Ross Flag

Over the following years, Congress passed acts to alter the appearance of the flag to allow for the admission of new states. The Act of 1794 provided for 15 stars and 15 stripes on the flag. This was the "Stars and Stripes" celebrated in the Star-Spangled Banner.

Star-Spangled Banner

Since 1818, the design has been fixed with 13 stripes for the original 13 colonies and a star for each state. A 48-star flag was flown from 1912 until 1959 when Alaska and Hawaii were admitted, the longest time any one flag design had been used until 2007.

48-star Flag

2008 #96
2020 #121

Since 1959, we have had the modern flag consisting of 13 stripes and 50 stars, one for each state. This is the flag the astronauts left on the moon on July 20, 1969. The colors used in the flag are the same as those in the

Today's 50-star Flag

2008 #97
2020 #122

Great Seal. The meaning of those colors was reported to Congress as: *"White signifies purity and innocence, Red, hardiness & valour, and Blue...signifies vigilance, perseverance & justice."*

Flag Act of 1818

This set the current policy of 13 stripes with one star for each state (before this act, the number of stripes had increased with each state). The new star would be added to the flag on the next 4th of July following the admission of the new state.

United States Flag Etiquette

U.S. Code, Title 4, Chapter i

Pledge of Allegiance

#52 2008
#66 2020

The pledge was written in 1892 by Francis Bellamy to celebrate the 400th anniversary of the voyage of Christopher Columbus. The pledge is recited at public events and in schools. The words "under God" were added in 1954. The pledge should be spoken while at attention, facing the flag, with the right hand over the heart. Non-religious headwear should be removed and held with the right hand. Uniformed personnel should face the flag and salute.

> I pledge allegiance
> To the flag of the United States of America
> And to the republic for which it stands,
> One nation under God,
> Indivisible, with liberty and justice for all.

Basic Economic Concepts

The success of the United States over the last 2½ centuries owes a lot to her form of government, her protection of personal freedoms, and her economic system. Important concepts are:

Capitalism: The means of production are privately owned and operated for profit. Production decisions are made based on the potential profits. Risk takers are often rewarded by large profits, but there is also no guarantee against failure and bankruptcy.

#11 2008
#12 2020

Free market system (market economy): Production, pricing, and distribution of goods and services are determined by the interactions of buyers and producers, with minimal government intervention, mainly in collecting taxes, enforcing contracts, and ensuring public safety. Prices are determined by the intersection of supply and demand curves (see below). Producers are not forced to make specific products, nor sell them at any specific price. Government attempts to circumvent this relationship, using price controls, subsidies, quotas, or rent controls, almost always results in failure. The free market is the optimal way to allocate scarce resources, which include time, labor, material, and money.

Laissez-faire: French meaning "leave it alone." This advocates minimal government intervention and taxation, usually only in enforcing contract and safety laws.

GREAT SEAL OF THE UNITED STATES

The Great Seal was first used in 1782. The front (obverse) is the national coat of arms used on passports, military insignia, and flags. The reverse is now used on the back of the one-dollar bill.

Front of the Great Seal

An American Bald Eagle supports a shield of thirteen stripes representing the original 13 colonies. Unlike the flag, the outermost stripes are white, not red, in keeping with heraldic rules. The stripes support a blue bar (chief) that contains no stars. This blue chief represents Congress supported by the states. The eagle holds a bundle of 13 arrows in its left talon and an olive branch with 13 leaves and 13 olives in its right, all representing the original colonies. The olives represent peace, while the arrows represent America's readiness for war. The eagle's head is turned towards the olive branch, symbolizing America's preference for peace.

The motto *E Pluribus Unum* alludes to the union of states: "Out of Many, One." The constellation of 13 stars above the eagle's head, arranged to form a small star, represents a new country taking its place among the powers of the world. The color white signifies purity and innocence; red represents hardiness and valor; and blue signifies perseverance and justice.

2020 #124

Reverse of the Great Seal

The pyramid represents strength and duration, and is composed of 13 layers to represent the colonies. The eye and the motto

"Annuit Coeptis" refer to the intervention of providence in favor of America. The date MDCCLCCVI (1776) on the pyramid is the date of the Declaration of Independence, and "Novus Ordo Seclorum" signifies the beginning of the new American era, roughly meaning "A New Order of the Ages."

American Inventions Lead the World

These items are from Encyclopedia Britannica's 2003 list of great inventions. Of the 321 world-wide inventions, half belonged to the United States. The United States comprises only a fraction of the world's population and is one of the newest countries, so you have to credit its free market system that encourages risk-taking but rewards success. Some were related to the government-funded space program, but the inventions were usually made by individuals and companies. Some inventors were extremely prolific, like Thomas Edison with 1093 patents. Many truly changed the world with their ideas.

Thomas Alva Edison
holder of 1,093 U.S. patents

#118 2020

Medicine/Health: *artificial heart; bifocals; defibrillator; pacemaker; laser vision correction; magnetic resonance imaging (MRI); oral contraceptives; Prozac; respirator; sunscreen; synthetic skin; tampon; Viagra*

Food: *Aspartame; beverage can; can opener; cereal flakes; chewing gum; Coca-cola; food irradiation; frozen foods; genetic engineering; hybrid corn; potato chips; prepared baby food; saccharin; sliced bread; supermarket; tea bag*

Technology: *air conditioning; airplanes; artificial diamond; assembly line; Astroturf; ATM; atomic bomb; auto airbag; bar code; barbed wire; brassiere; camera; carbon-14 dating; cash register; computer; computer mouse; corrugated cardboard; cotton gin; crayons; credit card; digital wristwatch; dishwasher; disposable diapers; electric guitar; electric iron; electric motor; electric razor; electric stove; e-mail; escalator; fiberglass; gas lawn mower; hand-held calculator; integrated circuit; Internet; jeans; jukebox; Kevlar; laser; laundromat; light bulb; light-emitting diode (LED); liquid crystal display (LCD); liquid-fueled rocket; loudspeaker; LP record; mechanical reaper; microwave oven; miniature golf; mobile home; mobile telephone; Morse code; motion-picture animation; movie camera; nuclear reactor; nylon; oil well; paper towel; parking meter; passenger elevator; phonograph; photocopying; photographic film; photography; Post-it Notes; radio; refrigerator; repeating rifle; revolver; revolving door; roller coaster; safety pin; safety razor; satellite; Scotch tape; sewing machine; skateboard; skyscraper; slot machine; smoke detector; stapler; steamboat; steel plow; Teflon; telegraph; telephone; television; tractor; traffic lights; transistor; tube lipstick; TV remote control; typewriter; video games; videotape; virtual reality; vulcanized rubber; washing machine; wire coat hanger; zipper*

Chapter 6

AMERICAN HEROES

❦

Benjamin Franklin *(1706-1790)*: Franklin was the quintessential American—inventor, writer, scientist, diplomat, and patriot. America would be a very different place without him. Besides experimenting with electricity, he researched

Franklin's Return to Philadelphia, 1785
by Jean Leon Gerome Ferris

2008 #68
2020 #85

the Gulf Stream and started a library system. He helped produce the Declaration of Independence, Articles of Confederation, and the Constitution. He was vital in getting French help to win the Revolution. His speech on the final day of the Constitutional Convention helped win overwhelming support from the delegates. He was the first Postmaster General and wrote Poor Richard's Almanac.

Alexander Hamilton *(1755-1804)*: Hamilton was crucial in the founding of our nation. Born in the British West Indies, he had one of the best minds of all founding fathers. He strongly believed in a strong central government and had a firm grasp of finances. He wrote the majority of the Federalist Papers that were vital in convincing the public of the importance of the Constitution. And aide to George Washington, he was the first Secretary of the Treasury and implemented the necessary financial systems that allowed the new country to prosper, such as having the federal government assume the war debts of the states and establishing the first bank of the U.S. Hamilton's belief in a strong federal government was at odds with Jefferson's belief in state and individual rights. Hamilton was killed in a duel with his rival Aaron Burr.

2020 #89

Alexander Hamilton in Uniform
by Alonzo Chappel

#77 2008
#99 2020

Susan B. Anthony: This leading civil rights leader played a key role in getting women voting rights. She co-founded the Women's Temperance Movement, but died before the 19th amendment gave women the vote. She was placed on the 1979 dollar coin.

#85 2008
#113 2020

Martin Luther King: The leading black leader of the civil rights movement in America. He led peaceful protests in the South before giving his famous "I Have a Dream" speech in 1963 at the Lincoln Memorial. He worked tirelessly for equality for all Americans. He received the Nobel Peace Prize before he was tragically assassinated in 1968 by James Earl Ray in Memphis, Tennessee. A national holiday was subsequently named in his honor in 1971.

#99 2020

Harriet Tubman: Born a slave in Maryland, she walked north to freedom in 1849. She spent the next years leading other slaves to freedom using the Underground Railroad, constantly putting her life at risk and earning the name of "Moses." She also worked in South Carolina as a spy for the Union. When the war ended, she continued helping other people and was active in the suffrage movement.

Chapter 7

PROCLAMATIONS AND SONGS

———————— ❦ ————————

THE EMANCIPATION PROCLAMATION

ABRAHAM LINCOLN   SEPTEMBER 22, 1862

Lincoln's main focus was always on keeping the Union together. Midway through the war, he felt it advantageous to formalize the government's position on slavery, and prepared a speech. He was advised to wait until the North achieved victory in battle. That victory finally came with the Battle of Antietam, and Lincoln released the proclamation officially freeing slaves only in the Confederate states in rebellion. He could not legally free the Northern slaves—that had to wait until future amendments to the Constitution. 200,000 blacks ended up fighting for the Union, while half a million fled the South to the North during the war. The proclamation went into effect on January 1, 1863.

2008 #76
2020 #95

Whereas, on the twenty-second day of September, in the year of our Lord one thousand eight hundred and sixty-two, a proclamation was issued by the President of the United States, containing, among other things, the following, to wit:

"That on the first day of January, in the year of our Lord one thousand eight hundred and sixty-three, **all persons held as slaves within any State or designated part of a State, the people whereof shall then be in rebellion against the United States, shall be then, thenceforward, and forever free**; and the Executive Government of the United States, including the military and naval authority thereof, will recognize and maintain the freedom of such persons, and will do no act or acts to repress such persons, or any of them, in any efforts they may make for their actual freedom.

"That the Executive will, on the first day of January aforesaid, by proclamation, designate the States and parts of States, if any, in which the people thereof, respectively, shall then be in rebellion against the United States; and the fact that any State, or the people thereof, shall on that day be, in good faith, represented in the Congress of the United States by members chosen thereto at elections wherein a majority of the qualified voters of such State shall have participated, shall, in the absence of strong countervailing testimony, be deemed conclusive evidence that such State, and the people thereof, are not then in rebellion against the United States."

Now, therefore I, Abraham Lincoln, President of the United States, by virtue of the power in me vested as Commander-in-Chief, of the Army and Navy of the United States in time of actual armed rebellion against the authority and government of the United States, and as a fit and necessary war measure for suppressing said rebellion, do, on this first day of January, in the year of our Lord one thousand eight hundred and sixty-three, and in accordance with my purpose so to do publicly proclaimed for the full period of one hundred days, from the day first above mentioned, order and designate as the States and parts of States wherein the people thereof respectively, are this day in rebellion against the United States, the following, to wit:

Arkansas, Texas, Louisiana, (except the Parishes of St. Bernard, Plaquemines, Jefferson, St. John, St. Charles, St. James Ascension, Assumption, Terrebonne, Lafourche, St. Mary, St. Martin, and Orleans, including the City of New Orleans) Mississippi, Alabama, Florida, Georgia, South Carolina, North Carolina, and Virginia, (except the forty-eight counties designated as West Virginia, and also the counties of Berkley, Accomac, Northampton, Elizabeth City, York, Princess Ann, and Norfolk, including the cities of Norfolk and Portsmouth[)], and which excepted parts, are for the present, left precisely as if this proclamation were not issued.

And by virtue of the power, and for the purpose aforesaid, I do order and declare that all persons held as slaves within said designated States, and parts of States, are, and henceforward shall be free; and that the Executive government of the United States, including the military and naval authorities thereof, will recognize and maintain the freedom of said persons.

And I hereby enjoin upon the people so declared to be free to abstain from all violence, unless in necessary self-defence; and I recommend to them that, in all cases when allowed, they labor faithfully for reasonable wages.

And I further declare and make known, that such persons of suitable condition, will be received into the armed service of the United States to garrison forts, positions, stations, and other places, and to man vessels of all sorts in said service.

And upon this act, sincerely believed to be an act of justice, warranted by the Constitution, upon military necessity, I invoke the considerate judgment of mankind, and the gracious favor of Almighty God. In witness whereof, I have hereunto set my hand and caused the seal of the United States to be affixed. Done at the City of Washington, this first day of January, in the year of our Lord one thousand eight hundred and sixty three, and of the Independence of the United States of America the eighty-seventh.

THE STAR-SPANGLED BANNER

SIR FRANCIS SCOTT KEY   SEPTEMBER 16, 1814

#98 **2008**

#123 **2020**

During the War of 1812, Key went aboard a British warship in an effort to secure the release of a friend who had been captured. He was still aboard when the British fleet shelled Fort McHenry, one of the many defenses of Baltimore. Key watched the flag flying during the night, and when it was still there in the morning, put together these lines as a tribute to the Star Spangled Banner. Congress waited until 1931 to officially make this our National Anthem.

O! say, can you see, by the dawn's early light,
What so proudly we hailed at the twilight's last gleaming—
Whose broad stripes and bright stars, through the perilous fight,
O'er the ramparts we watched were so gallantly streaming!
And the rocket's red glare, the bombs bursting in air,
Gave proof through the night that our flag was still there:
O! say, does that star-spangled banner yet wave
O'er the land of the free, and the home of the brave

On that shore dimly seen through the mists of the deep,
Where the foe's haughty host in dread silence reposes,
What is that which the breeze, o'er the towering steep,
As it fitfully blows, now conceals, now discloses?
Now it catches the gleam of the morning's first beam,
In full glory reflected now shines on the stream;
'Tis the star-spangled banner; O long may it wave
O'er the land of the free, and the home of the brave!

And where is that band who so vauntingly swore
That the havoc of war and the battle's confusion
A home and a country should leave us no more?
Their blood has washed out their foul footsteps' pollution.
No refuge could save the hireling and slave
From the terror of or the gloom of the grave;
And the star-spangled banner in triumph doth wave
O'er the land of the free, and the home of the brave.

AMERICA, THE BEAUTIFUL

KATHARINE LEE BATES   1895

Bates, a school teacher, was inspired by a trip to the top of Pike's Peak in Colorado, and wrote the words to this song when she returned home that night. It was published in 1895, and the music was later composed by Samuel A. Ward.

O beautiful for spacious skies,
　　For amber waves of grain,
For purple mountain majesties
　　Above the fruited plain!
America! America!
　　God shed His grace on thee
And crown thy good with brotherhood
　　From sea to shining sea!

O beautiful for pilgrim feet,
　　Whose stern, impassioned stress
A thoroughfare for freedom beat
　　Across the wilderness!
America! America!
　　God mend thine every flaw,
Confirm thy soul in self control,
　　Thy liberty in law!

O beautiful for heroes proved
　　In liberating strife,
Who more than self their country loved,
　　And mercy more than life!
America! America!
　　May God thy gold refine,
Till all success be nobleness
　　And every gain divine!

O beautiful for patriot dream
　　That sees beyond the years
Thine alabaster cities gleam
　　Undimmed by human tears!
America! America!
　　God shed His grace on thee,
And crown thy good with brotherhood
　　From sea to shining sea!

Unveiling the Statue of Liberty - 1886
by Edward Moran

ELLIS ISLAND IMMIGRATION STATION

In plain sight of the Statue of Liberty less than a mile away, this station served as a gateway for more than 12 million immigrants from 1892 to 1954. Up to 100 million Americans today may claim ancestors who arrived here.

———————————————— 🐚 ————————————————

And we should be a welcoming nation. Our identity is not based on race or ethnicity, it's based on a set of shared values. That's American citizenship.

—Jeb Bush

As long as I live, I will never forget that day 21 years ago when I raised my hand and took the oath of citizenship. Do you know how proud I was? I was so proud that I walked around with an American flag around my shoulders all day long.

—Arnold Schwarzenegger

What makes America special is that people come here, assimilate and become American with all of the rights and responsibilities citizenship bestows.

—Zoe Lofgren

Millions of us, myself included, go back generations in this country, with ancestors who put in the painstaking work to become citizens. So we don't like the notion that anyone might get a free pass to American citizenship.

—Barack Obama

KNOW YOUR GOVERNMENT

#55 2008
#69 2020

One of the most important duties of being an American citizen is staying involved in your government. You can join a political party, run for office, help a campaign, write letters to your newspaper...or just stay informed and vote in every election. Enter the names of your elected officials on this page, and hold them accountable for their actions. If you don't agree with their stances, vote them out at the next election. That is the purpose and the power of the ballot.

National Government

President: _____

Vice-President: _____

Secretary of State: _____

Secretary of Defense: _____

Speaker of the House: _____

Leader of the Senate: _____

Chief Justice: _____

State Government

State Name: _____

State Capital: _____

Governor: _____

Local Government

City Name: _____

Mayor: _____

WHO REPRESENTS YOU?

U.S. Senator #1: _____

U.S. Senator #2: _____

U.S. Representative: _____

State Senator: _____

State Representative: _____

Made in United States
Orlando, FL
07 March 2022

15502345R00162